The Pattern
of Responsibility

The Pattern
of Responsibility

Edited by McGeorge Bundy from
the Record of Secretary of State
Dean Acheson

Introduction by Douglas Southall Freeman

1 9 5 2

HOUGHTON MIFFLIN COMPANY BOSTON
The Riverside Press Cambridge

The Riverside Press

CAMBRIDGE · MASSACHUSETTS

PRINTED IN THE U.S.A.

PREFACE

THIS BOOK is an attempt to present the central public record of Dean G. Acheson as Secretary of State of the United States, from January, 1949, to August, 1951. Its method is mainly that of direct quotation; the principal witness is Mr. Acheson himself. He is a good witness, and with a few exceptions I have avoided any effort to provide more than such connecting comment and factual background as may recall the setting in which this public record has been made.

History is far more than the public statements of public officials, and it may well be asked why one should suppose that any important purpose is served by collecting a selected record of such comments. Obviously the public statements of Secretary Acheson cannot tell us all of what he is and does; neither can they give, of themselves, a full picture of American foreign policy. The full quality of any man is less than clear while he is still in office; soundly based biography comes well after the event.

To give the whole story of foreign policy, a man would need a wider and a longer view than can be found in the open words of a Secretary of State. He would also have to include the public record of the President, of military and Congressional leaders, and of many private citizens. He would need the cables still classified, the memoirs still unwritten, the whole vast collection from which written history is eventually fashioned.

Yet with all its limitations the method here chosen has certain advantages. The first is that we deal with open and verifiable fact — either Mr. Acheson did or did not say publicly, for the record, what is here attributed to him; the events recorded either did or did not happen, and they can be checked. Furthermore, the present selection (from a massive bulk of wordage, on great and small events of all descriptions) is either a fair or a distorted picture of the total public record. A characteristic of modern public debate is repetition. In order to spare the reader, I have omitted, condensed, and rearranged. For taking these liberties I owe an apology to Mr. Acheson, who is of course entirely without responsibility for what I have done with his record; he has not seen a word of it. I have tried to use those parts of the record which are truly representative, and I have made it a special point to omit nothing that has been the subject of major comment or criticism. I have noted every source, and both the accuracy and the representative character of my selection can be tested by any man with access to the *Department of State Bulletin* and the open hearings of the Congress. This advantage is of some importance in the case of a man who has been as widely misquoted and misrepresented as Mr. Acheson.

Mr. Acheson's public statements do not tell us all of what he is, but they make fairly plain a number of things he is not, and they do the same major job for American foreign policy. Since quite extraordinary charges have been leveled against both the man and the policy, these negative advantages are significant. They are, in a way, the initial motivation for this book. The publisher and I were agreed that in the hue-and-cry against Mr. Acheson, and against the whole course of our foreign policy, which characterized the last months of 1950, there was room for a book whose evidence might set the more irresponsible attacks in a perspective of fact, while providing Mr. Acheson's own answer on arguable matters. Now that the job of examination and editing is done, I am bound to say that I think it very hard indeed to square the record of man and policy with most of the charges that have been made.

There is one particular clarification which I hope this record may help to provide. It is a peculiarity of the criticism leveled at Mr. Acheson that in large degree it is contradictory. A particular example of this phenomenon comes in the conflict between the opinions of those who think him too soft and those who think him too hard. From one side we are told that he is an appeaser and a friend of the Reds, while from the other we hear that he has become a prisoner of his critics and is thus a tool of blind reaction. (This last opinion is particularly widespread among academic men-of-good-will.) My own view is that both of these charges are false. I think that Mr. Acheson's actions have been clearly and strongly anti-Communist, and that they have been governed, at each stage, by his own honest convictions, and by the facts. Thus, when he hardens his heart toward the Chinese Reds, in late

1950 and early 1951, I take it that this is because they are engaged in military aggression, not because the China Lobby has captured him. And I assume that when he agrees to support an effort to obtain military bases in Spain, it is primarily because he thinks that in 1951 such bases are needed, and not because he is in chains forged by Senator McCarran. I do not mean to suggest that domestic pressure has no effect on foreign policy; I do mean that those who think Mr. Acheson a prisoner of his critics have often mistaken for expediency what seems to me a real conviction. They would understand him better if they would get it through their heads that he simply does not agree with them on the issues. Then they could stop wailing about his "surrender to pressure" and straightforwardly attack him as wrong; this would be a good deal less easy, perhaps, but it would have the advantage of fairness.

I also hope this record may have a larger and more affirmative value, one for which I hardly looked when I began. Public statements and speeches are made for the moment, mostly; they are more acts than thoughts, and however valuable they may be as evidence, they tend to seem thin and a little wooden when they are lifted from the scene of action and imprisoned in bound volumes. No man's speeches are wholly free from this weakness, but what is striking in the case of Mr. Acheson is the high specific gravity of his public statements. It has seemed to me, in working with them, that as a body they succeed in presenting an unusually clear-cut analysis of the nature and purpose of American participation in world affairs as understood by the American Secretary of State. Taken together, the record seems to give with considerable clarity the pattern of a responsible foreign policy. It seems to present, to supporter and critic alike — and also to the fair-minded observer — a more substantial and rounded picture than any one speech or statement has done. I do not think this is an illusion, produced by my own contrivance. But if it is, the student can test it against his own view of the record.

The variety and complexity of modern American foreign affairs have forced me to limit this record to the central issues. I have tried to include the basic outlines of Mr. Acheson's policy toward the Russians, toward Europe, and toward Asia; I have also included a brief review of his position on matters of security and loyalty. While these areas are those of the greatest importance and the warmest debate, they obviously do not exhaust the subject. I have not considered specifically economic problems; I have not discussed American policy in the Western Hemisphere; I have skipped over the subject of information and intelligence, and even the large area of United

Nations' affairs has been considered only with reference to the "Acheson Plan." These and other omissions seemed inevitable if the central problems were to receive adequate treatment.

There is one omission, forced upon me by the inadequacy of the public record, which I greatly regret. Very near the heart of all foreign affairs is the relationship between policy and military power. Mr. Acheson has remarked more than once that in his view the principal American error after World War II was the extraordinarily rapid and helter-skelter demobilization in which nearly all of us joined so eagerly. Unofficial reporting from Washington indicates strongly that he has been a leading advocate within the government of extensive rearmament, and this well before the attack on South Korea crystallized public and official sentiment. Since in our government public statements of military policy are not considered to be the concern of the Department of State, the official record contains very little evidence on Mr. Acheson's position, and this question has therefore received inadequate treatment. This I think unjust to Mr. Acheson, for if his policy has been as it is reported, he clearly deserves high praise for realism and foresight.

Limited as it is by omission and compression, the "pattern of responsibility" sketched in this book covers a great deal of ground. To accept the general basis of this pattern, and to reject categorically the assertion that it is either soft or pink, is not at all to accept or underwrite every statement and every action. As Mr. Acheson himself has repeatedly stated, there is always room for honest differences, on foreign affairs as on anything else. In order to avoid misunderstanding, I enter here a summary list of my own more important disagreements with specific positions taken by Mr. Acheson.

I do not think that the State Department acted wisely in its démarche toward German rearmament in the fall of 1950.

I do not believe that our policy toward China, from 1945 to 1950, adequately assessed the probable character of a Communist régime in that country. That does not imply that I think Nationalist China could have been saved; I do not.

I do not entirely share the high opinion expressed by Mr. Acheson of the administrative skills of those in charge of the loyalty and security program of the State Department. I am persuaded that this program, while well intentioned, and certainly effective against genuine security risks, has been clumsily administered. I think that this clumsiness has produced some unfairness to individuals and has also redoubled unjustified attacks.

I think the Point Four Program has been badly mishandled — largely because it was launched without much thought or planning as an ornament to Mr. Truman's inaugural address.

Most of these points can be answered in part by pleas in extenuation, for all of them are in part the result of outside influences which bear on the Department of State, and especially of Congressional pressures, largely Republican. Few of them are among the usual complaints of Mr. Acheson's violent critics, and some run directly counter to these attacks. Moreover, all of them, in the larger context of foreign policy as a whole, are relatively small. Nor do they all involve personal mistakes by Mr. Acheson, any more than every failing of the armed forces in World War II could be personally assessed against Secretaries Stimson and Knox. No statesman is infallible, and none is omnipotent, although it is easy for critics and commentators to pretend that they ought to be.

There is one general point which does, I think, apply directly to Mr. Acheson. I think he has shown a tendency, at least until recently, to promise definite results in an indefinite world. The pressure to give such assurances weighs heavily on a modern Secretary of State. Members of the Congress are constantly eager for glowing assurances as to the result of this or that expensive action. Nevertheless, I have the impression that Mr. Acheson's natural zeal in advocacy has sometimes led him too far in responding to this pressure.

In the vexed issue of Alger Hiss, I think it entirely understandable that Mr. Acheson should have felt it right and necessary to say everything that he said, but I also think it plain that Alger Hiss, even on the difficult assumption that he was wrongly convicted, has not honorably or candidly repaid his friendship and compassion.

Finally, and this is merely a point which I note, without criticism, it is a natural part of Mr. Acheson's position that he should feel bound to put the best possible face on everything done by a Democratic Administration, at least since 1941. In particular, he has given to Mr. Truman not only official but personal loyalty, and I have no doubt that he has done so in complete sincerity of purpose. This position necessarily affects the conclusions he reaches, and the reader should be warned that Mr. Acheson, more than any other Secretary of State in recent history, has accepted the responsibility of acting as a personal advocate for his chief.

There is one general criticism of Mr. Acheson which this book makes no attempt to treat. If the charge against him is that in 1944 and early 1945 he was hopeful of Russian good intentions, then I believe he must plead guilty, along with most of his countrymen, myself among them. If it be further claimed that in this period Mr. Acheson was intolerant of many who did not share his hopes, I will still not complain. All that I would do is to point out three things.

First, to make this charge against Mr. Acheson the cause of a loss of confidence in his present policy would be to erect a bar which would exclude from public service that overwhelming majority of Americans (including many of Mr. Acheson's present enemies) who at one time shared these hopes and views in substantial measure. This we cannot afford to do. Second, the American position before the world would now be vastly weakened if no full, fair effort had been made to get along with Soviet Russia. Third, Mr. Acheson's record clearly demonstrates that he was quick to see that the Russians were breaking the spirit and letter of the bargains struck during the war, and to draw the necessary conclusions from this fact.

But my real objection to an indictment of *present* policy based on *past* attitudes is more deep-seated. I cannot escape the feeling that the attack on Mr. Acheson is largely motivated by two purposes which I think it fair to call sinister. On the one hand, it seems to me plain that there are men who are willing to wreck American foreign policy if in so doing they can advance their personal reputation or win an election campaign. And on the other, it seems quite clear to me that some who attack Mr. Acheson are using *ad hominem* insinuations and smears in an effort to discredit the whole course of policy developed and pursued by American political and military leaders since 1946.

These two attitudes run deeply and violently against everything that I believe about American foreign affairs. I hold, first, that the search for partisan advantage in foreign policy is a wholly destructive occupation; and second, that the main course of American policy — the course of energetic leadership in a partnership of free nations, building strength by sacrifice and effort to block the Kremlin without war — is our one hope for the survival of our civilization. I believe that Mr. Acheson's record plainly shows that he has been a devoted and skillful servant of this basic policy, and I believe that it is on this record, first and foremost, that he deserves to be judged.

These views I hold as a Republican; I have never voted for a Democratic candidate for any office higher than that of Mayor of Boston (where there is no choice), and I have worked actively on a full-time basis for Republican candidates. I think perhaps I believe what I do with particular vigor because I worked and studied at length under a great Republican, Henry L. Stimson. Colonel Stimson's last public statement, as it happens, defines precisely the line of thinking which has led me to undertake this task. The statement was made with particular reference to the charges of Senator Joe McCarthy, but I think it pertinent to the whole of the "get-Acheson" drive:

"It seems to me quite clear that the real motive of the accuser in this case is to cast discredit upon the Secretary of State of the United States. This man is not trying to get rid of known Communists in the State Department; he is hoping against hope that he will find some. Fortunately, the Secretary of State needs no defense from me. No one who knows his extraordinary record of able and disinterested public service can believe that he is in any danger from these little men. It is already obvious that in any test of personal confidence the men of honor, in both parties, will choose to stand with the Secretary.

"But there is more at stake in this matter than the rise or fall of individuals. What is at stake is the effective conduct of our foreign policy.

"Every Secretary of State, second only to his President, and alone among appointive officers of the Government, stands before the world as the representative of the United States of America. No man who holds this office can fail to feel the extraordinary responsibility he carries for service to the country and its peace. No man has a greater right to ask the sympathetic support and the cooperation of his fellow-citizens, and none is more properly exempt from the ordinary trials of politics. The man who seeks to gain political advantage from personal attack on a Secretary of State is a man who seeks political advantage from damage to his country." [1]

If I may add one further word, as a Republican, I do not agree with those who suppose that a defense of American foreign policy is somehow disloyal to the party. I do not suppose that because I consider Dean Acheson a good Secretary of State I must consider Harry Truman a good President or his Administration deserving of re-election. To put it mildly, I am of a wholly contrary mind; I think Mr. Truman an inadequate leader who is dangerously wrong on many major domestic matters. I also think that both Mr. Truman and Mr. Acheson have in the past played some politics with foreign policy, but two wrongs do not make a right, even in 1951, and it is with the greatest regret that I must admit this type of small-mindedness to be far more prevalent, at present, among Republicans than among Democrats.

---

[1] Letter to the *New York Times*, dated March 24, 1950, and appearing in the *Times* March 27, 1950.

Finally, and still as a Republican, I hold that the line of action typified by the drive to "get" Mr. Acheson is not good party policy. It is not the way to win in 1952.

I do not assert, as my own conviction, that Mr. Acheson must never resign. No man has a *right* to high office, and it is always possible in a republic for a first-rate man to lose his usefulness through no major fault of his own. Mr. Acheson is not frightened, I am sure, of the terrors of private life. What is important is that the general line of policy for which he has labored so hard should be understood for what it is. I think that he would be one of the first to recognize that there are others in the country who could carry on where he left off. But this is true only if as a people we do not turn our back on the course for which Mr. Acheson, among many others, but first among them, has labored for nearly three years.

For I will take a chance with history and bet that Mr. Acheson will be listed fifty years from now among the best of our American Secretaries of State. I think that on almost every big issue he has been at once right, energetic, and skillful.

The basic source for this record is the *Department of State Bulletin*, cited throughout as *Bulletin*. This official publication contains nearly all of Mr. Acheson's set statements on policy and a number of his extemporaneous comments, but occasionally additional material has turned up in the Department of State's Press Releases. The give-and-take of Congressional hearings has also produced a large body of material from which I have quoted extensively. Everything I have cited is of course in the public domain, but its accessibility is not automatic, and I must acknowledge with gratitude the debt which every student owes to all who help make these public records available — their editors and printers, the libraries that keep them, and the taxpayers who support their publication. I have tried to quote from these sources accurately, but in matters of punctuation and capitalization, finding that the sources themselves were far from uniform, I have sometimes pleased myself.

For help in understanding and briefly presenting the historical setting of Mr. Acheson's record, I have often turned to the serial publications of three great private organizations, and I am happy to express my debt to the World Peace Foundation, for its annual collection of *Documents on American Foreign Relations*, to the Council on Foreign Relations, for its annual account of *The United States in World Affairs*, and to the Brookings Institution, for its monthly record of *Current Developments in United States Foreign Policy*. It is also appropriate, in the year of its hundredth anniversary, to say that for the student of foreign policy the one indispensable newspaper is the *New York Times*. For several important quotations, failing to locate an official source, I have confidently cited the *Times*.

Finally, I owe much to the help of individuals. Leaving aside a great many men and women from whom I have learned in study and discussion of the issues with which this record deals, I have a special debt to the following: Paul Brooks and Austin Olney of Houghton Mifflin for encouragement, good counsel, and patience; Robert Osgood for a critical reading of the proofs and the correction of many slips; Margaret Brubeck for a skillful job on the index, and Helena Fiedler for efficient typing at all hours.

I must end with a declaration of personal interest. Mr. Acheson and my father have been close friends, across the party wall, for many years. More recently, to their shared pride, there has been a family connection. I hope to be understood when I say that I have undertaken to prepare this book not because of this connection, but in spite of it. I have done so because I really do not believe that friendship, or indirect family connection, is a bar to fair and honest defense, especially when that defense takes the form of allowing a man to speak for himself. Many men, in both parties, in the press, and even in the government, have been slow to defend Mr. Acheson, even though they know that as against those who would "get" him, he has been fundamentally right. These men have their reasons, which I do not here discuss, but I do not think that I should join their number because my brother had the good fortune to marry Mr. Acheson's daughter. Still, it is right that the connection should be stated, and having done so, I take the liberty of expressing my hope that this record may one day be read with satisfaction by a young man who is Mr. Acheson's grandson and my nephew.

McGEORGE BUNDY

Cambridge, Massachusetts
October 5, 1951

CONTENTS

INTRODUCTION

by D. S. Freeman

So MUCH MORE than the record of an individual is set forth in the pages of this volume that the reader will do well for himself if he disposes as quickly as his temperament permits of the personal element in the controversy over Secretary Acheson. Those who respect sound evidence, skillfully presented, will not be willing to close either the book or their minds until they have completed the greater part of the story. The type of American who reads history, as Wendell Phillips phrased it, not with his eyes but with his prejudices, will be in the easier position of deciding promptly whether Acheson is or is not a great Secretary, whether he should be dismissed or retained, and whether he cherishes or scorns sympathy with Communists.

When these considerations are out of the way, a student of American institutions will have time to reflect on the extent to which the unescapable expansion of the nation's foreign policy has changed the place the Department of State and its Secretary have in public administration. The background of this evolution may be followed through the ten volumes of Samuel F. Bemis's notable series *The American Secretaries of State and Their Diplomacy;* the crowded foreground begins in the fateful year 1933, when both Franklin Roosevelt and Adolf Hitler came to power.

Traditionally, the American President became his own Secretary of State in a serious crisis. Washington felt he had to take the helm in the storm raised by the affair of "Citizen Genêt" in 1793; almost every other Executive who faced a tempest did the same thing. On occasion, as in Woodrow Wilson's dealings with Secretary Lansing, this caused heartburning, but it appeared to be a policy as practicable as it was proper: If the President had to bear the responsibility, he should make the decision, and usually he could do so on the basis of what was, in appearances at least, ample and clear evidence. Such tangles as those that prompted the enunciation of the Monroe Doctrine were of rare occurrence. Within the narrow sphere of America's foreign interest or concern, comparatively brief study would give the President sufficient information with which to shape a conclusion that represented primarily sound judgment and a correct understanding of the extent to which Congress and the country would support a particular application of the principle of "no foreign entanglements."

This no longer is possible. America has assumed global responsibilities in an era of world wars. Our information must be as wide as our obligations. Otherwise we cannot cope with diplomacy more devious than that of Talleyrand, and with alliances more selfishly cunning and infinitely more dangerous than those of the eighteenth century. A statesman cannot take it for granted in 1951 that certain minimum standards of international honor will be observed by all the "European Powers." Repudiation of democracy by the dictators carried with it the abandonment of the ethics that made the crude processes of self-government safe. The "rule of the lie" succeeded the rule of law in a great part of the world. Mastery of the essential principles that should guide a few people's policy in dealing with even one of the totalitarian states has become a life work for any man. If a President is now to be his own Secretary of State he can be nothing else. All the "briefing" the ablest staff can give him may not suffice to prevent a ruinous blunder.

The Secretary must be, for these reasons, the active head of a large investigative and operating service, and not a chief clerk of a somnolent bureau. He must be Bishop, not curate. A President must have a Secretary of State whom he can trust and not one whom he easily may supersede in an emergency. Selection of a proper head of the State Department consequently is one of the most important single duties of the President. In the first seven decades of government under the Constitution of 1787, six of the fifteen Presidents had been Secretary of State under some other Chief Executive. Since James Buchanan, who served with Polk, no Secretary of State has become President, though at least half a dozen have sought, and several have won nomination. For the future, the probability is that the office will not have a corridor that leads to the White House. The unpopular character of much that a Secretary of State must do in an era of inflamed passions may destroy his political "availability." His duties, in addition, are going to absorb his energies so completely that he will not have time for "building fences." More fundamentally, the qualities of mind demanded of a competent Secretary of State must be so highly specialized that they literally may be a disqualification for the Presidency.

Many of the new requirements of the office are dangerous exactions. The Secretary must be independent but he cannot be detached. He must not be subservient to Congress, nor can he afford to be defiant of it. Superior ability must not be an affront. The Secretary must know thoroughly and must supervise vigilantly his incredibly expanded organization. At the same time that he encourages initiative, he cannot neglect discipline. He must be sure that he runs the machine and that the machine does not run him. These are things that must be regarded in every large administrative organization. They probably are no worse in the subordinate levels of the Department of State than in other major administrative agencies except insofar as intellectual endowment, untroubled tenure and official isolation may create a certain snobbery. The special problems a Secretary of State may be compelled to face in the future appear to an outsider to include, among others: (1) the continued maintenance of correct relations with the President; (2) co-operation with Congress; (3) a sound policy of recruitment; (4) the improved interpretation of intelligence reports; and (5) the establishment of a proper liaison with the Department of Defense.

On the first of these points, future Secretaries can scarcely hope for a better situation than has existed between Acheson and President Truman. The danger is that another President of loyalties less pronounced may seek once again to be his own Secretary of State, or that a Secretary of prestige, given a free hand, may have ambitions to manage his Chief. A second William H. Seward of the spring of 1861 might produce a like explosion.

Co-operation with Congress may be, in some respects, more difficult for the Secretary of State than for the head of any other Department, as distinguished from independent offices directly responsible to the President. In the Senate, not more than two or three members usually profess any specialized knowledge of such a matter as oil production, flood control, or the like, but nearly always there are at least twenty who consider themselves experts on foreign affairs. Senator William E. Borah, ambitious to run the State Department from the floor of Congress, has had many successors in spirit. A Secretary who has to deal with these gentlemen may expect his troubles to increase when partisan politics or national emotionalism becomes entangled in foreign policy.

In this respect, those who read this volume half a century hence will not be able to recapture the humor that observers found in Secretary Acheson's appearances before Congressional committees. Most of the members gave him a fair hearing and, when they questioned him, did so with consideration. A few had scant regard for the parliamentary counterpart of the Marquis of Queensberry's rules, yet they frothed in anger when Acheson found it difficult to conceal his contempt for the contemptible. Any distortion of statement was permissible if it was directed against him; but if he did not spell out the last letter of the obvious in answer, there were mumblings about half-truths. He had to fight, so to say, with one hand tied behind him. The handicap of being the gentleman cost him at least one lap before he got underway. Even at that, the only bet of any interest was on the time he would require to overcome that handicap and, with cold courtesy, to leave an adversary to swallow the dust of the dispute. Few of the critics who stood up to him through one committee hearing had particular relish for another bout. If they kept their grievance, they also kept their distance. A less able successor may find his road a little easier for the very reason that his intellectual level will not produce the familiar growl that "Acheson's too damned smart."

Wise recruitment is a continuing and complex problem for a country that has taken over most of Britain's police duties without having ready the equivalent of that nation's Colonial Service. There is danger, on the one hand, of enlisting persons of half competence and, on the other, of bringing into the Department highly intelligent men who by their very training may seem a supercilious class rather than a disciplined corps. It is not easy to find men who have uncommon ability but keep the common touch. Their competence may be their undoing. For this reason, among many, State Department bureau chiefs and directors of offices must not be "typed" as if they were blood donors.

The need of diversified equipment and varying outlook may become particularly evident in the analysis of "intelligence reports." The words are used deliberately because no agent behind the Iron Curtain can content himself with writing the leisured "dispatch" of calmer times that had a certain literary flavor and an eclectic range. Every such man is made to realize now, unhappily, that he is in the enemy's country and that what he reports differs only in emphasis from formal military intelligence. How inclusive and accurate this intelligence may be, the public does not and should not know, because if the location of peepholes in the curtain is a matter of general information, the identity of those who do the peeping may be discovered. It is not even prudent to probe the contributions the State Department makes to the Central Intelligence Agency, or vice versa. The point to stress is the necessity of a critical and cumulative analysis of this information by the employment of the methods that are themselves subject to constant review. The Intelligence Service of the United States Army never was quite so bad as when those who had charge of it thought they had an error-proof synthesis. This is a familiar weakness. Almost always, the public servant most apt to become slipshod and complacent is the one whose mistakes cannot be proven. Unguided, the wheels of bureaucracy find the rut of routine — and stay in it.

Determination of proper liaison with the Department of Defense may be one of the most difficult tasks ahead of the State Department. Aid given through American diplomacy is apt to be military for some years to come, with the result that the man in the Foreign Service is likely to find himself talking in terms of tanks and planes. The electronic may be the diplomatic. General Marshall's changing service as Army Chief of Staff, Ambassador at Large, Secretary of State and then Secretary of Defense may have dimmed the line between the Departments. Inclusion of representatives of the Department of State among the students of the National War College perhaps has led some men of each group to think the work of the others simpler than it actually is. "A little learning" still "is a dangerous thing" whether of war or of diplomacy. Liaison is no substitute for technical knowledge. America doubtless gains if the shoemaker knows the maker of skis, but when he goes to work, the shoemaker now as always should stick to his last.

Some of the light of these wide-angle responsibilities of the State Department is visible between the lines of Acheson's speeches as McGeorge Bundy here presents them with skill and candor. Still more light is projected. When the dispute over Acheson's alleged condonation of radicalism has been drowned, in public forgetfulness, the changes in the functions of the Department of State during his administration will remain. Should his labors for peace prove futile, Acheson will be made the scapegoat, as the Foreign Secretary often is when war comes. If the nation escapes that infinite catastrophe, Dean Acheson will receive credit from future historians not only for what he did in negotiation but also for his courage, his wisdom and his patience in administration.

DOUGLAS SOUTHALL FREEMAN

Westbourne
Richmond, Virginia
October 3, 1951

The Pattern
of Responsibility

CHAPTER ONE

The Office and the Man

THE PRESIDENT *has, in accordance with law and with the advice and consent of the Senate, appointed a man to serve as Secretary of State to assist him in the conduct of our foreign affairs.*[1]

1. The Office

Dean G. Acheson is the fiftieth American to hold the high office of Secretary of State. Like all his predecessors, back to Thomas Jefferson, he has held the chief responsibility, under his President, for the conduct of foreign affairs. What is this responsibility?

When Thomas Jefferson became Secretary of State, in 1790 (he was delayed in Paris, as Acheson has been, too), he had five men to help him. Together with a few ministers and clerks abroad, these men managed the foreign relations of the United States; the whole operation cost the taxpayer a grand total of less than one hundred thousand dollars a year.

When George C. Marshall resigned as Secretary of State, at the beginning of 1949, his Department employed about eight thousand people, and its missions abroad contained another thirteen thousand; expenditures directly charged to the Department were over three hundred million dollars a year. Under the Secretary were to be found specialists in nearly every field of human knowledge, and offices for the consideration of problems of the most bewildering variety. The growth of the Department of State, and

---

[1] Address at the University of California, Berkeley, California, March 16, 1950 (*State Department Bulletin*, XXII, p. 473).

1

the rapid expansion of American interests in world affairs, had brought with them a perennial problem of administration and organization.

Rapid and extreme as its growth had been, however, the Department of State remained one of the smaller agencies of Government, after Labor the smallest of Cabinet Departments. The real measure of growth was not in the numbers of its staff, but in the size of its problems. For these there is no ready measure. The money spent on defense and foreign programs in 1790 was perhaps a million dollars, and in 1948 it was well over twenty billions, but money is no true yardstick here. The difference to be measured is the difference between a small new nation, with a continent to win and a life to make, and a great world power, one of the greatest in history, increasingly committed to the leadership of free men in a contest with the slave power of Soviet Communism.

Yet this contrast, however striking, was perhaps of less importance than the basically unchanging character of the office of Secretary of State. Jefferson and his handful of clerks, and Marshall with his thousands of men and billions of dollars, separated by a century and a half of fantastic industrial and scientific change, were doing the same job. The administrative problems might grow, and the conditions of the work might vary — there remained a great constant: The Secretary of State was and still is senior member of the Cabinet, the chief adviser and spokesman on foreign policy, to and for the President, before the nation and the world. The heart of this great task has not changed since Thomas Jefferson's day. It is to define and point the course of policy — always under the President — so as to serve, in combination, the national interest and the national ideals; to define, to point, and then to carry out.

Diplomacy, some have thought, is the sum of the functions of the State Department, but the clear tradition is greater than diplomacy; it is a tradition of high policy, and those Secretaries who have tried to duck this duty are not the ones who are remembered. In high policy, diplomacy is one instrument — a great and often determining means to an end, having particular importance for the Department of State as an instrument for which it was directly responsible. But policy has, necessarily, other means; there is the economic — the ways and means of production, and the use of wealth in its broadest sense; there is the matter of information — what men know or think they know is often vital, and here too the maker of policy has an instrument that he dare not ignore. Finally, there is military strength, to deter, to encourage, to support, and if need be to defeat. These elements of action are so many and so closely entwined that in the end the decisions go back to the nation as a whole, and to its elected leaders, in Congress and in the White House. But the highest official who is called to give his whole mind and effort to these matters, the man whose very title is a mark of this concern and duty, is the Secretary of State.

The reader may think this a high estimate of the function of the Secretary of State in ordinary circumstances, more of a statement of theory than practice. Certainly he will be right if he remarks that the elevated description we have given does not always match the facts. He will be right too if he remarks that in America, a country famous for her jealousy of distinction, the man must make the office, more often than not; no one can claim for the office of Secretary of State the peculiar dignity that invests the Supreme Court and the White House. Yet even on this pragmatic test it is no small office; it has been held by men whose names ring with the authentic note of American greatness — Jefferson, Madison, J. Q. Adams, Clay, Calhoun, Webster, Seward, Fish, Hay, Root, Hughes, Stimson, Hull, and Marshall. And let us pause briefly with this last name, for no man in the history of the office has handed on a larger pair of shoes.

It was for his magnitude, indeed, that General Marshall was appointed. When Secretary Byrnes resigned, at the end of 1946, the Democratic President faced a world crisis and a Republican Congress. It was essential that his Secretary of State be a man commanding general confidence, and free from the contamination of energetic partisanship. The approval of his choice was overwhelming. For two years General Marshall was Secretary of State, and when he retired, in temporary but serious ill health, he still held the confidence of both parties in abounding measure. Moreover, he had turned the "patience and firmness" of his predecessor into firmness and action. This was of course not a purely personal achievement, but it is only the small-minded (and the General himself) who have ever objected to the fact that the great new step of these years was called the Marshall Plan. Not all of General Marshall's policies had full public approval, of course, and not all his public standing was extended to his Department — but it is hard to avoid the conclusion that the office of Secretary of State, as he left it, was a high one. Certainly this was the view of his successor and former subordinate.

It was to this office, with this tradition, and this last holder, that the President, on January 7, 1949, nominated Dean G. Acheson of Maryland.

2. Nomination and Confirmation

It has been remarked of Dean Acheson that he is the best prepared and least known man ever to be appointed Secretary of State. To the historian, recalling J. Q. Adams for preparation, and E. B. Washburne for obscurity, this may seem an extreme view, but the comment has its point. Acheson was not, in early 1949, a great public figure or a leading politician; he was primarily a professional — a professional lawyer, and by a series of government jobs, at least a semi-professional public servant. He had served in the State Department for six years, as Assistant Secretary and Under Secretary, and in those years he had been a participant in the forming of policies which by early 1949 were under retrospective debate. His appointment was greeted with approval by most of the sober press, but he had critics — indeed he had enemies. In the days after he was nominated these critics and enemies were not slow in expressing themselves, and the Senate Foreign Relations Committee decided to hold open hearings before reporting on his nomination. At these hearings Acheson himself was the first and only witness, except for a brief and energetic endorsement from his former superior, ex-Secretary Stettinius.

It is my purpose to consider this hearing in some detail, since it shows Acheson's own response to charges typical of a vast number which we shall not have time to discuss. The mud factories of politics are never shut down, and they have worked overtime on Dean Acheson, but no modern statesman has ever faced his critics more often or at greater length, and charges which have not been made to his face are hardly worthy of attention.[2]

The first questions at the hearing were simply biographical:

> The Committee met, pursuant to call, in room 318 of the Senate Office Building at 10.30 A.M., Senator Tom Connally (chairman of the committee) presiding.

[2] A good many of the more extreme and absurd accusations will be answered indirectly by the facts of the record that follow in later chapters, but it seems best to limit our direct attention, throughout, to those charges which Acheson himself has been called on to answer directly. Presumably those who have "lost confidence" in him — and many of his senatorial questioners have been among them — would not miss a chance to find out at first hand how much of what they believe is true; so if they do not discuss with Acheson the more fantastic charges, we may assume they do not believe them.

Present: Senators Connally (chairman), George, Thomas of Utah, Tydings, Pepper, Green, McMahon, Fulbright, Vandenberg, Wiley, Smith of New Jersey, Hickenlooper, and Lodge.

Also present: Senators Jenner, Thye, Knowland, and Mundt.

THE CHAIRMAN. Will the committee come to order, please?

This hearing is on the question of the nomination by the President of Mr. Dean Acheson as Secretary of State. . . .

. . . Mr. Acheson, will you detail to the committee your background and your former service in the Department, and briefly recount your qualifications from our viewpoint?

MR. ACHESON. Well, I can recount my experience, Mr. Chairman.

I was born in Connecticut. I was educated at Yale College; before that at Groton School, then at the Harvard Law School. After service in the Navy here in the first World War I was employed by the Department of Justice of the United States as law clerk to Mr. Justice Brandeis. After serving under him for two years, I entered the practice of law in Washington with the firm of which I am still a member.

In 1933, I left the practice of law from May to November to become Under Secretary of the Treasury. In November I returned to the practice of law.[3]

In 1939 and 1940 I served, at the request of the Attorney General of the United States, as the chairman of the Attorney General's committee on administrative procedure, which made its report in 1940, a report which was subsequently of some use to the Congress, I believe, in legislation on the subject of administrative procedure.

In 1941 President Roosevelt nominated me, and the Senate confirmed me, as Assistant Secretary of State. I was assigned the task of economic matters in the State Department. I continued in that work until December of 1944, when Secretary Stettinius assigned me to the work of representing the Department of State on the Hill in matters which came before the Congress.

In August 1945 I retired from that post and was nominated and confirmed as Under Secretary of State. I held that position until the 1st of July 1947, on which date I resigned and returned to private life. At the present moment I have no Government connection except the one on the Commission organized under an act of Congress at the last session

[3] Acheson resigned because of disagreement with the monetary policies of President Roosevelt.

called the Commission on the Organization of the Executive Branch of the Government. I was appointed a member of that Commission by President Truman, and am now serving as its Vice-Chairman under ex-President Hoover. . . .[4]

The most important question asked during the hearing was this one by Senator Vandenberg: "You are well aware of the fact that underlying this whole discussion is a rather universal debate regarding our policy toward Soviet Russia. I am wondering whether . . . you can draw on your own past record in making some sort of statement to the committee on the general subject."

Acheson's answer was a long one, and we must summarize it.[5] He began by noting that part of the concern people were feeling "has to do with the worry, the regret of many people, that the President must lose the powerful help and support of General Marshall . . . the great figure, as the President has said, of the war period." No one could take General Marshall's place, but "someone who has worked under him [as Acheson had done] can do his best, with the strength and ability which is given to him, to follow General Marshall's example." He went on to note that he thought he knew some thing "of the need in American foreign policy for steadiness and continuity," and that he had learned, in years of work in the State Department, "something about the function of an adviser to his chief — that that function was to be frank and forthright and vigorous in counsel; that it was to be energetic and loyal in accepting decisions and carrying them out."

Then, since he and the Senators agreed that he should not discuss future policy or problems he would face as Secretary, Acheson went back over his record, particularly with a view to answering charges that he had been an appeaser. These charges seemed to him "so incredible that I can't believe that even disinterested malevolence could think them up."

By quoting from speeches made in earlier years, he showed that for more than ten years he had been an outspoken opponent of appeasement; he had always urged strength, responsibility, and support for collective security. In 1939 he had said specifically that "the consequences of Russo-German and Japanese victories in terms of our own lives are too serious to permit indifference."

---

[4] This and following quotations in this section are from Hearing, *Nomination of Dean G. Acheson*, Senate, Committee on Foreign Relations, 81st Congress, 1st Session, January 13, 1949.
[5] For the full discussion see the *Hearing*, pp. 17–24.

It was true, of course, that he had hoped, in 1945, that there might be postwar cooperation with the Soviet Union, and he made no attempt to deny it. On the other hand he had been early with warnings of the danger posed by postwar Soviet attitudes and policies. He was able to show that a speech for which he had been criticized, delivered in November, 1945, had been regarded as hostile by the Communists, for while he had spoken of the fact that America and Russia could be friends, he had specifically warned that this fact did not make them so, and had appealed for a lifting of what later became known as the Iron Curtain. In early 1947, he had won a direct and official protest from Moscow when he publicly described Soviet policy as "aggressive and expanding"; this was the strongest statement made up to that time by a high official of the government. And Senators present knew (Acheson did not take time to tell them) that he had played a leading role in the formulation of the Truman Doctrine, under which America took her first firm stand against armed Communist subversion. Later, in executive session, he provided the Committee with a succinct statement of his current view of Soviet Communism; this statement will be found at the head of the discussion of this subject in the next chapter.

Acheson's view on Soviet Russia was almost the only subject discussed in the open hearing which bore directly on foreign policy. The rest of it was concerned with questioning on those parts of his opinions and associations from which critics had drawn the conclusion that he was not a fit nominee for the high office of Secretary of State. Probably the most explosive and sensational of the hostile charges was that he was in some way stained by association with Alger Hiss. Since the Hiss matter was revived in still more emotional fashion a year later, and since Acheson's supposed sympathy with the crime of which Hiss was convicted is still one of the major themes of his opposition, it seems well to leave the whole matter to later detailed discussion. Here it is enough to include that part of the testimony which turned on the general question of attitudes toward subversive activity in the Department of State.

SENATOR VANDENBERG. Several other Senators have said to me that the chief thing they want to know from this inquiry, and this relates in a corollary fashion to the Hiss matter, is whether unhampered efforts will continue to search out whatever may be left of subversive personnel, if any, in the State Department. One Senator [Mundt] has been publicly quoted as follows:

"I would like to be certain that Mr. Acheson would continue to give

Assistant Secretary of State John Peurifoy the free hand given by
Secretary Marshall in cleaning out of the State Department all remnants of the Communist cells now known to have been operating there."

That involves several assumptions which I do not ask you to pass on,
but you will gather from the inquiry what the general interest of these
Senators is, and I would be very glad to have you make your own comment as to your own interest, pro or con, in continuing an active effort of
this nature.

MR. ACHESON. I will be very glad to do so. I am interested in the
concern of the Senator that Mr. Peurifoy should not be hampered by
any action of mine. I think it might be of interest to the committee to
know that Mr. Peurifoy was my assistant prior to the time that I became
Under Secretary of State. It was on my recommendation to General
Marshall that he in turn recommended to the President that Mr. Peurifoy should be made an Assistant Secretary of State and put in charge of
this work. For the six months that he held that position while I was
Under Secretary of State, he reported to me, and the actions which he
took were actions which he and I worked out together.

So far as his future status is concerned, I think both he and I would
not care to make public commitments. I think Mr. Peurifoy has no
concern about his future.

Do you wish me to go further? Does that throw light on the matter?

SENATOR VANDENBERG. I think it throws light on the matter. Obviously the specific fundamental inquiry is whether you will have a
concern to persist in identifying any subversive or disloyal activities in
the Department such as are alleged in respect to some of these gentlemen, and whether or not your interest is to legitimately continue that
sort of screening for the purpose of totally protecting the loyalty character of the State Department.

I almost hesitate to ask you the question, lest it carry the inference
that you would not be interested.

MR. ACHESON. I think the simplest way to dispose of it is to say, of
course I would be interested in continuing it.

THE CHAIRMAN. In other words, you do not now, and have not in
the past, wanted any disloyal or subversive characters in the State
Department.

MR. ACHESON. That is true, Senator.

SENATOR VANDENBERG. But, Mr. Secretary, without prejudging the

Alger Hiss matter, it does develop, does it not, that things have happened in respect to State Department personnel which have been totally dumfounding to many officers of the Department, so that we are put on notice that everything always isn't quite as happy as it seems upon the surface?

MR. ACHESON. Senator, I agree with you that neither you nor I should comment in any way upon the matter of Mr. Alger Hiss, which is now before a United States court. I agree with you that the matters of security are of first importance, and that there is no step which should not be taken in order to make secure the State Department in its conduct of foreign affairs.

SENATOR VANDENBERG. That is a perfectly satisfactory answer.[6]

One other set of questions may be included here, simply because it shows Acheson's reaction to one of the more irresponsible charges against him. Here again it is noticeable that the Senator asking the question is careful not to associate himself with it:

SENATOR HICKENLOOPER. It has been claimed that in connection with the Marzani case, which I believe went to the Supreme Court — I do not make this as my statement — you were very much opposed to the prosecution of the Marzani case, and expressed yourself as hostile to the action.[7]

MR. ACHESON. That amazes me, because I didn't think I knew anything about the case. Do you mean that I was opposed to it when I was Under Secretary? I do not know what the case is, Senator, but I have no recollection of being opposed to it or for it, or of having anything to do with it.

One of the things I would like to state — whether this man has any connection with this I do not know — I have seen it stated in the press that I was opposed to and brought about the dismissal of some of the prosecutions in connection with the Amerasia case. Is that the matter you are discussing?

That statement is totally and completely untrue. That occurred

[6] *Hearing*, pp. 12–13.
[7] Carl Aldo Marzani was convicted in 1947 of falsifying his record as a Communist in obtaining a government job. He was originally an employee of the Office of Strategic Services, and when his office was transferred to the State Department, in 1946, he soon resigned.

when I was Assistant Secretary of State. Mr. Julius Holmes was then
Assistant Secretary of State in charge of administrative matters. He
consulted with me, and as a result of a lot of information which he received from the FBI he and I agreed that the only thing to do was to
request the FBI to proceed with great dispatch and arrest the people
involved, which was done.

The entire matter was then turned over to the Department of Justice
and from then on the action was in the hands of the Department of
Justice, and the grand jury here in the District of Columbia. I believe
two indictments were returned, and indictments were refused in other
cases. From that moment on the State Department had nothing to do
with those prosecutions of any sort whatever. If this is one of them,
that is my answer. If it is not, I do not know about it.[8]

A large part of the hearing was devoted to inquiries about Acheson's relationship to his law firm, a firm which had often engaged in work for foreign
clients. In particular it had been suggested that a loan granted to the
Polish government in 1946 involved some connection between Acheson as
Under Secretary and his former partners, who were counsel to the Polish
government at the time. This charge he categorically denied, noting that
the decision to grant the loan was not his alone, but that of all the interested
sections of the Department of State; it was also relevant to note that the
Polish government of this time was not the copper-bottomed Communist
régime that was later installed, but the Mikolajczyk government "and
there was, during that period, a hope that it might in some respects be free
from complete Russian domination." The loan moreover had been designed to advance economic recovery not only in Poland but in Western
Europe, which needed Polish coal. As for the fee paid to his former partners
by the Poles, it had been not $1,000,000, as one radio commentator had
said, but $50,000. The fee had been paid for technical legal work, and the
firm had had no connection whatever with the policy aspects of the matter.
And of course Acheson had not received one penny of this sum, since he had
entirely cut his connection with the firm on assuming public office.

Other questions had been raised as to the work of the firm between July,
1947 and the end of 1948, a time during which Acheson had resumed his
partnership and was practicing private law. He listed in detail all the cases
concerning foreign clients in which the firm had been concerned and pointed

[8] *Hearing*, pp. 27–28.

out that he himself had undertaken no work of this sort. Of these activities Senator Vandenberg remarked, "In that entire inventory, I find nothing which might be called lobbying employment." Acheson's reply is interesting:

> MR. ACHESON. No, Senator, you have not, and if you would permit me to make one statement, I should like to have this very clear. I have been twice in the Government of the United States, and twice returned to private life. It seemed to me mandatory on me that I should take no employment and engage in no activity which did not have the fullest possible publicity. I also felt that I should take no employment in which I had any relation with former colleagues, either in the department in which I was engaged or in any other department. That left only one resource for a lawyer, and that was to take cases which were before the courts. I did that in 1933, and I did that in 1947.
>
> It seems to me that there, everything I did or said was a matter of complete public knowledge under the supervision of a judicial officer, and although no one can ever be protected from criticism, at least you can be sure that the criticism is not just.[9]

After the public hearing, the Committee heard Acheson further in executive session, and we may suppose that the private questioning was directed more closely to questions of foreign affairs. The combined result of the public and private inquiry was favorable, for the Committee unanimously recommended his confirmation, and after a brief debate on the floor, the Senate agreed, with only six dissenting votes. We need not take time for this debate, but perhaps two statements by leading Republican members of the Committee are worth noting:

> SENATOR VANDENBERG. . . . In an unprecedented effort to make the record clear, the Senate Foreign Relations Committee in the present instance ordered a public hearing in which Mr. Dean Acheson, nominee, was asked to face all the objections which had been raised against him. He did so with what I believe his critics would concede was with complete and commendable candor. . . .
>
> Mr. Acheson has had a long and distinguished career in the public service, and particularly in foreign affairs. As a result he perhaps has a

[9] *Hearing*, p. 16.

greater and more reliable familiarity with all the vast details of our utterly complex current diplomatic problems than any other new Secretary who could be taken either from private citizenship or from another department of the Government. This is so essential a qualification that, taken by itself, it could be conclusive.

Mr. Acheson has also had a large experience in his contacts with Congress, where I believe it will again be generally conceded that he has proved himself to be one of the ablest advocates ever to appear before committees of the Senate and the House. We are all familiar with his habit of complete mastery of subjects which he brings to our attention. My own personal testimony is that in many dealings with him in the State Department, though we have had many differences of opinion, I have always found him reliable, helpful, co-operative, and trustworthy. . . . I think that Mr. Acheson's record and the committee record combine to affirmatively recommend Mr. Acheson's confirmation.[10]

SENATOR HICKENLOOPER. . . . So far as Mr. Acheson is concerned, there is not the slightest doubt in my mind as to his personal integrity. I believe it to be of an unusually high order. So far as his mental ability is concerned there is no question. I believe him to be a brilliant man. . . . He therefore brings to the office personal integrity, high ability, and unusual experience. . . . I am convinced that he is completely devoted to and is fully aware of the necessity of unswerving advancement of the principles by which our Government lives, and that he will defend these principles for us and for the world.[11]

3. The Man

We have considered the office, and we have watched the nomination and confirmation of Acheson as Secretary. Before we go on to consider his record on the job, we may stop a moment to consider the man. I have neither the skill nor the inclination to attempt a sketch of the character and quality of Acheson, and the scope of this study forbids it. Yet no record has full meaning if it is read without some picture of the person behind it, and that picture is pretty thin if all it contains is the bare facts of a career, and the praises of those who have inquired into fitness. The question re-

---

[10] *Congressional Record*, January 18, 1949, vol. 95, pt. 1, pp. 460–61.
[11] Same source, p. 466.

mains: What is he *like?* And if the careful and objective student can do without an invasion of the proper privacies of even a public man, the question has still this relevance — What is he like, as a public servant? How does he think about the problems with which he must now grapple?

"New occasions teach new duties," and so these questions never have a full answer ahead of time. In the case of Acheson, however, there is one document that repays attention — a speech delivered in 1946, which is full of the human being, yet directed to the problems of American foreign affairs. In 1946 the great problems of the postwar period were still incompletely evident; men still hoped for a real international control of atomic energy, and for a reasonably early and decent settlement with the Soviet Union. Yet what is remarkable about this particular speech is the degree to which it deals with persistent elements in the pattern of policy — with the questions of resolution, realism, and effort which are still so important. Still more striking, perhaps, is the speaker's discussion of the modern demagogue and his threat to freedom. And on all these points the tone and temper are personal. There is no need for me to apply adjectives to the mind that is here revealed; the reader can judge for himself. Acheson is talking to a meeting of the Associated Harvard Clubs in Boston, on June 4, 1946:

Life for all of us has been so concentrated on the immediate in these past years — each day with its pressing task; each meeting with its agenda; each conversation with its urgent need for relevancy — that one faces a gathering which is not going to end in a vote with a sense of emptiness. For it takes a wise man and the long habit of contemplation to spin threads from one's own innards. The rest of us can only splice those odd fragments of conclusion which this unaccustomed effort produces.

The first task is repression. One who has been serving in the field of foreign affairs must beware at a moment like this of those "pernicious abstractions," in the Lincolnian phrase, which rise in the heart and gather to the eyes — albeit only the mind's eyes. Sovereignty, security — in a curious way so many of them begin with "s" — selfishness, survival, sacrifice, self-executing, society, social significance, and suicide. The "inters" also dig a pit for the unwary — interdependent, international, inextricably intermingled. We turn to them from an almost biological urge to stretch from where we are to somewhere brighter, like a sprout coming through the earth. But speeches in which they appear usually portray a mood rather than a thought, and are apt to end with a paraphrase of the closing sentence of the Gettysburg address.

If one is to spin from his own visceral wisdom, he must say, first, "I shall not be a fake"; and, second, "What do I know, or think I know, from my own experience and not by literary osmosis?" An honest answer would be, "Not much; and I am not too sure of most of it."

One thing, however, seems pretty sure — that the tasks which grow out of the relations of our country with other countries are hard ones. This does not come from any lack of ideas and suggestions. These pour out on the unhappy laborer in this vineyard in a generous, if varied, flood. Mr. Morrow remarked that there were two classes of people: those who talked about things, and those who did things. And he added that the competition in the second group was not keen.

No, the difficulty does not come from any meagerness of choice of direction or method. It comes pretty directly from the medium with which one works, the human animal himself. Senator Barkley observes resignedly from time to time that one man has about as much human nature as another — and perhaps a little more. And so, when we tackle the fundamental task in the conduct of our foreign affairs, which Mr. Hull has described as focusing the will of a hundred and forty million people on problems beyond our shores, we find ourselves in trouble. The trouble comes from the fact that people are focusing on a hundred and forty million other things — or, more accurately not focusing on them, but getting very much mixed up with and about them — and the people in other countries are doing the same thing.

The reasons why this is so lie beyond the limits of my knowledge and so talk about them is banned by my self-restraining ordinance. But there is one contributing factor which I have observed and believe causes an immense amount of trouble. Man has been poking about with his own mind and has found out too much about it for his own wisdom to handle.

For a long time we have gone along with some well-tested principles of conduct: That it was better to tell the truth than falsehoods; that a half truth was no truth at all; that duties were older than and as fundamental as rights; that, as Justice Holmes put it, the mode by which the inevitable came to pass was effort; that to perpetrate a harm was always wrong no matter how many joined in it but to perpetrate it on a weaker person or people was particularly detestable; and so on.

Our institutions are founded on the assumption that most people follow these principles most of the time because they want to, and the institutions work pretty well when this assumption is true. More recently, however, bright people have been fooling with the machinery in the human head and they have discovered quite a lot. For instance, we know that association and repetition play a large part in the implanting of ideas. This has unexpected results. We no longer engage in the arduous task of making a better mouse trap to induce the world to beat a path to our door. We associate with our product a comely and exposed damsel, or a continued story which speeds daily through the air rejected only by the ionosphere.

So far the matter does not seem too serious. But when Hitler introduced new refinements they were serious. It appears to be true that people can be united most quickly by hatred of a comparatively weak group in the community and by the common sense of guilt which accompanies outrages against its members. We have had some experience of this ourselves. With this as a start and all the perverted ingenuity of propaganda, which uses familiar and respected words and ideas to implant the exact opposite standard and goal, a whole people have been utterly confused and corrupted. Unhappily neither the possession of this knowledge nor the desire to use it was confined to Hitler.

Others dip from this same devil's cauldron. The politician who knows that notoriety survives the context is anxious to be mentioned as often as possible. The perfect tool at hand is controversy. For controversy is far more diverting than exposition, and, therefore, the press and radio are more than willing to assist. They have been known to pitch some balls of their own. And no controversy is safer than one with the foreigner, the outsider. His defenders at once become suspect. So a field which is difficult enough, where more than anywhere widespread agreement is essential, becomes a peculiar prey to controversy.

There is also the new psychology of crisis — exemplified by the common expression, "to build a fire under him." Now in my archaic profession to do that is to commit arson; and the law takes a dim view of it. But abroad and at home it has been observed that to obtain relief from the unendurable produces a quite irrational sense of well-being. Therefore, the unendurable situation is created so that one may profit from the circumstances of relief.

It is, I believe, a Russian fable which recounts the advice given by a priest to a peasant who insisted that he was about to commit suicide because his life was so unbearable. The advice was for a week to move his goats and chickens into his own hut, and then to move them out. The advice, of course, was sound. Life took on a definitely rosier hue and the idea of suicide was abandoned. It is not recommended as a sound practice, like swinging two bats before going to the plate.

The evil is not merely that the perpetrator of the crisis misjudges his own skill and involves us all in disaster, but that, as with all these practices, a Gresham's law of politics and morals sets in. The baser practice drives out the better. The cheaper, the more fantastic, the more adapted to prejudice, the more reckless the appeal or the maneuver, the more attention, and excited attention, it receives. And the less chance there is that we shall listen to the often difficult analysis of the facts and the always difficult consideration of duty.

It is evil for shrewd men to play on the minds and loyalties and fears of their fellows as on an instrument. It produces not only the degradation of the democratic dogma about which Brooks Adams warned, but the degradation of all mankind everywhere, paralyzing the very centers of moral action, until these oceans of cunning words wash through the minds of men like the sea through the empty portholes of a derelict.

If the need for a remedy seems urgent, it might be sought both through attaining an intellectual immunity to this virus by identifying and isolating it and also by making it plain to its carriers at home and abroad by the plainest words and acts that they are not fit company for morally healthy people.

These practices, I said a moment ago, seemed to me a contributing factor in the trouble we have in focusing the will of people on problems beyond our shores. Perhaps, even more than this, they have contributed to those problems. If it is true, as I believe it is, that the continued moral, military and economic power of the United States is an essential factor in the organization of peace, then these matters about which we have been talking have greatly contributed to our troubles. They lie at the root of the hysteria which has wrought such havoc with our armed services, and continues to do so. They lie at the root, also, of the difficulty which we have in using our great economic power, in our own interest, to hasten recovery in other countries along lines which are essential to our own system. They have contributed largely to the weakening of our economic strength itself. The slogans, "Bring the Boys Home!" and "Don't Be Santa Claus!" are not among our more gifted or thoughtful contributions to the creation of a free and tranquil world.

This seems to me true for the simplest of all reasons, which is that the sensible way to strengthen a structure is not to weaken its most essential parts. I am often told that the way to solve this or that problem is to leave it to the United Nations. But it seems to me inescapable that if they are, or we hope will be, united, they are still nations; and no more can be expected of this forum for political adjustment than the sum total of the contributions. If these are wise and steadfast and supported by strength determined to organize peace, the results will be good. But, in the Arab proverb, the ass that went to Mecca remained an ass, and a policy has little added to it by its place of utterance.

So, when one sees our military forces disrupted, one is entitled to ask whether the considerations which led to this were more valid and urgent than the sense of steadiness and confidence which our forces gave and would have continued to give to millions all over a badly shattered and uncertain world. The answer which one most often gets does not go to the merits of the question. It goes to another of our devices for finding out what we think — opinion polls. It appears that we have become extroverts, if of a somewhat hypochondriac type, and ascertain our state of health by this mass temperature taking. Fortunately this was not one of the hardships of Valley Forge.

So, too, those who must labor daily at the crossings where the lives of many people meet understand better than they can expound that their tasks can be lightened but not performed by a resolution drafted and passed at Hunter College [where the Security Council was meeting]. These tasks are more deeply affected by how we and others master the intricacies of the production and movement of food and other goods, with how successfully we deal with labor problems and inflation, with credits, with the wise use of natural resources. They even involve the most national of all problems — the efficiency of the administrative and legislative processes.

At this point I am aware of voices which say that national sovereignty is the root of the whole trouble and that we must do away with all of that. It may be so, but to a sinking heart there comes the admonition of Old Hickory at the battle of New Orleans, apocryphally reported by Paul Porter — "Boys, elevate them guns a little lower." It may be that the way to solve a difficult problem is to transfer one's attention to an insoluble one. But I doubt it.

Rather it seems to me the path of hope is toward the concrete, toward the manageable, in the first instance. A forum there should be, and there is, for the adjustment, as best we can, of those critical issues which threaten the peace. But, when we come to tasks of common management, it seems wise to start with those which through hard and intelligent work can be reduced to manageable dimensions and governed by pretty specific rules and standards — like the monetary fund, the bank, the trade organization, and, if possible, the control of atomic energy. These are hard enough in all conscience. I have chewed on them and know their toughness and the frailty of the task forces and their plans. But the jobs are doable with good sense and good luck.

To do these jobs and conduct our own affairs with passable restraint and judgment — the type of judgment, as Justice Brandeis used to say, which leads a man not to stand in front of a locomotive — will be an achievement. Moreover, it will be an achievement which will profoundly modify many situations which now concern us, including — and I am now guessing — our relations with the Soviet Union. Problems which are difficult against a background of confusion, hesitation and disintegration may well become quite possible of solution as national and international institutions and activities become healthy and confident and vigorous in a large part of the world. Certainly our troubles will not increase.

But it is a long and tough job and one for which we as a people are not particularly suited. We believe that any problem can be solved with a little ingenuity and without inconvenience to the folks at large. We have trouble-shooters to do this. And our name for problems is significant. We call them headaches. You take a powder and they are gone. These pains about which we have been talking are not like that. They are like the pain of earning a living. They will stay with us until death. We have got to understand that all our lives the danger, the uncertainty, the need for alertness, for effort, for discipline will be upon us. This is new to us. It will be hard for us. But we are in for it and the only real question is whether we shall know it soon enough.[12]

[12] Address to the Associated Harvard Clubs, Boston, Massachusetts, June 4, 1946 (State Department Press Release 377, June 3, 1946).

CHAPTER TWO

The Soviet Threat
and the American Response

WE ARE FACED *with a challenge and a threat to the very basis of our civilization and to the very safety of the free world, the only kind of world in which that civilization can exist.*[1]

American foreign policy is a seamless web; no one place is the perfect starting point, and no one problem can be clearly distinguished from any other and considered solely "on its own merits." For this reason all attempts to treat the subject face a dilemma: if you try to cover it all at once, you become involved in indescribable confusion; if you try anything simpler, you inevitably oversimplify. Yet oversimplification is preferable to indescribable confusion, and so most students prefer to consider these matters one subject at a time. On this basis, the best place to begin is with the Soviet Challenge. Acheson himself has stated a good reason:

> The main obstacle to peace is easy to identify, and there should be no mistake in anyone's mind about it. That obstacle has been created by the policies of the Soviet Government.[2]

In this chapter then, we shall be concerned with Acheson's view on two matters — first, the Soviet threat, and second, the basic outlines of the American response.

[1] Address to the American Society of Newspaper Editors, April 22, 1950 (*Bulletin,* XXII, p. 674).
[2] Address to the General Assembly of the United Nations, September 20, 1950 (*Bulletin,* XXIII, p. 523).

1. The Nature of Soviet Communism

Communism as a doctrine is fatal to a free society and to human rights and fundamental freedoms. Communism as an aggressive factor in world conquest is fatal to independent governments and to free peoples.[3]

Because so much of American policy is governed by the great threat from Soviet Russia, Acheson has talked more on this topic than on any other. There is, therefore, almost no need for any editorial service other than that of condensation and selection. The following passages give the basic pattern of views expressed with the greatest frequency.

A little over thirty years ago there came into power in one of the great countries of the world a group of people who ... claim the right to speak on your behalf. That claim was based not on any constitutional procedure, or on any expression of the will of those whose representatives they professed to be. It was based on a claim which those men made to a monopoly of the knowledge of what was right and what was wrong for human beings. They further profess that their claim is based on a body of thought taken over in large part from the writings of a mid-nineteenth-century German economist and theorist, Karl Marx.

I have no desire to debate here the errors of one version or another of what is today called "Marxism." But I think it must be recognized, in the light of the experience of the last hundred years, that many of the premises on which Marx based his thought have been belied by the known facts of what has actually happened in the decades since Marx made his studies. Marx's law of capitalist accumulation, his law as to the rate of profit, his prediction of the numerical decline of the middle classes and of the increase of the class struggle: none of these calculations had been borne out by the experience of the societies of the West. Marx did not foresee the possibility of democratic solutions.

Furthermore, the body of doctrine now professed by the Moscow-controlled Communists is only tenuously identified with Marx's writ-

[3] To the Senate Committee on Foreign Relations, in executive session, January 13, 1949, quoted to the Senate by Senator Arthur H. Vandenberg, January 18, 1949 (*Congressional Record*, vol. 95, pt. I, p. 460).

ings and is largely overlaid with Russian imperialism.[4] We certainly cannot accept the thesis that such a doctrine can serve as the justification for the right of a small group of individuals to speak for the great masses of human beings who have never selected them as their spokesmen and whose own opinions they have never consulted.

Now, for three decades this group of people, or their successors, have carried on as the rulers of that same great country. They have always, at the same time, maintained the pretense that they are interpreters of the aspirations of peoples far beyond their borders. In the light of that professed philosophy, they have conducted, as masters of the Russian state, a foreign policy which now is the center of the most difficult and troublesome problems of international affairs, problems designed to keep the peoples of the world in a state of deepest apprehension and doubt. In addition to this, they have operated within the limits of the Soviet state on the basis of a domestic policy founded, they say, on the same philosophy.[5]

Soviet Communism does not permit diversity of ideas. Freedom, this doctrine says, is an evil thing. It says that people who exercise freedom of thought, people who dare to depart from the doctrine laid down in the Kremlin in Moscow are criminals. It puts such people behind bars or it puts them to death. . . .[6]

[Similarly] no state is friendly which is not subservient. An official report to the Cominform defines an internationalist as one who "unreservedly, without any hesitation, and unconditionally, is ready to defend the U.S.S.R." Anyone who rejects this notion is a warmonger. Even a Communist state cannot live on friendly terms with the Kremlin unless it shows complete subservience and submission. . . . The very prospect of peaceful cooperation among non-Soviet states to defend their own interests and solve their own problems is anathema to the Kremlin. . . .[7]

[It is] made amply clear in Bolshevist political writings that the holding

[4] For further emphasis on the component of old-fashioned Russian imperialism in the Soviet threat, see pp. 33–34 and 291–92 below.

[5] Address at the University of California, Berkeley, California, March 16, 1950 (*Bulletin*, XXII, pp. 473–74).

[6] Address to American Society of Newspaper Editors, April 22, 1950 (*Bulletin*, XXII, p. 674).

[7] Statement before the Senate Foreign Relations Committee and the House Foreign Affairs Committee, February 21, 1950 (*Bulletin*, XXII, p. 403, and Senate Hearings, *Extension of European Recovery*, p. 13).

of power by the rulers of the Soviet Union requires the complete sub-version or forcible destruction of the countries now free of their control. They are encouraged to act on this belief by the illusion that, in so doing, they are helping along the inevitable course of history. According to the Bolshevist interpretation, history points to the collapse of non-Soviet states and their replacement by Soviet-style and Soviet-controlled states. Conflict is anticipated in Bolshevik theory as an inevitable part of the process. . . .[8]

This fanatical doctrine dominates one of the great states in the world, a state which, with its satellites, controls the lives of hundreds of millions of people, and which today possesses the largest military establishment in existence. . . .[9] The hostility of Soviet intentions, if taken alone, would not produce so grave a threat. But the combination of these intentions and Soviet military power creates very grave danger to the survival of free nations and free institutions, a danger which must not be underestimated. . . .[10]

The Soviet Government raises five barriers to peace.

First, Soviet efforts to bring about the collapse of the non-Soviet world, and thereby fulfill a prediction of Soviet theory, have made genuine negotiation very difficult. The honorable representative of Lebanon, Dr. Charles Malik,[11] stated it precisely at our last Assembly when he said: "There can be no greater disagreement than when one wants to eliminate your existence altogether."

Second, the shroud of secrecy which the Soviet leaders have wrapped around the people and the states they control is a great barrier to peace. This has nourished suspicion and misinformation, in both directions. It deprives governments of the moderating influence of contact between peoples. It stands in the way of the mutual knowledge and confidence essential to disarmament.

Third, the rate at which the Soviet Union has been building arms and

---

[8] Address to the National Council of Churches of Christ in the United States, November 29, 1950 (*Bulletin,* XXIII, p. 964).

[9] Address to American Society of Newspaper Editors, April 22, 1950 (*Bulletin,* XXII, p. 674).

[10] Address to the National Council of Churches of Christ in the United States, November 29, 1950 (*Bulletin,* XXIII, p. 964).

[11] Charles Malik, a distinguished diplomat and student of philosophy, has the misfortune to share his surname, though nothing else, with Jacob Malik, the Soviet representative in the Security Council.

armies, far beyond any requirement of defense, has gravely endangered peace throughout the world. While other countries were demobilizing and converting their industries to peaceful purposes after the war, the Soviet Union and the territories under its control pushed preparation for war. The Soviet Union has forced countries to rearm for their self-defense.

Fourth, the use by Soviet leaders of the international Communist movement for direct and indirect aggression has been a great source of trouble in the world. With words which play upon honest aspirations and grievances, the Soviet leaders have manipulated the people of other states as pawns of Russian imperialism.

Fifth, the Soviet use of violence to impose its will and its political system upon other people is a threat to the peace. There is nothing unusual in the fact that those who believe in some particular social order want to spread it throughout the world. But as one of my predecessors, Secretary Adams, said of the efforts of an earlier Russian ruler, Czar Alexander, to establish the Holy Alliance, the Emperor "finds a happy coincidence between the dictates of his conscience and the interests of his empire." The combination of this international ambition and the Soviet reliance on force and violence — though it be camouflaged as civil war — is a barrier to peaceful relations. . . .[12]

[And finally,] those who hold and practice this doctrine pick out our country as the principal target of their attack. From their point of view they pick it out rightly. It is our country, with its belief in freedom and tolerance, its great productive power, its tremendous vitality, which stands between the Kremlin and dominion over the entire world. We must not forget that it is we, the American people, who have been picked out as the principal target of the Soviet Communists.[13]

2. What To Do About It

The times call for a total diplomacy equal to the task of defense against Soviet expansion and to the task of building the kind of world in which our way of life can flourish.[14]

[12] Address to the United Nations General Assembly, September 20, 1950 (*Bulletin,* XXIII, p. 524).
[13] Address to American Society of Newspaper Editors, April 22, 1950 (*Bulletin,* XXII, p. 674).
[14] Address at the University of California, Berkeley, California, March 16, 1950 (*Bulletin,* XXII, p. 478).

The response to the Soviet challenge takes many shapes in many places, but the basic outline of Acheson's policy toward the Soviet Union remains the same — and he has stated it clearly in a general form.

What course of action will enable us to maintain our freedom and bring about a peaceful resolution of this world crisis; or, if despite our best efforts aggression does take place, will provide a basis for defeating it? . . . The course of action we have chosen is to join with our allies in building the strength of the free world as a bulwark against Soviet aggression. The purpose of this strength is not aggression. It is the very opposite. It is to deter such aggression. This involves building military strength, but it requires no less the buttressing of all the other forms of power — economic, political, social and moral — and the utmost resolution and unity among the free nations of the world.[15]

In adopting this line of policy, Acheson has rejected three others. First, there is no answer in isolation.

There are several ways we could go about meeting these problems. One way would be to pull down the blinds and sit in the parlor with a loaded shotgun, waiting. I think, however, that most of us have learned that isolationism is not a realistic course of action. It does not work, and it is not cheap.

There are some who argue that isolationism would offer us a bargain-basement security. But, in the long run, it would, in fact, cost us much more to keep up that level of armament which would be required if we were to try — and it would be a vain attempt — to remain an island of security in a Soviet-dominated world.

I think the best short answer to this line of thinking was given by General George Marshall [who has] said that such a policy as this would be "psychologically wrong, militarily wrong, and just wrong generally." [16]

Second, there is no answer in appeasement.

The policy of appeasement of Soviet ambitions, which might con-

---

[15] Address to the National Council of Churches of Christ in the United States, November 29, 1950 (*Bulletin*, XXIII, pp. 964–65).
[16] Address before the Civic Federation of Dallas and the Community Course of Southern Methodist University, Dallas, Texas, June 13, 1950 (*Bulletin*, XXII p. 1038).

ceivably be another course of action open to us, is in fact an alternative form of isolationism. The result of such a policy would be to encourage Soviet aggression. It would lead to a final struggle for survival in which our moral position and our military position would have been seriously weakened. . . .[17] We must not, in our yearning for peace, allow ourselves to be betrayed by vague generalities or beguiling proffers of peace which are unsubstantiated by good faith solidly demonstrated in daily behavior. We are always ready to discuss, to negotiate, to agree, but we are understandably loath to play the role of international sucker. . . . We want peace, but not at any price.[18]

Third, there must be no "preventive war."

There is a third course of action which might be considered in earlier times and by another type of government and people than ours. That is that we should drop some atomic bombs on the Soviet Union. This course is sometimes called by the euphemistic phrase of "preventive war." All responsible men must agree that such a course is unthinkable for us. It would violate every moral principle of our people. Such a war would necessarily be incredibly destructive. It would not solve problems, it would multiply them. . . .[19]

This whole idea that war is inevitable seems to me to be completely wrong and very vicious. I remember looking back over the history of the United States not long ago and reading the terrible things that were said in the 1850's about the irrepressible conflict. It's talk like that, talk of an irrepressible conflict, talk about war being inevitable which tends to make it so. . . .[20]

War is not inevitable. It is our responsibility to find ways of solving our problems without resort to war and to exhaust every possibility in in that effort. This is what we intend to do.[21]

Thus Acheson repudiates isolationism, appeasement, and preventive war, clearly and repeatedly. Instead he has presented, and regularly argued for,

[17] Same, p. 1038.
[18] Address at the University of California, Berkeley, California, March 16, 1950 (*Bulletin*, XXII, pp. 477–78).
[19] Address before the Civic Federation of Dallas and the Community Course of Southern Methodist University, Dallas, Texas, June 13, 1950 (*Bulletin*, XXII, p. 1038).
[20] A television interview released September 10, 1950 (*Bulletin*, XXIII, p. 460).
[21] Address before the Civic Federation of Dallas and the Community Course of Southern Methodist University, Dallas, Texas, June 13, 1950 (*Bulletin*, XXII, 1038).

a fourth line of policy. This policy has a number of elements, and it does not lend itself to simple condensation. But basically the position can be summarized in the following propositions: Resist communism, and build "situations of strength"; work for an eventual settlement without war, accepting the fact that the course ahead is long, hard, and dangerous; stick to our own ideals. Each of these notions he has spelled out in some detail.

3. Resist Communism and Build Situations of Strength

The concept of resistance to Communist expansion is not complicated, but it is important to observe that Acheson has been wholly firm in this attitude throughout his term as Secretary of State (and for a long time before). Given his assessment of the nature of communism, it is not a surprising attitude, and two short quotations will be enough to make it plain:

> We are . . . determined that communism shall not by hook or crook or trickery undermine our country or any other free country that desires to maintain its freedom. . . .[22]
> Our best hope of peace lies in our ability to make absolutely plain to aggressors that aggression cannot succeed.[23]

The record on this policy is clear, and the point itself is simple. A somewhat more complex line of thought is involved in Acheson's emphasis on "situations of strength." This phrase is in some ways the key to his thinking about policy toward the Soviet Union. Acheson himself has undertaken to explain it mainly in terms of the experience of the first years after World War II.

> Let me go back a little way and give you some background to this basic premise of our foreign policy. After the war, we all hoped and believed that it was going to be possible to create a rule of law among nations by establishing a great international institution, the United Nations, which would be based on law, which could be based on the idea of

[22] Address to the American Society of Newspaper Editors, April 22, 1950 (*Bulletin*, XXII, p. 676).
[23] Address to the General Assembly of the United Nations, September 20, 1950 (*Bulletin* XXIII, p. 524).

preventing aggression and insuring the independence and right of each people to live its own independent existence. . . .[24]

It was essential to the success of this organization, as Mr. Cordell Hull had said on April 9, 1944, that the major powers recognize and harmonize their basic interests.

The foreign policy of the United States was firmly founded on the belief that this could be done. We hoped that the union of our efforts with those of our allies in time of war could be continued. To this end, we were determined to accommodate our basic interests with those of other powers.

That determination found expression in our actions.

Differences there were, but that was to be expected. We were prepared to look upon them as the natural residue of years of mutual mistrust. We were prepared to honor our wartime commitments and the security requirements of other nations. The overwhelming sentiment of our people favored settlement of our points of friction, as we regarded them, the immediate demobilization of our armed forces, and the inauguration of the new era of peace.

But, as the ominous portents grew, doubt also grew as to whether one of our late allies was, in fact, intent on co-operation. . . .

The year of the San Francisco conference was also the year in which the Soviet Union renewed intimidating pressures upon its neighbors, Iran and Turkey. It was the year in which the Soviet Union, in violation of agreements on which the ink was scarcely dry, imposed governments of its own choosing on Bulgaria and Rumania and supported the imposition of a minority régime in Poland. . . .[25]

When this drive upon Iran occurred in '45–'46 President Truman instructed the then Secretary of State, Mr. Byrnes, to go to the Security Council and fight this thing out. Mr. Byrnes did that and it resulted in the withdrawal of Soviet troops from Northern Iran and the collapse of the puppet régime which had been set up in Azerbaijan. . . .[26]

In the following year, 1946, the sequence of Soviet actions filled out an unmistakable pattern. This was the year in which the head of the Soviet state made it clear in a speech to his people that the wartime

---

[24] A television interview released September 10, 1950 (*Bulletin*, XXIII, p. 460).
[25] Address before the Harvard Alumni Association, Cambridge, Massachusetts, June 22, 1950 (*Bulletin*, XXIII, p. 14).
[26] A television interview released September 10, 1950 (*Bulletin*, XXIII, p. 461).

alliance with the non-Communist world was at an end. This speech was followed by a propaganda campaign of unrestrained hostility against our country, which has continued to this day. . . .[27]

In 1946 the President instructed the Secretary of State to support Turkey with the aid of the British and French and resist the attempt to gain control of the Straits. . . .[28]

This was the year when Soviet action in Germany foreshadowed its intention to break up the four-power control arrangement and to Sovietize the Eastern zone, which it controlled. . . .[29]

When the troubles in Germany began we started the program of unifying Germany. First of all unifying what we could by putting together the British and the American zones and then bringing the French zone in and finally creating the Republic of Western Germany. . . .[30]

The pattern was plain. Wherever the force of Soviet arms prevailed, the Soviet Union would take over virtual control. Where Soviet armed forces could not reach, the international Communist movement was used to gain control by subversion.

Three events which took place in 1947 helped to crystallize the American response to Soviet conduct.

The first of these was President Truman's message to Congress of March 12, requesting funds for the Greek-Turkish Aid Program. In his message, the President declared it to be the policy of the United States —

" . . . to support free peoples who are resisting attempted subjugation by armed minorities or by outside pressures.

" . . . We must assist free peoples to work out their own destinies in their own way." [This is the Truman Doctrine.]

The second event of 1947 was the speech of General Marshall on June 5th. [This speech was foreshadowed, in large part, by a speech delivered by Under Secretary Acheson. See pp. 46–50 below.]

Its purpose was the revival of the working economy of the world so that free institutions could exist.

Less than 1 month later, the Soviet Foreign Minister, Mr. Molotov,

[27] Address before the Harvard Alumni Association, Cambridge, Massachusetts, June 22, 1950 (*Bulletin*, XXIII, p. 14).
[28] A television interview released September 10, 1950, (*Bulletin*, XXIII, p. 461).
[29] Address before the Harvard Alumni Association, Cambridge, Massachusetts, June 22, 1950 (*Bulletin*, XXIII, p. 15).
[30] A television interview released September 10, 1950 (*Bulletin*, XXIII, p. 461).

walked out of the conference at Paris at which the European Recovery Program was launched.

That the Soviet Union would not only refuse to participate in the European Recovery Program but would also sabotage the effort was made explicit two months later at the founding of the Communist Information Bureau.

There, the Soviet delegate announced that the Soviet Union would bend every effort in order that the European Recovery Program be doomed to failure.

The Soviet effort to defeat the program did not succeed. But its decision to obstruct rather than participate did much to sharpen the cleavages of a divided world.

The third event in 1947 which helped to mark and to crystallize a development in American thinking was the London meeting of the Council of Foreign Ministers and General Marshall's report to the American people upon his return, on December the 19th.

In analyzing the reason for the frustration we had encountered in our efforts to reach an agreement with the Soviet Union on Germany, General Marshall concluded — and this was a significant step in the development of our thinking — that until the political vacuum created by the war had been filled by the restoration of a healthy European community, we would not be able to achieve any genuine agreements with the Soviet Union.

Agreements between sovereign states, General Marshall reminded us, are usually the reflection and not the cause of genuine settlements.

This was the issue, he said: We would not have a settlement until the coming months had demonstrated whether or not the civilization of Western Europe would prove vigorous enough to rise above the destructive effects of the war and restore a healthy society.[31]

Historically, then, it has been impossible to reach enduring agreement with the Soviet Union as long as Soviet leaders saw a chance to exploit "situations of weakness." And for this reason it is pointless to hope for any true settlement with the Soviet Union as long as these situations remain. It is on this line of argument that Acheson has been firm in his opposition to the notion that somehow if we only tried hard enough we could get agreements with Stalin.

[31] Address before the Harvard Alumni Association, Cambridge, Massachusetts, June 22, 1950 (*Bulletin*, XXIII, p. 15).

It has been hard for us to convince ourselves that human nature is not pretty much the same the world over. We hear it said that if we could only get Harry Truman to "get his feet under the same table" — that is the phrase used — with Joe Stalin, we would be able to iron out any international difficulty. Our own experience with people in our own communities has been such that it has seemed to us that good intentions must, in the long run, prevail — and if one proposition didn't meet with acceptance, all we had to do was to think up a better one. . . .

We must realize, however, that the world situation is not one to which there is an easy answer. The only way to deal with the Soviet Union, we have found from hard experience, is to create situations of strength. Wherever the Soviet detects weakness or disunity — and it is quick to detect them — it exploits them to the full. A show-down, in the brutal and realistic sense of resort to a military decision, is not a possible policy for a democracy. The Kremlin knows that.

We are struggling against an adversary that is deadly serious. We are in a situation where we are playing for keeps. Moreover, we are in a situation where we could lose without ever firing a shot.[32]

I don't need to go over again with you the fact that, growing out of the last war and other conditions before the war and between the wars, there have been created all over the world these situations of weakness. Every time one of those situations exists — and they exist in Asia and they exist in Europe — it is not only an invitation but an irresistible invitation for the Soviet Government to fish in those troubled waters. To ask them not to fish and to say we will have an agreement that you won't fish is like trying to deal with a force of nature. You can't argue with a river — it is going to flow. You can dam it up, you can put it to useful purposes, you can deflect it, but you can't argue with it. Therefore, we go to work, as I said, to change those situations of weakness so that they won't create opportunities for fishing and opportunities for trouble.[33]

So building situations of strength is the main business of American foreign policy as Acheson understands it. The remaining chapters of this book are

[32] Remarks made at a meeting of the Advertising Council at the White House, February 16, 1950 (*Bulletin*, XXII pp. 427–28).

[33] Extemporaneous remarks made at a press conference, February 8, 1950 (*Bulletin*, XXII, p. 274).

all concerned, in one way or another, with the varying ways and means of doing this job. Taken together, these ways and means make up what Acheson has called the Strategy of Freedom. Our present task is to connect this general undertaking with Acheson's view of long-term policy toward the Soviet Union.

4. Work for an Eventual Settlement

The situations of strength must come before the agreement. The next question is whether there is any chance of agreement even then. On this point Acheson has consistently maintained that *in the long run* the Communist and non-Communist worlds may be able to live together in the same world, without war. In other words, his anti-communism does *not* include the notion of a necessary crusade to bring about the overthrow of the Soviet régime. This aspect of his thinking and policy has been severely criticized by men who stop short of calling him a Communist sympathizer; it deserves detailed analysis. Obviously there is a basic difference between a policy which hopes for an eventual settlement and one which rests on the assumption that the world is too small for both Communists and anti-Communists.

Yet before we enquire into the affirmative aspects of this hope it will be useful to narrow the issue by pointing out two things it does *not* mean. It does not mean moral compromise; it does not mean that a peaceful settlement is certain.

There are many points in [Soviet] philosophy, and particularly in the way in which it has already been applied in practice in the Soviet Union and elsewhere, which are not only deeply repugnant to us, but raise questions involving the most basic conceptions of good and evil — questions involving the ultimate moral nature of man. There is no use in attempting to ignore or gloss over the profundity of this conflict or view.

The free society values the individual as an end in himself. It requires of him only that self-discipline and self-restraint which make the rights of each individual compatible with the rights of every other individual. Individual freedom, therefore, implies individual responsibility not to exercise freedom in ways inconsistent with the freedom of other individuals, and responsibility positively to make constructive use of freedom in the building of a just society.

In relations between nations, the prime reliance of the free society is on the strength and appeal of its principles, and it feels no compulsion sooner or later to bring all societies into conformity with it.

It does not fear, rather it welcomes, diversity and derives its strength from freedom of inquiry and tolerance even of antipathetic ideas.

We can see no moral compromise with the contrary theses of international communism: that the end justifies the means, that any and all methods are therefore permissible, and that the dignity of the human individual is of no importance as against the interest of the state.

To our minds, these principles mean, in their practical application, the arrogation to individual human leaders, with all their inevitable frailties and limitations, of powers and pretenses which most of us would be willing to concede only to the infinite wisdom and compassion of a Divine Being. They mean the police state, with all that that implies; a regimentation of the worker which is hardly distinguishable from slave labor; a loss to society of those things which appear to us to make life worth living; a denial of the fundamental truths embodied in all the great religions of the world.

Here is a moral issue of the clearest nature. It cannot be evaded. Let us make no mistake about it. . . .

It also does not follow . . . that the two systems will necessarily be able to exist concurrently. That will depend largely on them.[34]

The meaning of this last proposition is obvious. In its sharpest terms, it means that it is always possible for the Soviet Union to choose war and not co-existence. And American foreign policy must be conducted accordingly; nowhere has Acheson stated this point more forcefully and simply than in his appearance before the Russell Committee in June, 1951: "We stand ready to defend our future by force of arms if that necessity is forced upon us. But we seek to deter war if we can. . . ."[35]

If war can be averted, strength may lead to a gradual improvement in relations with the Russians.

When we have reached unity and determination on the part of the free nations — when we have eliminated all of the areas of weakness

[34] Address at the University of California, Berkeley, California, March 16, 1950 (*Bulletin*, XXIII, p. 474).

[35] Hearings, *Military Situation in the Far East*, Senate, Committee on Armed Services and Committee on Foreign Relations, 82d Congress, 1st Session, June 1, 1951, p. 1714.

that we can — we will be able to evolve working agreements with the Russians. We will not have to keep our ears to the ground in order to know when the Russians are prepared to recognize that they cannot exploit a situation to their own benefit. In the case of Berlin, when they realized that the airlift had prevented them from ousting the Allies, we had no difficulty in learning when they came to that conclusion. . . .[36]

This perspective takes into account the possibility that the Soviet Government may not be inherently and unalterably committed to standing in the way of peace, and that it may some day accept a live-and-let-live philosophy.

The Soviet leaders are realists, in some respects at least. As we succeed in building the necessary economic and defensive military strength, it will become clear to them that the non-Soviet world will neither collapse nor be dismembered piece-meal. Some modification in their aggressive policies may follow, if they then recognize that the best interests of the Soviet Union require a cooperative relationship with the outside world.

Time may have its effect. It is but thirty-three years since the overthrow of the Czarist régime in Russia. This is a short time in history. Like many other social and political movements before it, the Soviet revolution may change. In so doing, it may rid itself of the policies which now prevent the Soviet Union from living as a good neighbor with the rest of the world.

We have no assurance that this will take place. But as the United Nations strengthens its collective security system, the possibilities of this change in Soviet policy will increase. If this does not occur, the increase in our defensive strength shall be the means of ensuring our survival and protecting the essential values of our societies.

But our hope is that a strong collective security system will make genuine negotiation possible, and that this will in turn lead to a cooperative peace.[37]

One factor which may make an eventual settlement possible in Acheson's view is the fact that Soviet imperialism is closely connected with the Russian character. In one sense this connection merely reinforces the expansionism

[36] Remarks to Advertising Council, February 16, 1950 (*Bulletin*, XXII, p. 429).
[37] Address before the United Nations General Assembly, September 20, 1950 (*Bulletin*, XXIII, p. 525).

of Stalinist doctrine: Acheson pointed out in June, 1951 that, "Historically the Russian State has had three great drives — to the west into Europe, to the south into the Middle East, and to the east into Asia." But he at once added that, "Historically also the Russian State has displayed considerable caution in carrying out these drives. The Russian rulers liked to bet on sure things . . . the Polit-bureau has acted in this same way . . . Russian policy makers, Czarist or Communist have always taken a very long view. They think in generations where others may think in terms of a few years or a decade at most . . . yet the ruling power in Moscow has long been an imperial power and now rules a greatly extended empire. It cannot escape the consequences that history teaches us befall all empires." [38]

The implication of this analysis is that there is good reason to suppose that neither Communist nor Russian attitudes require any early showdown. If this is true, there is obviously time for the building of strength from which an eventual bargain may be struck.

Another factor which improves the prospect of an eventual settlement is that the impossibility of moral compromise does not imply that political compromise is impossible:

It does not follow from this [moral conflict] that the two systems, theirs and ours, cannot exist concurrently in this world. Good and evil can and do exist concurrently in the whole great realm of human life. They exist within every individual, within every nation, and within every human group. The struggle between good and evil cannot be confined to governments. That struggle will go on, as it always has, in the wider theater of the human spirit itself. . . . However much we may sympathize with the Soviet citizens who for reasons bedded deep in history are obliged to live under it, we are not attempting to change the government or social structure of the Soviet Union. . . .[39] We do not propose to subvert the Soviet Union. We shall not attempt to undermine Soviet independence.[40]

This disclaimer of any effort to destroy Soviet independence should not be taken as a refusal to employ certain methods of political and psychological

[38] Hearings, *The Mutual Security Program*, House, Committee on Foreign Affairs, 82d Congress, 1st Session, June 26, 1951, pp. 11 and 12.

[39] Address at the University of California, Berkeley, California, March 16, 1950 (*Bulletin*, XXII, p. 474).

[40] Address to the American Society of Newspaper Editors, April 22, 1950 (*Bulletin*, XXII, p. 676).

pressure to weaken Soviet totalitarianism. The public record on this subject is necessarily and properly obscure, but it would be rash to assume that in the present phase of Soviet imperialism Acheson has rejected the notion of acting where possible to weaken the Kremlin's grip on the Russian people.

Eventual improvement in relations is a hope, not a certainty, but it is a hope of great importance; the simplest way to see its importance is to observe the consequence of giving it up. If there is no way to achieve some sort of peaceful coexistence, then there is no alternative to war, for nothing short of war can be expected to destroy the Soviet system. If we are to avoid war, we must be ready to "live and let live."

As a part of this readiness, the United States must always be ready to negotiate; this is a point Acheson constantly repeats; once, after expressing his doubts about the present intentions of the Soviet Union, he put it this way:

> This does not mean that discussion should not take place or that every effort should not be made to settle any questions which are possible of settlement.
>
> It is our policy to be, as General Marshall put it, the first to attend at international conference tables and the last to retire.[41]

A readiness to negotiate and, "even to take the initiative in efforts to bring about honest negotiation" is matched in Acheson's mind by a certain caution about the prospect of any successful settlement until a real change is produced in the minds of Soviet leaders. He has been particularly cool to proposals for very general negotiations between heads of state, remarking on one occasion that, "Such an effort on our part would raise false hopes among some people and fears among others." [42]

This cautious view of the possibility of top-level negotiations sets Acheson apart from another notable anti-Communist leader. In several major addresses in the last few years, Winston Churchill has appealed for negotiations "upon the highest level," with the object of driving a bargain — reaching an overall settlement — between East and West, while time remains. Mr. Churchill has never spelled out in any detail the possible content of such a settlement, and it may be significant that he has been spared, as Acheson

---

[41] Address before the Harvard Alumni Association, Cambridge, Mass., June 22, 1950 (*Bulletin*, XXIII, p. 17).

[42] Remarks to the Advertising Council, February 16, 1950 (*Bulletin*, XXII, p. 429).

has not, the direct experience of efforts to negotiate with the Russians since 1945. Probably the basic difference between the two men is in their estimates of present Russian willingness to make a large-scale settlement of any kind. In this sense, for what it may be worth, Acheson is not soft; he is harder than Mr. Churchill.

One basic reason for this caution toward the possibility of a general settlement is Acheson's view that any real improvement in the relations of the west with the Soviet Union will require a great change in Soviet policies. Specific agreements on specific subjects may become possible at any time, but a general settlement is a different matter. In his remarkable address on Soviet problems, delivered in March, 1950 at the University of California, he spelled out in some detail the things that the Soviet Union would have to be willing to do in order to make possible a real change of feeling in the free world. Although on several points it is already dated, this passage is of the greatest value as a measure of his basic thought on the issues between East and West.

If the two systems are to co-exist, some acceptable means must be found to free the world from the destructive tensions and anxieties of which it has been the victim in these past years and the continuance of which can hardly be in the interests of any people.

I wish, therefore, to speak to you about those points of greatest difference which must be identified and sooner or later reconciled if the two systems are to live together, if not with mutual respect, at least in reasonable security. What is it which the leaders of international communism could do to make such co-existence more tolerable to everyone? . . .

One. Definition of Terms of Peace

It is now nearly five years since the end of hostilities, and the victorious Allies have been unable to define the terms of peace with the defeated countries. This is a grave, a deeply disturbing fact. For our part, we do not intend nor wish, in fact we do not know how, to create satellites. Nor can we accept a settlement which would make Germany, Japan, or liberated Austria satellites of the Soviet Union. The experience in Hungary, Rumania, and Bulgaria has been one of bitter disappointment and shocking betrayal of the solemn pledges by the wartime Allies. The Soviet leaders joined in the pledge at Teheran that they looked forward "with confidence to the day when all peoples of the world may live free lives, untouched by tyranny, and according to their varying desires and their own consciences." We can accept treaties of peace which would give reality to this pledge and to the interests of all in security. . . .

Two. Use of Force

With regard to the whole group of countries which we are accustomed to think of as the satellite area, the Soviet leaders could withdraw their military and police force and refrain from using the shadow of that force to keep in power persons or régimes which do not command the confidence of the respective peoples, freely expressed through orderly representative processes. In other words, they could elect to observe, in practice, the declaration to which they set their signatures at Yalta concerning liberated Europe.

In this connection we do not insist that these governments have any particular political or social complexion. What concerns us is that they should be truly independent national régimes, with a will of their own and with a decent foundation in popular feeling. We would like to feel, when we deal with these governments, that we are dealing with something representative of the national identity of the peoples in question. We cannot believe that such a situation would be really incompatible with the security of the Soviet Union.

This is a question of elementary good faith, and it is vital to a spirit of confidence that other treaties and other agreements will be honored. Nothing would so alter the international climate as the holding of elections in the satellite states in which the true will of the people could be expressed.

Three. Obstruction in the United Nations

The Soviet leaders could drop their policy of obstruction in the United Nations and could instead act as if they believe the United Nations is, as Stalin himself has recently called it, a serious instrumentality for the maintenance of international peace and security. They are simply not acting that way now.

Their policy of walk-out and boycott is a policy that undermines the concept of majority decision. Indeed, they seem deliberately to entrench themselves in a minority position in the United Nations. . . .

A respect for the expressed will of the majority is as fundamental to international organization as it is to democracy. We know that a majority of the General Assembly has generally not agreed with the Soviet Union, whereas we ourselves have generally been on the majority side. There is nothing artificial about this situation. It has not been the result of any sleight of hand or pressures on our part. We do not have any satellites whose votes we control. The significant fact is that proposals which have commended themselves to a majority of the members of the United Nations have also commended themselves to us.

Let the Soviet Union put forward in the United Nations genuine proposals conducive to the work of peace, respectful of the real independence of other governments, and appreciative of the role which the United Nations could and should play in the preservation of world stability and the cooperation of nations. They will then doubtless have a majority with them. We will rejoice to see them in such a majority. We will be pleased to be a member of it ourselves.

Four. Effective Control of Atomic Energy

The Soviet leaders could join us in seeking realistic and effective arrangements for the control of atomic weapons and the limitation of armaments in general. We know that it is not easy for them under their system to contemplate the functioning on their territory of an authority in which people would participate who are not of their political persuasion.

If we have not hesitated to urge that they as well as we accept this requirement it is because we believe that a spirit of genuine responsibility to mankind is widely present in this world. Many able administrators and scientists could be found to operate such an authority who would be only too happy, regardless of political complexion, to take an elevated and enlightened view of the immense responsibility which would rest upon them. There are men who would scorn to use their powers for the negative purpose of intrigue and destruction. We believe that an authority could be established which would not be controlled or subject to control by either ourselves or the Soviet Union.

Five. Attempts at Undermining Established Governments

The Kremlin could refrain from using the Communist apparatus controlled by it throughout the world to attempt to overthrow, by subversive means, established governments with which the Soviet Government stands in an outward state of friendship and respect. In general, it could desist from, and could cooperate in efforts to prevent, indirect aggression across national frontiers — a mode of conduct which is inconsistent with the spirit and the letter of the United Nations Charter.

Six. *Proper Treatment of Diplomatic Representatives*

The Soviet leaders could cooperate with us to the end that the official representatives of all countries are treated everywhere with decency and respect and that an atmosphere is created in which these representatives could function in a normal and helpful manner, conforming to the accepted codes of diplomacy. . . .

When we now find our representatives treated as criminals, when we see great official propaganda machines reiterating that they are sinister people and that contact with them is pregnant with danger — we cannot believe that such insinuations are advanced in good faith, and we cannot be blind to the obvious implications of such an attitude.

Seven. *Distortion of Motives of Others*

In general, the Soviet leaders could refrain, I think, from systematically distorting to their own peoples the picture of the world outside their borders, and of our country in particular. . . .

What are we now to conclude from the morbid fancies which their propaganda exudes of a capitalist encirclement, of a United States craftily and systematically plotting another world war? They know, and the world knows, how foreign is the concept of aggressive war to our philosophy and our political system. They know that we are not asking to be the objects of any insincere and effusive demonstrations of sentimental friendship. But we feel that the Soviet leaders could at least permit access to the Soviet Union of persons and ideas from other countries so that other views might be presented to the Russian people.

These are some of the things which we feel that the Soviet leaders could do, which would permit the rational and peaceful development of the co-existence of their system and ours. They are not things that promise the Kingdom of Heaven. They have been formulated by us, not as moralists but as servants of government, anxious to get on with the practical problems that lie before us, and to get on with them in a manner consistent with mankind's deep longing for a respite from fear and uncertainty.[43]

These seven issues indicate the magnitude of the problem, and as **Acheson** himself has repeatedly pointed out, the resort to open aggression in Korea adds a further and still more important issue to those on which a basic change is required. Yet the Korean war has not changed the basic problem, and it is a fair guess that he would still stand today on a summary analysis made in April, 1950:

> One thing is clear. There can be no agreement, there can be no approach to agreement unless one idea is done away with, and that is the idea of aggression. And that word "aggression" includes not only military attack but propaganda warfare and the secret undermining of free countries from within. . . . If, as, and when that idea of aggression, by one means or another, can be ruled out of our relations with the Soviet Union, then the greatest single obstacle to agreement will be out of the way.[44]

Whether stated at length, in seven points, or in brief, as an end of aggression, the requirement for a general settlement is a great change in Soviet policy. Acheson has regularly warned that there are no easy solutions, that the way ahead is long and difficult, and that we must be willing to support a great program of "total diplomacy." A single sample of this line of thought will give its flavor. In the speech at Berkeley quoted above, after detailing the practical steps the Soviet Union could take, he continued,

> I fear, however, that I must warn you not to raise your hopes. No one who has lived through these postwar years can be sanguine about reaching agreements in which reliance can be placed. . . . I see no evidence that the Soviet leaders will change their conduct until the progress of the free world convinces them that they cannot profit from a continuation of these tensions.
>
> So our course of action in the world of hard reality which faces us is not one that is easily charted. It is not one which this nation can adopt without consideration of the needs and views of other free nations. . . .

[43] Address at the University of California, Berkeley, California, March 16, 1950 (*Bulletin*, XXII, pp. 474–77).

[44] Address to the American Society of Newspaper Editors, April 22, 1950 (*Bulletin*, XXII, p. 676).

The times call for a total diplomacy equal to the task of defense against Soviet expansion and to the task of building the kind of world in which our way of life can flourish. We must continue to press ahead with the building of a free world which is strong in its faith and in its material progress. The alternative is to allow the free nations to succumb one by one to the erosive and encroaching processes of Soviet expansion.[45]

5. Our Own Ideals Come First

There remains one last general point without which this discussion of the Soviet problem would be incomplete. Acheson is not one of those who think that anti-communism, in and of itself, is a sufficient basis for foreign policy.

We frequently hear that the United States is striving to halt the spread of communism. That is far too negative a way of putting it. . . .

The American people have been the leaders in a revolution that has been going on for a century and a half, a revolution by the common people. And the basic objective of American foreign policy is to make possible a world in which all peoples . . . can work, in their own way, toward a better life. That is why we are opposed to the spread of communism . . . It is because this tool of Soviet imperialism perverts the real democratic revolution that has been going on all over the world since long before communism as a world conspiracy had been thought of. This is why we must unceasingly in all we do and say affirm the positive goals of free peoples. We are for something positive, for the most fundamental urges of the human spirit. We are not and must not allow ourselves to appear merely negative, even though that negation is directed against the most corrupting force now operating in the world.[46]

Following his own injunction, Acheson has repeatedly insisted on the positive aspects of American policy, and upon the basic affirmations from which it proceeds. The following three quotations show this thought in three different contexts, first in purely American terms, second in the context of the Atlantic community, and lastly on the scale of the United Nations and the world. They speak for themselves.

[45] Address at the University of California, Berkeley, California, March 13, 1950 (*Bulletin*, XXII, p. 478).
[46] Address at San Francisco, March 15, 1950 (*Bulletin*, XXII, p. 472).

Our first line of action — and this seems to me the basis of all the others I shall discuss — is to demonstrate that our own faith in freedom is a burning and a fighting faith. We are children of freedom. We cannot be safe except in an environment of freedom. We believe in freedom as fundamentally as we believe anything in this world. We believe in it for everyone in our country. And we don't restrict this belief to freedom for ourselves. We believe that all people in the world are entitled to as much freedom, to develop in their own way, as we want ourselves.

If we are clear about this, if we are full of passion about this, then we have in our hearts and minds the most dynamic and revolutionary concept in human history and one which properly strikes terror to every dictator, to every tyrant who would attempt to regiment and depress men anywhere. . . .[47]

It is a fact of considerable importance, although hardly recognized, that much of what the free world has been doing to build its strength has been in itself a great creative effort. The means by which free men have sought to strengthen their defenses have led, perhaps to some degree unconsciously, to a community sense among free nations. Both the North Atlantic Community and the community of the American states are institutions founded on principles which must eventually prevail in a wider world.

Unlike the alliances of a former day, these associations among states produce a community of peoples where no dominance exists, a community which is based on generous and willing cooperation and on the primacy of individual liberty. These are communities in which rules of mutual aid and self-help are cardinal and in which the duty and responsibility of aiding other free peoples to achieve their own development in their own way are fully recognized.

Thus, the weaving of a community sense among the nations who have joined their strength in these common efforts is a substantial step toward the realization of a world order based on consent and dedicated to peace and progress. It has accomplished, in a great area of the world, a fuller realization of the principles of the Charter of the United Nations since it has advanced international cooperation to maintain the peace, to advance human rights, to raise standards of living, and to promote respect for the principle of equal rights and self-determination of peoples.

[47] Address to the American Society of Newspaper Editors, April 22, 1950 (*Bulletin*, XXII, p. 675).

The great effort in which we are engaged to build a North Atlantic Community is not merely a means. It is in itself a creative act of historic significance.

It is often true in history that men acting under immediate compulsion are only partly aware of the great consequences of what they have set in motion. Measures taken to suit a narrow purpose, if conceived in harmony with man's moral nature, may leave a great creative legacy....[48]

In building a more secure and prosperous world, we must never lose sight of the basic motivation of our effort: the inherent worth of the individual human person. Our aim is to create a world in which each human being shall have the opportunity to fulfill his creative possibilities in harmony with all.

It is our hope that the relaxation in international tension, which we seek, will be accompanied by a great restoration of human liberty, where it is now lacking, and progress everywhere toward the "larger freedom."

But the safeguarding of human freedom is not a distant goal, nor a project for the future. It is a constant, immediate and urgent concern of the United Nations....

We speak here as the representatives of Governments, but we must also speak the hearts of our countrymen. We speak for people whose deep concern is whether the children are well or sick, whether there is enough food, whether the roof leaks, whether there will be peace.

But peace, for them, is not just the absence of war.

The peace the world wants must be free from fear — the fear of invasion, the fear of subversion, the fear of the knock on the door at midnight.

The peace the world wants must be free from want, a peace in which neighbors help each other, and together build a better life.

The peace the world wants must be a moral peace, so that the spirit of man may be free, and the barriers between the hearts and minds of man may drop away and leave men free to unite in brotherhood.

This is the task before us.[49]

[48] Address before the Harvard Alumni Association, Cambridge, Massachusetts, June 22, 1950 (*Bulletin*, XXIII, p. 17).

[49] Address to the General Assembly of the United Nations, September 20, 1950 (*Bulletin*, XXIII, p. 529).

CHAPTER THREE

The Atlantic Community

THE PEOPLES *of the North Atlantic Community value peace and freedom above all other things, and they are determined to take whatever measures may be required to preserve them. In the world today, this depends upon their being strong and joining their collective strength in support of the cause of peace and freedom.*[1]

Having considered the basic problem — the problem of Soviet imperialism — we come to the detailed issues of policy in different areas of the world. Acheson has regularly resisted the view that any one area of the world is all-important, emphasizing that in the end the whole is one, and all its problems interlocking. Still, it is necessary to start somewhere, and it seems proper to begin with Europe. At least until the outbreak of aggression in Korea, in June, 1950, the major part of American attention and effort and outlay went to Europe, and certainly we can say that in Acheson's policy no part of the world is of *greater* importance to the United States. He has given his own explanation of this point:

The twelve nations that compose the North Atlantic Community include some three hundred and thirty-seven million people,[2] about one-sixth of the earth's population. Within this area is the world's greatest concentration of industrial and technical skills. This community of

[1] Statement on signing of Mutual Defense Assistance Agreements, January 27, 1950 (*Bulletin*, XXII, p. 199).

[2] These figures include the United States; the twelve nations referred to are the original parties to the North Atlantic Treaty.

44

nations is also brought together by a common political experience, the growth of the idea of freedom and the rights of man.

So geography, political experience, and industrial capacity join to make the North Atlantic Community a natural and a critically important grouping of states By common action on their mutual problems of defense, economic development, and political cooperation, the North Atlantic states can achieve a substantial increase of their combined strength. In so doing, they increase the strength of the entire free world.

Our support for the strengthening of the North Atlantic Community does not imply any lessening of our interest in, or our commitments toward, other parts of the world. Rather, it reflects the keystone role which this combination of states must play in strengthening the security and the welfare of the entire free world.[3]

Within the subject of American policy toward Europe, we might begin at many places, but the easiest way is to start at the beginning. And the beginning of the policy of "situations of strength" in Europe is to be found in two undertakings launched when General Marshall was Secretary of State — the Marshall Plan and aid to Greece and Turkey. The Greek-Turkish Aid Program is a somewhat special case and can best be treated in a later section, but the Marshall Plan is a central matter; it is the first of the three fundamental pillars of American policy in Europe. If we begin with the Marshall Plan, it will be easy and natural to move on to the other two, the North Atlantic Treaty and the defense of the Atlantic Community.

1. The Marshall Plan

The European Recovery Program lights a path to a future to which men can look with confidence for peace and order in a system based on freedom and justice.[4]

The Marshall Plan, or European Recovery Program, was launched in June, 1947 and became a going concern about a year later. When Acheson became Secretary of State, it was in full course, operating outside the State

[3] Address before the Civic Federation of Dallas and the Community Course of Southern Methodist University, Dallas, Texas, June 13, 1950 (*Bulletin*, XXII, p. 1039).

[4] Address at the Mid-Point Anniversary of E.C.A., April 3, 1950 (Department Press Release 307, 1950).

Department under the direction of Paul G. Hoffman. Acheson's responsibility, as Secretary, has been that of general cooperation and policy coordination, and specific credit for specific accomplishments clearly belongs to the men of the Economic Cooperation Administration.

At the same time the Marshall Plan has been a vital element in over-all foreign policy, and as such it cannot be omitted here. The planning and operation of matters for which Acheson has had more direct and continuous responsibility cannot be sensibly considered except in the context of a working recovery program. Moreover the Marshall Plan itself, almost as a result of its initial successes, has posed a number of problems that reach out into the field of broad policy. And finally, it can fairly be claimed that Acheson himself, as Under Secretary of State in the spring of 1947, had a significant role in the thinking which produced the program.

On May 8, 1947, he delivered a speech at Cleveland, Mississippi. This speech has often been described as the forerunner of General Marshall's famous address at Harvard the next month. Whether or not this description is accurate, the reader can perhaps judge for himself from the extracts which follow; at the least he should find this address a useful statement of the general situation which the Marshall proposals were designed to meet.

When Secretary of State Marshall returned from the recent meeting of the Council of Foreign Ministers in Moscow he did not talk to us about ideologies or armies. He talked about food and fuel and their relation to industrial production, and the relation of industrial production to the organization of Europe, and the relation of the organization of Europe to the peace of the world.

The devastation of war has brought us back to elementals, to the point where we see clearly how short is the distance from food and fuel either to peace or to anarchy.

Here are some of the basic facts of life with which we are primarily concerned today in the conduct of foreign relations:

The first is that most of the countries of Europe and Asia are today in a state of physical destruction or economic dislocation, or both. Planned, scientific destruction of the enemy's resources carried out by both sides during the war has left factories destroyed, fields impoverished and without fertilizer or machinery to get them back in shape, transportation systems wrecked, populations scattered and on the borderline of starvation, and long-established business and trading connections disrupted.

Another grim fact of international life is that two of the greatest workshops of Europe and Asia — Germany and Japan — upon whose production Europe and Asia were to an important degree dependent before the war, have hardly been able even to begin the process of reconstruction because of the lack of a peace settlement. As we have seen, recent efforts at Moscow to make progress towards a settlement for Germany and Austria have ended with little accomplishment. Meanwhile, political instability in some degree retards revival in nearly every country of Europe and Asia.

A third factor is that unforeseen disasters — what the lawyers call "acts of God" — have occurred to the crops of Europe. For two successive years unusually severe droughts have cut down food production. And during the past winter storms and floods and excessive cold unprecedented in recent years have swept northern Europe and England with enormous damage to agricultural and fuel production. These disasters have slowed down the already slow pace of reconstruction, have impeded recovery of exports, and have obliged many countries to draw down irreplaceable reserves of gold and foreign exchange, which had been earmarked for the importation of reconstruction materials, for the purchase of food and fuel for subsistence.

The accumulation of these grim developments has produced a disparity between production in the United States and production in the rest of the world that is staggering in its proportions. The United States has been spared physical destruction during the war. Moreover, we have been favored with unusually bountiful agricultural crops in recent years. Production in this country is today running at the annual rate of two hundred and ten billion dollars.

Responding to this highly abnormal relationship between production in the United States and production in the rest of the world, the United States Government has already authorized and is carrying out an extensive program of relief and reconstruction. We have contributed nearly three billion dollars to foreign relief. We have taken the lead in the organization of the International Bank for Reconstruction and Development and the International Monetary Fund, and have subscribed to these two institutions to the extent of almost six billion dollars. We have increased the capacity of the Export-Import Bank to make loans abroad by almost three billion dollars. We have made a direct loan of three and three quarter billion dollars to Great Britain. We are proposing this year to contribute a half billion dollars for relief and reconstruction in the Philippines, and a billion dollars to relief in occupied areas. The President's recommendations for aid to Greece and Turkey to the extent of four hundred million dollars and for post-UNRRA relief to the extent of three hundred and fifty million dollars are still under consideration by Congress. And there are a few other smaller items.

These measures of relief and reconstruction have been only in part suggested by humanitarianism. Your Congress has authorized and your Government is carrying out a policy of relief and reconstruction today chiefly as a matter of national self-interest. For it is generally agreed that until the various countries of the world get on their feet and become self-supporting there can be no political or economic stability in the world and no lasting peace or prosperity for any of us. Without outside aid, the process of recovery in many countries would take so long as to give rise to hopelessness and despair. In these conditions freedom and democracy and the independence of nations could not long survive, for hopeless and hungry people often resort to desperate measures. The war will not be over until the people of the world can again feed and clothe themselves and face the future with some degree of confidence.

The contribution of the United States towards world livelihood and reconstruction is best measured today not in terms of money but in terms of the commodities which we ship abroad. It is commodities — food, clothing, coal, steel, machinery — that the world needs, and it is commodities that we must concentrate our attention upon. . . .

In return for the commodities and services which we expect to furnish the world this year, we estimate that we will receive commodities and services from abroad to the value of about eight billion dollars. This is just about half as much as we are exporting. This volume of imports is equal to about two weeks' work of all the factories, farms, mines, and laborers of the United States, and consists largely of things which are not produced in this country in sufficient quantity. We wish that the imports were larger, but the war-devastated world is just not able to supply more.

The difference between the value of the goods and services which foreign countries must buy from the United States this year and the value of the goods and services they are able to supply to us this year will therefore amount to the huge sum of about eight billion dollars.

How are foreigners going to get the U.S. dollars necessary to cover this huge difference? And how are they going to get the U.S. dollars to cover a likely difference of nearly the same amount next year? These are some of the most important questions in international relations today. . . .

The facts of international life . . . mean that the United States is going to have to undertake further emergency financing of foreign purchases if foreign countries are to continue to buy in 1948 and 1949 the commodities which they need to sustain life and at the same time rebuild their economies. Requests for further United States aid may reach us through the International Bank, or through the Export-Import Bank, or they may be of a type which existing national and international institutions are not equipped to handle and therefore may be made directly through diplomatic channels. But we know now that further financing, beyond existing authorizations, is going to be needed. No other country is able to bridge the gap in commodities or dollars. . . .

Since world demand exceeds our ability to supply, we are going to have to concentrate our emergency assistance in areas where it will be most effective in building world political and economic stability, in promoting human freedom and democratic institutions, in fostering liberal trading policies, and in strengthening the authority of the United Nations.

This is merely common sense and sound practice. It is in keeping with the policy announced by President Truman in his special message to Congress on March 12 on aid to Greece and Turkey. Free peoples who are seeking to preserve their independence and democratic institutions and human freedoms against totalitarian pressures, either internal or external, will receive top priority for American reconstruction aid. This is no more than frank recognition, as President Truman said, "that totalitarian regimes imposed on free peoples, by direct or indirect aggression, undermine the foundations of international peace and hence the security of the United States." . . .

Not only do human beings and nations exist in narrow economic margins, but also human dignity, human freedom, and democratic institutions.

It is one of the principal aims of our foreign policy today to use our economic and financial resources to widen these margins. It is necessary if we are to preserve our own freedoms and our own democratic institutions. It is necessary for our national security. And it is our duty and our privilege as human beings.[5]

To the general argument expressed by Acheson at Cleveland, Secretary Marshall at Harvard added two specific points which turned a general analysis into a great new hope.[6] First, he called for a program that would "provide a cure rather than a mere palliative," and second, he called for a European initiative in preparing a combined plan for the area. The response in Europe was immediate and effective. By midsummer it was clear that there would be presented a long-term program of European co-operation to which the United States could contribute with reasonable confidence that it was working toward a real reconstruction of this vital area, and there were also at work, on the American side, a quite extraordinary group of committees representing the executive branch, the Congress, and the public.

And one further point had become clear. General Marshall's original proposal was "directed not against any country or doctrine but against hunger, poverty, desperation and chaos." It was open to all European countries, and in the initial European discussions the Soviet Union was included. At the same time General Marshall's speech had contained this warning: "Any government which maneuvers to block the recovery of other countries cannot expect help from us. Furthermore, governments, political parties or groups which seek to perpetuate human misery in order to profit therefrom politically or otherwise will encounter the opposition of the United States." Thus the speech left it an open question whether or not the Marshall Plan would proceed with Soviet participation. But the answer was not long in coming, and Acheson has described it in interesting terms:

We did not limit the scope of our offer of cooperation.

The sufferings and the destruction left by the war were not confined to any one area. All over the Continent people were longing to rebuild a useful and orderly existence after the long misery and violence of the war. They wanted to restore their homes and farms and workshops. They wanted to plan for the futures of themselves and their families; they wanted to move toward a more promising day, toward a world in which peace might endure.

We in America wanted this too. And so General Marshall proposed that all European countries should participate in a joint recovery pro-

[5] Address at Cleveland, Mississippi, as Under Secretary, May 7, 1947 (*Bulletin*, XVI, pp. 991–95).
[6] The text is in *Bulletin*, XVI, pp. 159–60.

gram, to which each would contribute in the measure of its ability. In this way and with our aid, we hoped that the weak and war-wracked organism of Europe could regain strength and health.

We were rebuffed by a small group of men who stood to profit from Europe's misery and who have never viewed the United States with anything but envy and hostility. More important, the principle of international cooperation was scorned. As a result of an arbitrary and selfish attitude on the part of some, the program was limited to that half of Europe where men were at liberty to choose the path of cooperation. . . .[7]

It can be argued that the ruthless opposition of the Soviet Union and the Cominform was the one thing needed to make the Marshall Plan a reality. Certainly it is true that the rape of Czechoslovakia in February, 1948 did much to stiffen American and European determination to get on with this and other jobs. But at this time Acheson was a private citizen, and his participation in the launching of the European Recovery Program was that of an ardent individual advocate; there is not space here for this advocacy, which closely paralleled that of the Administration

The Economic Cooperation Act was approved April 3, 1948. Under that law and succeeding acts of authorization and appropriation, the United States in the next three years spent something over eleven billions of dollars on European recovery, acting in co-operation with some seventeen European nations. In the course of these three years, Acheson has regularly appeared before the appropriate committees of the Congress to urge continuation of the program.

His basic assessment of the program as a whole appeared very clearly in testimony to a joint meeting in February, 1949, just after he had been sworn in as Secretary:

To estimate honestly and accurately the degree to which we are achieving the objectives we set ourselves in the recovery program, we must not merely return to the situation in the free community of Europe at the time of the adoption by the Congress of the Foreign Assistance Act of 1948. It is necessary to go back to the situation at the time the program was first proposed by Secretary Marshall in June 1947.

[7] Address at the Mid-Point Anniversary of E.C.A., April 3, 1950 (Department of State Press Release No. 307, 1950). For a further description of Soviet attitudes toward the Marshall Plan, see p. 29 above.

The response among the European democracies to the suggestion which he put forth at that time and the reaction of those who did not share the desire to see European recovery accomplished marked, without question, a climactic point in postwar history.

The mere suggestion of a constructive program of international cooperation, dedicated to reconstruction, recovery and peace, was sufficient to alter the political atmosphere of an entire continent. Apathy and despair were replaced by renewed hope and confidence among the free countries of Europe — hope and confidence in the possibility of jointly working out, with American assistance, the staggering problems of reconstruction which had descended upon them in the aftermath of war. The peoples of the European democracies saw in this suggestion the possibility of demonstrating that economic recovery could be achieved without sacrifice of the freedom which formed part of their traditional vitalization and ours. Their response to Secretary Marshall's suggestion, in itself, was an impressive demonstration of their will to reconstruct their national lives on a basis of free institutions.

Events have proved that the hopes reposed in this program, both here and abroad, have not been misplaced.

The sixteen nations which were willing and able to meet together to act upon this suggestion are all still to be counted in the ranks of the democracies. There has been no advance in totalitarianism on the continent of Europe.

It cannot be claimed, and I shall not attempt to do so, that this result is solely due to the recovery program. But, without it, the situation would probably have been very different. As it is, the free community of Europe has not only held its own, but it has, during this period, made great strides forward.

The situation today on that continent is vastly more encouraging than it was two years ago. Within the participating countries there has been a rebirth of faith in the vitality of the democratic system and its ability to deal with their postwar problems.

In every important election held in these countries since the inception of this program of recovery, the people have more vigorously reaffirmed their adherence to the principles of individual freedom and governments based on constitutional restraints. Those elements within the countries who, by deliberate choice or foreign inspiration sought — in the words of Secretary Marshall — "to perpetuate human misery in order to profit therefrom politically," have been checked and forced into retreat.

The enemies of recovery have, by no means, confined their activities to the political field.

In both France and Italy, Communist-inspired attempts to defeat recovery and sabotage domestic production have been met with energy and courage by the governments of those countries with the full support of the great majority of their people.

In the free countries of Europe, labor, on whom so much depends for the success of this program, has not permitted itself to be misled by foreign dictation into the sabotage of its own well-being. It has become increasingly aware of the aims of those who have, for political ends, seized upon grievances — in many instances legitimate grievances — for the purpose of disrupting progress in recovery.

Improvements can be noted in almost every phase of the national life of the participating countries. Increased production and greater economic stability have been stimulated by renewed hope and confidence in the future, and hope and confidence in turn have been augmented by increased economic recovery. . . .

The European recovery program was presented and adopted by the Congress as a calculated risk. The results of the first year of its operation definitely establish that the measure was sound. Therefore, the President has recommended that the program be continued. Of course there are difficulties and problems ahead. But the outstanding fact which emerges from this first appraisal is that the program is succeeding. Every sound precept calls upon us to press that success. The worst of all courses would be to relax our efforts and allow the momentum of achievement to diminish. To do so would be to lose all that has been gained, and to lose also the opportunity to bring the program to full completion.[8]

This general satisfaction has continued throughout the program; in the spring of 1950, at the halfway point, there is a further statement of the matter, with a specific statement of achievements and a specific tribute to some of the architects of the program:

Two years ago the American people, acting through their Congress

---

[8] Statement to the Senate Committee on Foreign Relations and the House Committee on Foreign Affairs, February 8, 1949 (Hearings, *Extension of European Recovery*, Senate, Committee on Foreign Relations, 81st Congress, 1st Session, pp. 16–19).

and the President, began a "heroic adventure" with the people of Europe. The phrase is not mine — it belongs to that valiant worker for peace, Senator Vandenberg. . . .

The recovery plan has now operated for two years under the direction of the European countries, working with Mr. Hoffman and Mr. Harriman and the splendid team they have organized and led. This combination has been unbeatable. This has been the kind of a constructive job that arouses the enthusiasm and spirit and devotion of free men.

Great progress has been made in Western Europe. Over-all industrial production in 1949 was 15 percent above the 1938 level. Coal production was 434,000,000 metric tons in 1949 — in 1948 it was 398,000,000 tons. Steel output in 1949 was 46,000,000 metric tons — one-sixth more than in 1948. The production of bread grains has risen by more than half in the period from 1947 to 1949.

And these gains will continue, for the farmers and workers have more and better tools and machines. In 1949 the average factory worker produced 25 percent more than he did in 1947.

It would be incomplete if I spoke of European recovery as though it mattered only to that one continent. Western Europe is one of the world's great workshops and one of the world's great markets. The recovery which has been made there has extended its influence to many other countries — to the countries of South America, to Africa, and to Southern Asia. It is greatly to the interest of all of us to have Western Europe strong and healthy.

This illustrates what has been accomplished through the Marshall Plan. This is the exciting record of recovery. These statistics are alive with hope. . . .

When the European recovery program began, the Communists filled the air with dire predictions that the European countries could not cooperate in this way without its ending in their domination by the United States. The experience of the European recovery program has shown how dishonest and insubstantial this propaganda was. No country has lost anything but poverty; no country has gained domination, but all have gained in self-respect and have won a new confidence and a strengthened independence. . . .[9]

[9] Address at the Mid-Point Anniversary of E.C.A., April 3, 1950 (Department Press Release 307, 1950).

The first great objective of the European Recovery Program was the revival of European production. By the spring of 1950, as the last selection shows, this goal had in the main been achieved, at least in the sense that inability to produce was no longer the central problem. But as Acheson is fond of pointing out, one problem solved in international affairs usually brings another in its place. The very fact of increasing European production brought to the foreground, in 1950, two additional problems, one primarily European and the other primarily American. Neither was new, and on both Acheson had strong opinions.

The European problem was that of trade and integration.

The Europeans must not only expand their productive capacities but must, through greater efficiency, through lower costs and improved marketing methods, improve the competitive position of their products in the markets of the United States and the rest of the world.

This is the reason why we favor the closer association of the free countries of Europe in the economic field, as we do in the political and military fields. Such association is necessary if they are to put their economies on a sound, competitive, self-supporting basis. If Germany, instead of being a threat to world peace, is to be a constructive partner in Europe, it is necessary to build a European framework within which her skills and energies can be used for the benefit of all. We hope this drawing together of the European countries will take place within a framework of closer association of all the free countries of the world, including our own. Unity in Europe requires the continuing association and support of the United States. Without it free Europe would split apart.[10]

The specific proposal for increased integration which was being supported by the American government in the spring of 1950 was the plan for a European Payments Union, which was in fact established the following July. The specific details of this mechanism need not concern us, but during the discussion of it in Committee there is an exchange of views which illuminates a larger problem in the American relationship to European developments:

[10] Statement to Senate Foreign Relations Committee and House Foreign Affairs Committee, February 21, 1950 (Hearings, *Extension of European Recovery, 1950*, Senate, Committee on Foreign Relations, 81st Congress, 2d Session, p. 15).

MR. RICHARDS. . . . What do you think about the idea of putting an amendment in this bill making this thing mandatory, making these seventeen countries do these things that Mr. Hoffman suggests should be done before the Administrator makes an allocation to them? . . .

SECRETARY ACHESON. . . . I think there are several reasons why it is better to leave the thing in Mr. Hoffman's hands to work out rather than make it mandatory.

In the first place, this is not altogether an easy thing to accomplish. There are many interests which have to be reconciled in Europe and there are many interests which have to be reconciled outside of Europe. For instance, the British have serious problems which have to be worked out in a cooperative way before they can make their full contribution to this scheme. I think if we say this is mandatory, you will find first of all that there will be a period where nobody could have the use of these very necessary funds while it was being worked out and, in the second place, instead of having this done on an entirely cooperative, voluntary basis it would be done under the coercion of this requirement of the act. This would make it more difficult to work with our friends in Europe and would give considerable ammunition to the propaganda of the Communists who would say that this was an example of American imperialism and that we were dictating. . . .[11]

Thus the use of American assistance, even to produce economic changes, is a ticklish matter. And this difficulty, in Acheson's view, is compounded when the problem is more political than economic. "We favor the closer association of the free countries of Europe" in all fields, but we cannot force them to it:

While there is growing popular debate in Europe on the problem of federation, neither the people nor their governments appear ready for this step. We recognize their right to decide democratically as our founding fathers did, when, how and whether they will federate. We reserve the same right for ourselves, as we approach, on a step-by-step basis, a closer association with other nations, through the UN, the North Atlantic Treaty and other arrangements. . . .

The progress which has been made in the direction of a closer drawing

[11] Hearings, *To Amend the Economic Cooperation Act of 1948, as Amended*, House, Committee on Foreign Affairs, 81st Congress, 2d Session, pp. 17–18.

together in Europe would have been regarded as quite extraordinary at any other time. At the present time, it has to be regarded as disappointing progress, because the pressures are so great and the time is so short within which to do these things. If you ask whether our sights are high enough, that is a real question. It could be stated that they are not. A good argument can be made for the position that economic integration is very difficult if it is tackled on its own side alone, and experience in other countries at other times have shown that you have to precede economic unity with some political decisions. . . .

All in all, it would seem to me that if we could go forward with the steps which [these] countries have already stated they were willing to take, and if this could work for a few years, it might pave the way to very much closer political arrangements, and if at the same time that was going on we could press on with the North Atlantic Treaty arrangements, and under the auspices of that treaty consider some of these questions which have a very great bearing on security, that might be a way of helping to go forward, too, but it is extremely difficult on a democratic and voluntary basis to overcome a couple of thousand years of history. . . .

We must not put ourselves in a position of even appearing to subvert authority in any of these friendly countries with which we work. The French people, the British people, the German people, and the Italians have worked out a system by which they create a governmental authority. We are trying to help and not subvert or go around or in any way make the task of that governmental authority any more difficult. We have been able, through such things as the UN organization, UNESCO, the Social and Economic Council of Europe, to meet with leaders in these various countries who are not necessarily governmental authorities — the ECA, for instance, has established ways by which we can meet with businessmen in these countries. Through this new international trade union which has just been set up, we have made very great progress in having American labor leaders meet with the labor people of other countries. But all the time we must be very clear that nobody has the slightest suspicion that we are trying to build a fire under some government or get it to do something which it does not want to do. . . .

SENATOR LODGE. If the United States placed itself under the suspicion of trying to pull the rug out from under those governments, why, you might create a worse situation and get yourself into more trouble, might you not?

Secretary Acheson. I think you most certainly would, and it would backfire on you very badly.[12]

The integration of Europe has the special complication that it cannot be accomplished simply by American say-so, but this does not make it, in the end, any more difficult or testing than the side of the problem which is particularly American. This is the problem of American imports:

> Readjustments of United States economic policies will be necessary. The problem which confronts us can be stated very simply: to maintain the volume of American exports which the free world needs and which it is in our national interest to supply as a necessary part of building a successfully functioning political and economic system, the free world must obtain the dollars to pay for these exports. They can be obtained in only three ways: By our imports of goods and services from them, by our public and private loans and investments abroad, and by continued gifts. In the long run, the only reliable and desirable way is to increase our imports, but that is a big job and until it has been done we have to continue assistance to countries which need it and which it is in our national interest to help. Whatever we can do to build up our imports from abroad and to make our exports available at reasonable prices contributes to the success of ERP and more broadly to the building of a successful free world enterprise.[13]

This problem, which seemed particularly urgent in early 1950, became less immediately pressing after the attack in Korea, for with that attack the American demand for strategic imports greatly increased, and so did the need for continued foreign aid. As a basic problem, however, it remains unsolved; the point Acheson made was one with which America must eventually come to terms. Acheson's own suggestion, advanced in these same hearings, was that some means must be found, as American imports increased and tariff barriers came down, for sharing the burden which would fall on a few American producers who could not meet foreign competition.

---

[12] Hearings, *Extension of European Recovery, 1950*, Senate, Committee on Foreign Relations, 81st Congress, 2d Session, pp. 15, 106–7.

[13] Statement to Senate Foreign Relations Committee and House Foreign Affairs Committee, February 21, 1950 (Same hearings, p. 16).

But it is time, now, to move on to the other focal elements in American policy toward Europe. The Marshall Plan, by its first successes, led on to other problems. At the same time, by its incompleteness, it required additional acts of policy in other fields, and to these we now turn.

2. The North Atlantic Treaty

We must make it clear that armed attack will be met by collective defense, prompt and effective. That is the meaning of the North Atlantic Pact.[14]

The North Atlantic Treaty was negotiated in the winter of 1948–49, and signed at Washington, April 4, 1949. When its text was agreed upon and made public, at the end of March, there began a "great debate" of the sort which has punctuated the development of American foreign policy in recent years.

In this debate Acheson naturally had a part, and two of his statements are of particular importance. In the first he explains the historical background of the treaty. He is speaking to the Senate Committee on Foreign Relations, as first witness in the hearings on the Treaty:

SECRETARY ACHESON. Mr. Chairman and members of the committee, I welcome this opportunity to discuss with you the North Atlantic Treaty signed on April 4. That treaty is no new document to you. It has been developed, to an extent without parallel in my knowledge, as a cooperative enterprise between the executive and legislative branches of the Government and particularly between the Department of State and this committee. Without the vision and assistance of your chairman [Senator Connally], of your former chairman [Senator Vandenberg], and the members of this committee, this treaty could never have been concluded. The text embodies many constructive suggestions from the members of the committee. . . .

If I may use an understatement, the sense of insecurity prevalent in Western Europe is not a figment of the imagination. It has come about through the conduct of the Soviet Union. Western European countries have seen the basic purposes and principles of the [United Nations] Charter cynically violated by the conduct of the Soviet Union with the countries of eastern Europe. Their right to self-determination has been

[14] Radio address, March 18, 1949 (*Bulletin*, XX, p. 388).

extinguished by force or threats of force. The human freedoms as the rest of the world understands them have been extinguished throughout that whole area. Economic problems have not been solved by international cooperation but have been dealt with by dictation. These same methods have been attempted in other areas — penetration by propaganda and the Communist Party, attempts to block cooperative international efforts in the economic field, wars of nerves, and in some cases thinly veiled use of force itself. . . .

For more than a year the members of the committee and officers of the Department of State have been in consultation as to the nature of the problems involved, how they might best be met, and how the influence of the United States might best be brought to bear in the cause of peace. Throughout the negotiation of this treaty the United States negotiators have been guided by the wishes of the Senate as expressed in Resolution 239. . . .[15]

Following the resolution of the Senate, Mr. Lovett [then Under Secretary of State] undertook to explore the matter with the Ambassadors of Canada, the United Kingdom, France, Belgium, the Netherlands, and Luxemburg. The objective of this Government and of the other governments participating in these discussions was to establish an arrangement which would:

First. Increase the determination of the parties to resist aggression and their confidence that they could successfully do so;

Second. Promote full economic recovery through removing the drag of a sense of insecurity;

Third. Stimulate the efforts of the parties to help themselves and each other and, through coordination, to achieve maximum effectiveness for defense; and

Fourth. Contribute to the maintenance of peace and reduce the possibility of war by making clear the determination of the parties jointly to resist armed attack from any quarter.[16]

From these considerations, and a series of complex and delicate negotiations, there emerged the North Atlantic Treaty. Its members are twelve:

[15] This was the Vandenberg Resolution, passed on June 11, 1948, by a vote of 64–4. Half of this Resolution supported the existing American position in favor of a stronger United Nations; the other half urged the "progressive development" of just such special arrangements for security as the North Atlantic Treaty.

[16] Hearings, *North Atlantic Treaty*, Senate, Committee on Foreign Relations, 81st Congress, 1st Session, April 27, 1949, pp. 4, 7–8, 9–10.

the United States and Canada in North America; Britain, France, Belgium, the Netherlands, and Luxemburg, in the center of Western Europe; Denmark, Norway, and Iceland in northern Europe; Italy in the Mediterranean, and Portugal in the southwest corner of Europe. Only four nations in Western Europe were omitted: Germany, Sweden, Switzerland, and Spain. Sweden and Switzerland preferred to maintain their traditional neutrality; Spain and Germany are discussed in later chapters.

But what is the Treaty? Most Americans know "in a general way," but the following analysis is still of interest. It is from the speech in which Acheson first discussed the Treaty with his fellow citizens.

The paramount purposes of the pact are peace and security. If peace and security can be achieved in the North Atlantic area, we shall have gone a long way to assure peace and security in other areas as well. . . .

The Atlantic Pact is a collective self-defense arrangement among the countries of the North Atlantic area. . . .

It is important to keep in mind that the really successful national and international institutions are those that recognize and express underlying realities. The North Atlantic community of nations is such a reality. It is based on the affinity and natural identity of interests of the North Atlantic powers.

The North Atlantic Treaty, which now formally unites them, is the product of at least three hundred and fifty years of history, perhaps more. There developed on our Atlantic coast a community, which has spread across the continent, connected with Western Europe by common institutions and moral and ethical beliefs. Similarities of this kind are not superficial, but fundamental. They are the strongest kind of ties, because they are based on moral conviction, on acceptance of the same values in life. . . .

Added to this profoundly important basis of understanding is another unifying influence — the effect of living on the sea. The sea does not separate people as much as it joins them, through trade, travel, mutual understanding, and common interests.

For this second reason, as well as the first, North America and Western Europe have formed the two halves of what is in reality one community, and have maintained an abiding interest in each other.

It is clear that the North Atlantic pact is not an improvisation. It is the statement of the facts and lessons of history. We have learned our history lesson from two world wars in less than half a century. That experience has taught us that the control of Europe by a single aggressive unfriendly power would constitute an intolerable threat to the national security of the United States. We participated in those two great wars to preserve the integrity and independence of the American half. It is a simple fact, proved by experience, that an outside attack on one member of this community is an attack upon all members.

We have also learned that if the free nations do not stand together, they will fall one by one. The stratagem of the aggressor is to keep his intended victims divided or, better still, set them to quarreling among themselves. Then they can be picked off one by one without arousing unified resistance. We and the free nations of Europe are determined that history shall not repeat itself in that melancholy particular. . . .

What are the principal provisions of the North Atlantic Pact? I should like to summarize them.

First, the pact is carefully and conscientiously designed to conform in every particular with the Charter of the United Nations. . . .

The second article is equally fundamental. The associated countries assert that they will preserve and strengthen their free institutions and will see to it that the fundamental principles upon which free institutions are founded are better understood everywhere. They also agree to eliminate conflicts in their economic life and to promote economic cooperation among themselves. Here is the ethical essence of the treaty — the common resolve to preserve, strengthen, and make understood the very basis of tolerance, restraint, and freedom — the really vital things with which we are concerned.

This purpose is extended further in Article 3, in which the participating countries pledge themselves to self-help and mutual aid. In addition to strengthening their free institutions, they will take practical steps to maintain and develop their own capacity and that of their partners to resist aggression. . . .

Successful resistance to aggression in the modern world requires modern arms and trained military forces. As a result of the recent war, the European countries joining in the pact are generally deficient in both requirements. The treaty does not bind the United States to any arms program. But we all know that the United States is now the only democratic nation with the resources and the productive capacity to help the free nations of Europe to recover their military strength.

Therefore, we expect to ask the Congress to supply our European partners some of the weapons and equipment they need to be able to resist aggression. We also expect to recommend military supplies for other free nations which will cooperate with us in safeguarding peace and security. . . .

Article 5 deals with the possibility, which unhappily cannot be excluded, that the nations joining together in the pact may have to face the eventuality of an armed attack. In this article they agree that an armed attack on any of them, in Europe or North America, will be considered an attack on all of them. . . .

This does not mean that the United States would be automatically at war if one of the nations covered by the pact is subjected to armed attack. Under our Constitution, the Congress alone has the power to declare war. We would be bound to take promptly the action which we deemed necessary to restore and maintain the security of the North Atlantic area. That decision would be taken in accordance with our constitutional procedures. The factors which would have to be considered would be, on the one side, the gravity of the armed attack, on the other, the action which we believed necessary to restore and maintain the security of the North Atlantic area. That is the end to be achieved. We are bound to do what in our honest judgment is necessary to reach that result. If we should be confronted again with a calculated armed attack such as we have twice seen in the twentieth century, I should not suppose that we would decide any action other than the use of armed force [would be] effective either as an exercise of the right of collective self-defense or as necessary to restore the peace and security of the North Atlantic area. That decision will rest where the Constitution has placed it.

This is not a legalistic question. It is a question we have frequently faced, the question of faith and principle in carrying out treaties. Those who decide it will have the responsibility for taking all appropriate action under the treaty. Such a responsibility requires the exercise of will — a will disciplined by the undertaking solemnly contracted to do what they decide is necessary to restore and maintain the peace and security of the North Atlantic area. That is our obligation under this Article 5. It is equally our duty and obligation to the security of our own country. . . .

Anyone with the most elementary knowledge of the processes of democratic government knows that democracies do not and cannot plan aggressive wars. But for those from whom such knowledge may have been withheld I must make the following categoric and unequivocal statement, for which I stand with the full measure of my responsibility in the office I hold:

This country is not planning to make war against anyone. It is not seeking war. It abhors war. It does not hold war to be inevitable. Its policies are devised with the specific aim of bridging by peaceful means the tremendous differences which beset international society at the present time. . . .[17]

The speech just quoted gives Acheson's basic reasoning on the Atlantic Pact. It does not cover all the questions that were raised in the public and Senatorial discussion of the Treaty. For a more detailed discussion of some of these tough points, we turn again to the Hearings.

The toughest problem in negotiation, and in the Senate, was the problem of Article 5, often called the heart of the Treaty. In this Article the United States and all other members agreed "that an armed attack against one or more of them in Europe or North America shall be considered an attack against them all," and "that, if such an armed attack occurs each of them . . . will assist [those] so attacked by taking forthwith, individually and in concert with the other parties, such action as it deems necessary, including the use of armed force, to restore and maintain the security of the North Atlantic area."

This language is the product of much discussion and compromise among foreign diplomats, the State Department, and members of the Senate Committee. The central difficulty was this: the European parties to the Treaty wanted an unconditional guarantee of unlimited American support in the event of Soviet aggression, but under the American Constitution — at least in the traditional opinion of the United States Senate — no such prior guarantee is possible. The problem, then, was to find language for Article 5 which would give adequate assurance to both the Europeans and the Americans. The somewhat cumbersome result has, so far, satisfied both parties. The speech quoted above contains a brief gloss on Article 5; the remarks which follow are additional evidence of Acheson's thought on the matter:

SECRETARY ACHESON. The provision of Article 5 of the North Atlantic Treaty states, first of all, that an attack upon one is an attack

[17] Radio address, March 18, 1949 (*Bulletin*, XX, pp. 384–88). The italics appear in the original mimeographed release of the speech.

upon all. That is to make clear that there is collective self-defense involved. The article then goes on to spell out what happens when that occurs. . . .

That might be a declaration of war and the use of all the resources of the country. It might be something much less, depending on what happens as a result of the attack. If the attack is something which has not been deliberately planned but has flared up in some way, it might be dealt with by means not involving the use of armed force. It might be dealt with by reason, and that sort of thing.

If, however, it were a deliberate plan, a highly mobilized attack upon the whole area, then I assume that the only thing that could possibly have any effect in restoring and maintaining the security would be every possible physical effort on the part of the country. . . .

SENATOR DONNELL. If I may give you an illustration, Mr. Secretary: If Norway were to be attacked, six months after this treaty were ratified, by a force of 500,000 Russians, this pact would constitute, in your opinion, would it not, an absolute engagement on the part of this country to go to war?

SECRETARY ACHESON. My judgment would be that the only way to restore peace and security would be by the use of armed force. You might differ with me on that.

SENATOR SMITH OF NEW JERSEY. . . . Would you or would you not consider this an extension, for example, of our original foreign policy of noninterference in the affairs of the world and the Monroe Doctrine, and so forth? In other words, is it really an extension of exactly the same principle on exactly the same basis that we laid down when we made the unilateral declaration of the Monroe Doctrine that now we have extended in the Rio Pact into a collective responsibility of the same principle for this hemisphere? Now in this treaty we have extended our vision because of world conditions, World War II and threats to peace, to include these Atlantic Pact countries? The same principle is involved that we had in mind when we did set the Monroe Doctrine?

SECRETARY ACHESON. I think you are entirely right, Senator Smith. This is the recognition and enunciation of something which has happened twice before in our history. It lays down principles on which we have acted in this hemisphere since the statement of President Monroe which developed into a similar treaty within the hemisphere. . . .[18]

---

[18] Hearings, *North Atlantic Treaty*, Senate, Committee on Foreign Relations, 81st Congress, 1st Session, April 27, 1949, pp. 28, 29, 30.

Another problem which concerned some Senators, though not those on the Foreign Relations Committee, was whether the treaty could in fact be considered an aggressive anti-Soviet alliance, as the Soviet Government had officially claimed. Acheson had already made a most emphatic declaration on this point, but Congressional hearings are no place for a man who is unwilling to repeat himself, and the following passage shows that something is often gained, in clarity and pungency, by such repetition:

> THE CHAIRMAN [Senator Connally]. . . . Now, Mr. Secretary, you brought out rather clearly — it won't hurt to reiterate it a little — that this treaty is not aimed at any nation particularly. It is aimed only at any nation or any country that contemplates or undertakes armed aggression against the members of the signatory powers. Is that true?
>
> SECRETARY ACHESON. That is correct, Senator Connally . . . and it seems to me that any nation which claims that this treaty is directed against it should be reminded of the Biblical admonition that "The guilty flee when no man pursueth." . . .[19]

The debate on the North Atlantic Treaty was long, and not always cool, but from the beginning it was plain that it would eventually be ratified. The Senate of the United States will not be rushed, and its consent did not come as quickly as most supporters of the Treaty would have liked. But it came, and its coming was the product of a national debate and a national decision. For fundamental authority and leadership in the debate itself, one would have to turn to a wider circle than any one man or group, but the fundamental reasoning behind this nearly all-American decision was, for other leaders as for Acheson, much as it has been presented above. Europe and America were indivisibly connected; their common defense was a common problem; war in one place would mean war for all. Why not say so clearly, and act on the statement, in the hope that any would-be aggressor would learn in time what was learned too late by Imperial Germany and by Adolf Hitler? It was a great and far-reaching decision, a reversal of ancient objections to foreign entanglement. The vote in the Senate was 82 to 13, and since the Treaty became law, some of its thirteen opponents have come to think it valuable.

[19] Hearings, *North Atlantic Treaty*, Senate, Committee on Foreign Relations, 81st Congress, 1st Session, April 27, 1949, p. 17.

3. For the Common Defense

The United States, as the most popular member of the North Atlantic Community and the one with the largest and most productive plant, has necessarily a leading role in building balanced collective forces.[20]

Treaties are as treaties do — however pretty the words, their real meaning comes only in action. This is particularly true of the North Atlantic Pact, which contains much more than a simple mutual guarantee of support in the event of aggression. If Article 5 is its heart, the bone and sinew is to be found in what is done under Article 3 and Article 9. Article 3 provides that "the Parties, separately and jointly, by means of continuous and effective self-help and mutual aid, will maintain and develop their individual and collective capacity to resist armed attack." Article 9 establishes a council to recommend measures "for the implementation of Articles 3 and 5." A very large part of Acheson's time and effort as Secretary of State can be described as falling under these two articles, and his public discussion of this activity and its objectives provides a good running account of the matter.

On August 8, 1949, he appeared before a Joint Hearing of the Foreign Relations and Armed Services Committees. He was the first witness for the Administration in the presentation of a bill providing military assistance to various countries important in the defense of the free world. The bulk of the authorization for which he was pleading concerned the North Atlantic Treaty countries, for whom somewhat over a billion dollars was requested, in addition to the power to release substantial surplus stocks of military equipment. The first point he made about this military program is that it was a direct outgrowth of the measures discussed in preceding sections of this chapter.

With respect to Europe, primary emphasis has been placed upon the revival of the economies of the free peoples as the necessary foundation of their social structure and political organization. The European Recovery Program has in fact achieved a gratifying degree of economic rehabilitation. It also has produced salutary results in the form of greater political stability and renewed confidence in the future.

[20] Address to Members of the Senate and the House of Representatives, May 31, 1950 (*Bulletin*, XXII, p. 935).

Yet, it has become increasingly clear that economic measures alone are not enough. Economic recovery itself depends to a considerable degree upon the people being inspired by a sense of security and the promise of the future to put forth their best effort over a long period. This sense of security and faith in the future in turn depends upon a firm belief in the ability of the free nations to defend themselves against armed aggression. Such a belief is notably lacking in Western Europe today. Therefore, the capacity of mutual self-defense on the part of the free nations of Europe must be increased, largely by their own effort, without [impeding] progress toward economic recovery. We must not now, by failing to recognize fully the fear of security which is growing out of the clear pressures [exerted] from the East, lose the gains already made. Prompt action is imperative to create the conditions that will allay that fear and will erase the conditions that might encourage an aggressor to resort to military force.

It is for these reasons that the European Recovery Program, the North Atlantic Treaty, and the proposed military-assistance program are elements of a broad and soundly conceived policy with definite and attainable objectives. Two of the pillars are in place. Favorable action on the military-assistance program is vitally necessary now as an essential element of the structure. . . .

The nations of Western Europe, with the exception of Great Britain, were virtually disarmed as a result of enemy occupation during the war. They have begun to rebuild their defenses but have made barely a beginning, because . . . the greater part of their resources has properly gone into economic recovery. Meanwhile, the Soviet Union has continued to maintain the largest armed forces in the peacetime history of any country, has substantially expanded the areas under its control, and has used or attempted to use its obvious military superiority to intimidate and coerce smaller nations. The serious imbalance of military strength in postwar Europe has exposed the nations of Western Europe to the constant danger of aggression and has created a widespread sense of insecurity which has impaired confidence in the future and impeded the recovery effort.

What is the meaning of this situation for our own country? It is important that the American people fully realize the extent to which the circumstances I have outlined have radically altered the security position of the United States. In both of the two world wars in which we have engaged, our allies in Western Europe were relatively strong — in fact, at the outset they possessed more military power than the United States. They grappled first with the enemy and fought the early stages of both wars with comparatively little help from us. In each case, only after a period of intensive training and rearming were we able to throw our full weight into the struggle and tip the scales on our side.

The first line of defense is still in Europe, but our European allies today do not have the military capacity to hold that line. The shield behind which we marshaled our forces to strike decisive blows for the common cause no longer exists. In that sense, the United States is open to attack on its own territory to a greater extent than ever before.

But in a broader sense this weakness in the front line of defense in Europe produces not only strategic dangers to our own country — it increases the danger of war itself. In and of itself it is an invitation to aggression and hence a threat to the maintenance of peace. The dictators of recent times have become involved in war when, in their belief, their intended victims would fall easy prey without substantial risk to the aggressor. The strengthening of the defenses of Western Europe is designed to prevent a repetition of the tragic consequences of such dangerous self-deception. Its first objective, like that of the North Atlantic Treaty, is peace.

Thus, history and common sense dictate the wisdom that the preservation of peace and of our own security is immeasurably advanced by the strengthening of Western Europe to resist aggression. The North Atlantic Treaty, reflecting this wisdom, is based on the concept of the common and collective defense of that area by the member nations. This purpose is in turn advanced as the members progressively become more able to play their parts in collective action.

The treaty does not contemplate that one nation undertake the defense of the area, but that all do. The nations of Western Europe have every desire to play their full part. Their peoples passionately want to avoid the indignities and suffering of another occupation. . . . They want to be able to defend themselves if attacked and to be able to hold the aggressor at bay until we can come quickly to their aid. They can realize this purpose only if they actually possess adequate defense forces in being, not planned on paper for some future date or concentrated three thousand miles away on this side of the Atlantic. . . .[21]

[21] Joint Hearings, *Military Assistance Program*, Senate, Committees on Foreign Relations and Armed Services, 81st Congress, 1st Session, August 8, 1949, pp. 6–8.

This last point is really the central one in Acheson's mind, and it may be useful to emphasize it by adding a comment from an earlier hearing:

> These nations are anxious to join with us. They say the signing of this pact means that we are all together. They say, as we look at the situation, if there were a really serious, all-out attack, we know that in the long run, probably, the great strength of the United States would end in the defeat of the aggressor.
>
> But in the meantime, they say, "we would be overrun. Most of us," they say, "would be dead; our countries would be destroyed. The final outcome would be that the United States would be liberating a corpse."
>
> "Now," they say, "we want a chance to fight with you; we want a chance to protect ourselves; we want to join in the effort. If you can help us in bringing the equipment of our admittedly small forces to a more competent level, then the will of those forces to fight will be great, the will of the countries to resist will be great; and any would-be aggressor will know that he will be faced with immediate resistance, not only ultimate defeat, but immediate resistance, so that he cannot accomplish his results by some kind of coup or some kind of a push which is all over before he starts. . . ." [22]

Acheson continued his presentation of the military assistance program by pointing out that the planning and effort of a joint defense program were already well under way in Europe. But even here he came back in the end to the basic issue of hope against fear:

> We must never forget that we are dealing not with abstractions, but with people. Our allies in Western Europe are human beings, with human hopes and fears. Because of the constructive and productive efforts which we and they have put forth together in recent months, their hopes today are greater than their fears. We must keep their hopes in the ascendancy. [23]

Having laid out the background, he stated the terms of the bill, and then continued with a general argument for the program:

[22] Hearings, *North Atlantic Treaty*, Senate, Committee on Foreign Relations, 81st Congress, 1st Session, April 27, 1949, pp. 43–44.

[23] Joint Hearings, *Military Assistance Program*, Senate, Committee on Foreign Relations and Committee on Armed Services, 81st Congress, 1st Session, August 8, 1949, p. 10.

Under the proposed legislation, the United States would meet this situation by authorizing the President to supply military assistance heretofore requested by nations which have joined with us in the North Atlantic Treaty for purposes of collective defense, on the basis of self-help and mutual aid. The amount of assistance proposed by these nations is approximately 1.1 billion dollars for the period ending June 30, 1950. . . .

I am convinced that this program is the most logical and effective way of dealing with a major problem which cannot be ignored or allowed to go unchallenged, but must be recognized and met with firm and forthright measures. If the job of assisting the free nations to strengthen their defense against aggression is worth doing, it is worth doing well. When the stakes fundamentally at issue are our own freedom and security, I do not believe the American people will be satisfied to settle for half measures.

I think we can put this proposal in proper perspective by considering what its practical effects are likely to be. . . .

Would it strengthen or weaken the security of the North Atlantic Community? Western Europe is now an organism with a soft shell, and as such it invites attack from the predatory. It must develop a hard shell of adequate defense forces to discourage such an attack. . . .

A realistic understanding of the nature of the struggle being waged in Europe warns us that we must consider the ever-present possibility of aggression and take effective action to forestall it. Whatever the Communists may claim for the supposedly superior appeal of their ideology to the minds of men, the record shows that no Communist government has come to power in any country by the free choice of the people, openly expressed in an honest election. The pressure of the large military forces maintained in readiness at all times behind the iron curtain is the club in the closet of every Communist government in Europe, and there is little effort made to keep the weapon concealed.

The record also shows, notably in the cases of France and Italy, that if strength in the hands of democratic governments is resolutely and wisely used, they can prevent aggressive Communist minorities from seizing power by force. The military assistance proposed for Western Europe would go to governments which have already proved themselves capable of dealing with subversion. The further strengthening of their defenses would make them still less vulnerable to internal threats to their security and more capable of resisting aggression against their frontiers.[24]

This last argument has not always been persuasive to critics of the policy of military aid. Their claim and his answer to it were given by Acheson in a statement to the House committee:

> It is contended by some that, in any event, there is no way to create a defense which would protect Western Europe from invasion once such an invasion had been launched. This is the counsel of despair. It is like arguing that because burglars can break into houses we should not put locks on our doors. We do not believe that to discourage military aggression it is necessary to create Western European defensive forces which are by virtue of their size capable of successfully resisting an all-out attack. What is required is rather sufficient strength to make it impossible for an aggressor to achieve a quick and easy victory. The dictators of recent times have become involved in war when, in their belief, their intended victims would fall easy prey without substantial risk to themselves. The strengthening of the defenses of Western Europe is designed to prevent a repetition of the tragic consequences of such dangerous self-deception.[25]

So he rejected the notion that Russian strength was too great to make it worth while to strengthen Western Europe. And he argued further that the assistance program was in the interest not only of the North Atlantic Community but of the United States itself, and the cause of peace:

> Even though our defenses in this country may be strong, we are only partly protected as long as the European members of the Atlantic Community are woefully weak. The transfer of some of our military potential to Western Europe, without weakening us at home, is a form of insurance which is soundly conceived and which we can afford. It is simply common sense to shift part of our strength, which at the moment is the major element of strength of the Atlantic Community, to the point where it may be needed first and can be used with quick effectiveness. . . .

[24] Same hearings, pp. 10, 12–13.
[25] Hearings, *Mutual Defense Assistance Act of 1949*, House, Committee on Foreign Affairs, 81st Congress, 1st Session, July 28, 1949, p. 16.

Would military assistance strengthen or weaken the chances of world peace? The greatest danger to world peace today is the possibility that an aggressor, in an ill-considered attempt at easy conquest, might launch an attack on an intended victim which would draw other forces into the conflict and precipitate an all-out war. The military assistance program is designed to preclude that possibility by providing free nations under pressure the means to defend themselves effectively and thus to discourage a potential aggressor from making the attempt.[26]

We have treated these arguments at some length, because they have remained a part of Acheson's policy continuously since they were first expressed. They are, of course, not his alone; this is much the same case that was made for the first military assistance program by other members of the Administration and by both Democrats and Republicans in the Congress. The bill for which this argument was made passed with the support of a strong bipartisan majority in both houses, though there was real debate and a close fight on the amount to be provided (the House at one stage cut the amount requested in half). In the end a flat billion was appropriated for aid to North Atlantic Treaty members, but the use of most of it was made conditional upon the development of a truly unified defense plan for the area.

Acheson's next business was the direction of American diplomacy in working out such a plan and the machinery for its operation. Here we move into a part of history the details of which are not yet on the public record. From August, 1949, to December, 1950, there were six meetings of the North Atlantic Council, which is the senior controlling body of the North Atlantic Treaty Organization. This Council is composed of the foreign ministers of the member nations, and during its first year of operation Acheson was its chairman. In September, 1950, he provided a useful summary of the early work of the Council:

I think in looking at the whole North Atlantic Treaty one needs to get a little perspective. . . .

The first thing that had to be done was to set up the framework of the organization. That was done at the meeting of September 17, 1949. They there created the main structure of the North Atlantic Organization: defense under a committee of defense ministers; finance under a

[26] Joint Hearings, *Military Assistance Program*, Senate, Committees on Foreign Relations and Armed Services, 81st Congress, 1st Session, August 8, 1949, pp. 13–14.

committee of finance ministers; production and supply under another group; a military committee made up of professional military people; a standing committee, which was made up of French, British, and American Chiefs of Staff — that was the organization.

The next thing they had to do was to devise the fundamental strategic concept which was called for, particularly in relation to the U. S. military defense assistance program, which is based on agreed collective . . . plans rather than on unintegrated aid to individual nations. That was worked out and was approved in our meeting in the first of the year. . . . It then went to the President and was approved by him and became the basis for operations under the Mutual Defense Assistance Program. Now, that was an important accomplishment.

The defense ministers then got to work on the implementation of this strategic concept — what were the forces to be, and how were they to be organized. That came before the defense ministers in their meeting in April on a report from the military regional planning groups. At that time it was a tentative report. They sent it on to the Council with their approval. The Council approved it at its meeting in London in May and asked them to take hold of it and with all possible speed try to shake it down into minimum terms to get it down into something that just could be done. In the meantime the Council asked all the member governments to get on with their programs, because whatever they did immediately was certain to be far less than the long range requirements.

Among other things we did at the May meeting, besides take that action was to get estimates of the financial magnitude of the task and then to center upon this idea of balanced collective strength with available resources. . . . [27]

The agreement on the notion of "balanced collective forces" was indeed the fundamental achievement of the London meeting of the Council, in May, 1950. On his return from this meeting Acheson addressed a meeting of members of the House and Senate; a major element of the address was an exposition of the new notion:

Perhaps the most important action of the Council was the recommendation of . . . the creation of balanced collective forces, rather than

[27] Remarks at press conference, September 6, 1950 (Department Press Release No. 911, 1950).

the duplication by each nation in a large or small way of what every other nation was doing. . . .

This principle of balanced collective forces is of great and perhaps revolutionary significance. It has its legislative origin, so far as this Government is concerned, in the Mutual Defense Assistance Act of 1949 which stipulated that the assistance to be granted by the United States to other North Atlantic Treaty countries, should be used to promote "the integrated defense of the North Atlantic area." It demonstrates that each country will rely on every other member of the community, and that the community will look to each country to contribute what it is best able to contribute to the common defense in accordance with a common plan. It demonstrates that each country recognizes that its own security is no better than the security of the community as a whole. It will give tangible proof to an aggressor that he must face the combined resources of the community, and there will not be opportunities to pick off one member at a time.

The United States, as the most populous member of the North Atlantic Community and the one with the largest and most productive plant, has necessarily a leading role in building balanced collective forces. If we faithfully observe this principle and direct our energies to the creation of such forces, we will find a corresponding response from the other Treaty members. . . .[28]

In line with the agreements and the basic principle worked out in these early meetings, the American government proceeded, in the spring of 1950, with plans for a second year of military assistance; the program was to include for the following year a level of appropriations and effort almost exactly the same as that approved the year before. Acheson's testimony before the joint committees of both houses, in early June, 1950, emphasized in about equal proportion the gains which had been made and the need for continued progress. Questioned about the prospect of an eventual decrease in the level of military assistance, he was a little less optimistic than he had been the previous year. In 1949 he had thought it possible that the natural development of defensive strength in Europe would permit a fairly early decrease in American help, although he carefully pointed out that no clear-cut prediction was possible. In 1950, even before Korea, he was somewhat less hopeful:

[28] Address to members of the Senate and the House of Representatives, May 31, 1950 (*Bulletin*, XXII, p. 935).

The effort which we are going to have to make here, and abroad, is going to be considerable. We are a long way from having an adequate security force for the North Atlantic Treaty, and I think that all the members of the Treaty and the United States have got to face the fact that unless there is a very considerable change in the international climate and actions of certain other powers, we may have to put more, rather than less effort into the defense field.[29]

Thus in early June, 1950, the North Atlantic Treaty nations, including the United States, were engaged in strengthening their collective defenses by stages which seemed slow, casual, and insufficient a few weeks later.

It remained a fact that in a little over a year there had been established a quite unprecedented organization for the planning and control of this collective defense. Acheson pointed out, even in early June, that the program in contemplation "comes far from meeting the total bill," but he also believed that "we have accomplished more than I thought it would be possible to do."[30] At the very least, there had been established the framework for a rapid reaction to the open challenge laid down to the free world by a flagrant act of armed aggression on June 25, 1950, in Korea. And it may be worth remarking that no Senator or Congressman, at least in the published hearings, raised any question with Acheson as to the adequacy of the program presented in early June; all the questions on size were aimed in the opposite direction.

4. After Korea

The immediate, urgent need is for all of us to step up our defenses.[31]

When the Communist army of North Korea undertook to "liberate" the southern half of that unhappy land, on June 25, 1950, the face of the world changed. The years since 1945 often appear, looking back, as no more than a series of crises, and the vista is not entirely appetizing to a people slowly coming to believe that the end is still far away. But Korea was not just

[29] Hearings, *Mutual Defense Assistance Program, 1950*, Senate, Committee on Foreign Relations and Committee on Armed Services, 81st Congress, 2d Session, June 2, 1950, p. 12.
[30] Hearings, *To Amend the Mutual Defense Assistance Act of 1949*, House, Committee on Foreign Affairs, 81st Congress, 2d Session, June 5, 1950, pp. 6, 10.
[31] Statement to the Armed Services Sub-Committee of the House Committee on Appropriations, August 2, 1950 (*Bulletin*, XXIII, p. 249).

another ordinary crisis; it was the first clear-cut act of military aggression since the fall of the Axis, and as such it had an immediate and spreading impact. The direct course of events and policy in the Far East must be reserved for later discussion; what is important here is the way in which American policy toward Europe, and indeed the policy of the Atlantic Community as a whole, was sweepingly modified by a new sense of danger and urgency. Partly because this change has been so obvious, perhaps, and partly because it is a change in tempo and magnitude, not one of basic purpose or method, it has been surprisingly little discussed. Yet a clear understanding of American policy in the last year cannot be achieved without a recognition that in a very few weeks after June 25 the whole pattern of thought changed. This was true of the public, of the Congress, and of the Administration.[32]

A simple but striking example of this change is to be found in the shift which occurred in the Mutual Defense Assistance Program between Acheson's appearance before the committees in early June and his reappearance at the end of August. In June the Administration had been asking for a billion dollars for European military aid, and the pressure of questioning, together with the temper of the Congress generally, made it seem doubtful that all of this would be granted. In August the Administration asked for an additional three and a half billions. The Congress responded at once, almost without debate, and its final vote was overwhelming — 311 to 1 in the House, and unanimous in the Senate. For the moment at least, the legislature seemed to share the Administration's view that military aid abroad was a part of our own national defense, and the aid appropriation received the same eager support as the enormous new appropriations for the American armed services.

[32] There is no doubt that Korea thus marks a turning point, but it is also likely that for some Administration leaders, and in particular for Acheson, it was in part simply an opportunity to adopt openly a policy urgently recommended in private for some months previously. On this analysis, for which I am unable to present official documentation, the Soviet mastery of atomic energy, signalized by an atomic explosion in August or September, 1949, was a turning-point as important as Korea. It seems certain that for some months before Korea Acheson was a leader in demanding a higher level of American and Allied armament, and it seems a good guess that this advocacy was based in essence on the line of reasoning at which he hints in the testimony quoted below on pages 92–93. All this, however, was behind the scenes, and there is no official record from which to describe it. Indeed, the official position of the Administration was that the Soviet bomb did not make any difference. I have never been convinced that this outward attitude was either genuine or wise. By the same token I think it plain that Acheson was right and brave to urge rearmament so early.

The hearings on the vastly expanded aid program, though short and to the point, brought out several aspects of the new tenor of policy. Perhaps the most important development was the evidence of a new attitude toward the place of Germany in the defense of the West, but this problem deserves separate treatment. Three other aspects of the matter can be treated here; they were well covered by Acheson. The first is simply the new need for speed:

> The international Communist movement has shown that it does not hesitate to use force to conquer a sovereign and independent nation, where it can hope to do so successfully. . . .
>
> The strength of the free nations is potentially great — more than enough to deal with this threat. But we must translate that potential into defense in being, with the greatest speed.
>
> The capabilities of the Communist movement for further acts of aggression must be the measuring rod by which we judge the adequacy of our defensive strength. By this measurement, it is evident that a forced-draft effort on a very large scale is required.
>
> It takes time to create defense in being. To build up armies, and to equip them with tanks and planes, takes many months after the necessary decisions are made.
>
> The magnitude of the task before us is apparent. It is also apparent that we cannot wait for the complete refinement of plans before beginning to increase necessary production of equipment. . . .[33]

The second point is a little more tricky, and somewhat less explicitly brought out in the hearing. It is that before Korea the pace was too slow, even for the somewhat less tense situation of that time.

> There was an effort to equip the forces which were called for by the existing budgets of the European treaty members. Those forces conformed to the strategic concept.
>
> It was recognized by everyone, by the Europeans, by the military side of the treaty organization, and by the Council, that the forces which were called for by these budgets were only a beginning. [But] even these small forces had not been adequately armed, so we had to press forward to provide them with equipment.

[33] Hearings, *Supplemental Appropriations for 1951*, Senate, Committee on Appropriations, 81st Congress, 2d Session, August 31, 1951, pp. 268–69.

Since we have received the Defense Ministers' more detailed plans, it has been perfectly clear to the Council, and through them it has been reported to the governments, that the rate of progress was not sufficient. . . .

SENATOR SALTONSTALL. Is their failure to go forward due to lack of morale, lack of spirit to fight? . . . Or is it a lack of confidence in us, or what?

SECRETARY ACHESON. I do not think it is any of those things. I think it has been in part that they have been trying to get centered on exactly what should be done, so that you would not waste time doing the wrong thing.

In part, they have not until recently had the sense of urgency which is necessary. In part, also, it is because the size of effort required, raises very severe economic problems for them. These problems can be worked out, but it takes some time to adjust their attitudes of mind to it. . . .

It is a struggle.[34]

The American government, even before Korea, was disturbed by the rate of progress in creating an effective defense force. To the degree that this is true, the attack in Korea may have had advantages for the West. Certainly the Americans did not find themselves alone in a changed attitude after that attack:

In response to our inquiries, most of the North Atlantic Treaty countries have indicated their intentions to increase their defense efforts and have indicated the general magnitude of the efforts which they feel they should undertake.

The speed with which they have replied has been most gratifying and has reflected a sense of urgency on their part, which we welcome. Their projected plans are now under active study in this Government and are also being discussed in the current session of the Deputies of the North Atlantic Council.[35]

The third general result of the Korean attack was to shift the balance of priorities between military and economic aid. Until Korea, Americans

---

[34] Same hearings, pp. 278–79.
[35] Same hearings, pp. 269–70. The Deputies of the North Atlantic Council are a group who sit more regularly than the foreign ministers are able to do; the American representative is Charles Spofford.

and Western Europeans were agreed that economic recovery should have priority; Acheson himself made the point repeatedly, and it was formally embodied in the preamble to the Mutual Defense Assistance Act. But with Korea the emphasis changed; economic strength was still important, but it could no longer have, in and of itself, an absolute priority; it was now primarily important as a part of the pattern of defense. The following passage shows fairly the new attitude:

> We must recognize, in the administration of the mutual defense assistance program, that the health and vitality of the economies of the countries associated in this effort are a fundamental part of the defensive strength of this group of nations. . . .
>
> The security of our country, and of the free world, of which we are a part, will depend upon the speed and the cooperation with which this program is put into effect.
>
> The defense effort required is tremendous, but we cannot afford to do less.[36]

Finally, the new urgency and the new call for action necessarily imposed a new load on American leadership. This is not a pleasant thought for many Americans, but Acheson did not duck it:

> We recognize that commensurate efforts by the other nations, whose total economy is roughly forty percent of ours, impose burdens more than comparable with ours, and we recognize therefore that we have special responsibilities toward the common effort. . . .[37]

The primary emphasis thus shifted to the defense effort; within the defense effort the emphasis shifted from plans to action; and as the need for effort increased, a new and special responsibility passed to the richest and least burdened of the Atlantic partners. Yet in the summer of 1950, there remained a number of important matters still unplanned, and a number of weaknesses of organization. Not until December, after two further meetings of the North Atlantic Council, was Acheson able to discuss the defense set-up in terms which indicated that the planning phase was coming to an end. Is

---

[36] Same hearings, p. 271.

[37] Statement to the Armed Services Sub-Committee of the House Committee on Appropriations, August 2, 1950 (Department Press Release No. 797, same date).

there a hint of impatience in the following résumé, presented at a press conference after the Brussels meeting of the Council in December?

This meeting at Brussels was the conclusion of a chapter in a long book, a book in which the chapters which lie behind us are history, and the chapters that lie before us are plans for dynamic action.

So far as the North Atlantic Treaty organization is concerned, that is only one part of this book. It is an important part. That part of the chapter which lay before Brussels was a period and a very important and necessary period of planning and organization. We were thinking to draw up the structure of this organization before we could go to work to put real muscle and real bone into it.

Brussels brought the culmination of that part of the North Atlantic Treaty work. We have finished the matter of organization. Now we have taken the first step in the field of action. From now on it is action which counts and not further resolutions or further plans or further meetings, although there will be all of those.

The important thing now in the future is action. At Brussels we did several things. We took recommendations which had come from the meetings immediately preceding in London and acted on those recommendations. They had to do with the creation of the united, unified, integrated army which is to provide for the defense of Europe. The papers which came to us laid out the structure of that army, how should it be composed, of what troops, where should the troops come from, how should it be organized, what was its command structure, what was the higher command structure which would give that army its direction and how should the Supreme Commander be selected and appointed. . . . All of those matters were acted upon.

The structure was agreed upon and the force was created. The Council unanimously asked the President of the United States to select a United States officer to be the Supreme Commander. A specific recommendation was made as to who it was hoped that officer would be. The President responded at once, and that officer, General Eisenhower, was unanimously appointed the Supreme Commander.

The creation of a supreme commander and the selection of General Eisenhower is an essential step and a most vital step in galvanizing into action the actual translation of these papers into terms of men with guns and materiel and air forces and naval forces into being.

There must be this one dynamic figure to give all of our allies the guidance, the direction, the inspiration which will lead to the translation of papers into people and things and organized people and organized things. General Eisenhower, more than any living soldier, has got the capacity, the prestige, the imagination which can bring that about. His appointment is in itself a great act in Europe, which has completely revolutionized the attitude of people toward the problems ahead of them and given them the sense that it can be done and it will be done and here is the leadership and here is the spirit with which to do it. . . .

This force which is now in being means several concrete things. It means, first of all, that our forces in Europe will be, and they now are, under the command of General Eisenhower. It means that the British and French and Italian and Dutch and Belgian and all the other forces of all the other North Atlantic Treaty nations which are now in existence for the defense of Europe will be, and many of them now are, under his command. It means also that those forces must be increased. They are not now adequate for their mission. They will be increased and steps are in process now by which they will be increased in France and in England and in other countries of Europe, *and in the United States additional forces will be placed at General Eisenhower's disposal in Europe.*[38]

And with this last sentence we move on to another Great Debate.

[38] Remarks at a news conference, December 22, 1950 (*Bulletin*, XXIV, pp. 3–4). Italics added.

CHAPTER FOUR

The Great Debate on Troops to Europe

AT THIS MOMENT, *there could be no greater contribution to the cause of peace than for the Government of the United States, in all its branches, to reaffirm the course of action on which we are moving.*[1]

Between December, 1950, and April, 1951, the people of the United States held a broad discussion on the ways and means of American policy toward the world crisis, and in particular toward Europe. This discussion gradually came to a focus on the relatively narrow question of the attitude which the Senate should take on President Truman's decision to strengthen the American ground forces in Western Europe, but its origin and its significance were considerably wider. In essence, this was a re-examination of the basis of policy toward the North Atlantic community, deriving special point and energy from two events which, on the surface, seemed to have only a tangential relevance to the issue: serious reverses in Korea, and a marked Republican gain in the mid-term elections. Since Acheson's part in this debate was that of defender, not an attacker, we must briefly outline some of the attacking positions. Perhaps the most notable opposition leaders were ex-President Hoover and Senator Robert Taft. In this discussion we omit the Republican attack upon Acheson as an individual.

It was Mr. Hoover who opened the debate. In a radio address delivered on December 20, he argued for a policy less reliant upon allies, and more reliant upon a defense of the Western Hemisphere. "The foundation of our

---

[1] Hearings, *Assignment of Ground Forces of the United States to Duty in the European Area,* Senate, Committee on Foreign Relations and Committee on Armed Services, 82d Congress, 1st Session, February 16, 1951, p. 86.

national policies must be to preserve for the world this Western Hemisphere Gibraltar of Western civilization." He agreed, in a later statement, that "We are vitally interested not only in carrying out the North Atlantic Pact, but [also] in the preservation of Europe as a part of civilization itself." Still he remained very doubtful of the will and spirit of Europe, and he did not think it America's business to create their spiritual forces for them. In particular, he was opposed — and here he was clearly affected by the reverses in Korea — to any important commitment of American ground forces to the defense of Europe. America's reliance must be on overwhelming air and naval strength; America's only really reliable ally in Europe was Great Britain; the deterrent to Soviet aggression in Europe must be the deterrent of overwhelming air and naval strength, American and British. At all costs the country must avoid "Operation Land War in Europe." [2]

Mr. Taft's opinions were similar but not identical. He too was disposed to rely chiefly on air and naval strength; he too was opposed to any American leadership in organizing direct defense of Europe, and in particular he was opposed, though not violently, to the appointment of an American as the Supreme Commander in Europe. Yet he was not opposed to the commitment of "some limited number of American divisions," under certain conditions, and in the end he supported the President's decision to send four more. Mr. Taft's real zeal and ardor were directed to his basic mistrust of the President and the Secretary of State, and to his clearly sincere conviction that matters of this sort must be decided by Congress and not by the President alone. A scarcely concealed undercurrent in all his statements was his feeling that the whole course of American policy in recent years had been fuzzy, untrustworthy, and overexpensive. This was not surprising, because Mr. Taft had been either sceptical of or directly opposed to each successive step in policy toward Europe, from the Marshall Plan through the North Atlantic Treaty and the Mutual Defense Assistance Program. And Mr. Taft thought his smashing victory in Ohio was largely the result of the fact that the public shared these views. Immediately after the election, he called for a re-examination of the scope, methods, and character of American aid to Europe. Yet he specifically repudiated the concept of isolationism, which he thought a meaningless notion with no adherents.

[2] Mr. Hoover's views were stated in a series of public addresses and statements, most of which were very fully treated in the *New York Times*. The quotations in this paragraph are from his address of December 20 and his statement to the Joint Committee on troops to Europe, February 27, 1951.

Mr. Taft had often stated his view that the Administration was "soft" on communism, and that the State Department, particularly under Acheson, was a hotbed of unreliability, or worse.[3]

It will already be clear to the reader that the opinions of Mr. Taft and Mr. Hoover did not commend themselves to Acheson. He lost no time in making his position clear, and for this some even among his supporters have criticized him, suggesting that it would have been better to make a great effort to co-operate and compromise with such leading figures. Acheson evidently believed that the differences were too deep for compromise, and I leave to the reader the question whether the basic attitudes of Mr. Taft and his friends were or are compatible with the basic principles of policy toward Europe as Acheson understood them. With this indecisive comment, let the Secretary speak for himself. The first, and perhaps the least important of his replies to Mr. Taft came very shortly after the elections in November. Mr. Taft had said isolationism was dead, but he had called for a re-examination of foreign policy; Acheson's reply was prompt:

I should like to discuss with you something which has to do with the natural history of public life. I read in the papers, and I'm sure you do too, that there is a species of *Homo sapiens* which has now become extinct; very recently, only in the last few weeks, has it become extinct. That is the isolationist.

We are told there aren't any more. And we are told it is very rude to refer to anybody as an isolationist, and it hurts the feelings of people to use that phrase since all isolationists are now extinct. They are just as dead as the dodo or the saber-toothed tiger.

But there is a new species which has come on the horizon. This new species I call the re-examinist, because the re-examinist says, "I want to re-examine all our policies and all our programs."

I was very much puzzled when I heard about this new species of re-examinist coming on. I thought to myself of how we are all affected by advertising slogans. There is an advertising slogan which says "some words fool you." I don't want this word to fool us. We need to look at this re-examinist and see what kind of a person he really is.

[3] Mr. Taft's opinions on foreign policy can be found most handily in the *Congressional Record*. His major address in the Great Debate was delivered on January 5; subsequent addresses of interest were delivered outside the halls of Congress on January 15 and February 10. Mr. Taft also testified at length during the hearings on sending troops to Europe. His views on the significance of the November election can be found, among other places, in *U.S. News & World Report*, November 17, 1950.

If to re-examine what we are doing means to do what we do every single year of our lives, which is to go before the Congress and explain every single item of every policy and every program and to justify every dollar for which we ask the Congress, then this can't be a new species. There is nothing new about it, because we all belong to that school; we all re-examine our progress. We all find out what our failures have been. We all look at what new actions we should take. We all justify what we have been doing.

But is that what this really means? Is that what this re-examinist wants? Because it might be something different. And if it's something different we ought to know that.

Now, it's possible that a re-examinist might be a farmer that goes out every morning and pulls up all his crops to see how they have done during the night. It might be that that is what it means. Or it might be that this kind of a re-examinist is someone who comes down to breakfast in the morning and looks at his wife or at her husband and says, "Do I really love that man or woman? How did I ever turn up here with her or him?" Or he can put on his hat and go down to the office and look around and say, "Am I really in this business? Are these my partners? How did I get mixed up with these people? I wonder if I shouldn't have been an atomic scientist after all?" Is that what it means?

When we re-examine, does it mean that we are like the sound navigator who, on a long flight or a long voyage, checks his course by the sun and stars every day? Or does it mean that the navigator says, "How did I ever get started on this? Do I really want to take this trip after all?"

What does it mean? It is very important for us to find out. If it means any of these things that I have suggested, then it is something very serious in terms of our whole life. It is serious because it means that the person who has the views of the farmer who tears up the crops every morning, the man who doesn't know whether he really loves his wife, or the wife who doesn't know whether she really wants to live with her husband, or the navigator who doesn't know whether he has started on the right course — if that is what it means — then that person, or a nation which takes that view, puts him or itself in the center of its map of the world. He or it is the center, and the map goes out from there. If that is so, then that person is sitting in isolation. That person or that nation is isolationist, because everything has to originate from him or from it. That person is incapable of constancy of purpose. That person is incapable of the very foundations of leadership, and a nation which accepts that view cannot associate itself in the larger groupings of people where mutual confidence is required.

Now, if that is true, it is very important. We have it on the highest of all possible authority that no man, having put his hand to the plow and looking back, is fit for the Kingdom of God. No nation and no group of people who wish to lead a nation in this day and age in which we live are worthy of leadership, if at every moment they wish to tear up and examine the very roots of the policies upon which the whole future of the free world depends.[4]

These remarks, of course, are both clever and cutting, and most of the press, in reporting them, gave primary emphasis to the obvious fact that the Secretary was scoring off an old opponent; much less attention was given to the basic argument behind the wit (and perhaps Acheson should have foreseen that this would be the result). Yet the speech in fact contained an argument which went to the roots of his disagreement with Taft: in the struggle for freedom, the one sure way to lose was by adopting an attitude of niggardly, fearful, doubting mistrust, of self, of national purpose, and of friendly countries. This argument was re-emphasized later in the same talk:

The United States has gone forward in the economic field, gone forward in the human rights field, gone forward in the effort to prevent war. The Soviet Union has been frustrating these efforts from the very beginning. And so we have come to another series of ideas — we must carry on these efforts within the free world and also, within the free world, we must build up a military shield. We cannot any longer count upon the good faith of nations to settle their disputes amicably.

When we see what happened in Korea, when we see what has happened in other parts of the world which are exposed to Soviet threats, we know that we cannot count upon restraint and on obedience to law and good will. And so through the North Atlantic Treaty and through the Military Assistance Pact and through the whole conception now of a unified force in the Atlantic community, we are building up a shield for the protection of free men. This is the center of the whole force of free-

---

[4] Extemporaneous remarks to the National Council of Negro Women, November 17, 1950 (*Bulletin*, XXIII, pp. 839-40).

dom. Behind this shield, free men can continue to build up their economic power and their economic welfare. And that has resulted in programs which are going forward in the Western World.

At the same time this has happened, we have seen the great surge of nationalism in the Far East. We have seen the great desire of the peoples of the Far East to free themselves from the misery under which they have lived and to build lives which will be worthy of human beings. We have done our best to help that.

Here is something of great complexity. Here is a thing which requires constancy of purpose. Here is a thing which requires year after year after year of effort. It requires building our own force, being faithful to our allies and to our friends, and never allowing discouragements to deflect us from our course, never allowing irritations between free nations to build up into friction which will divert us from our ends. It requires the greatest patience, the greatest courage, the greatest determination, to carry this forward.[5]

To an argument like this Mr. Taft might give no violent opposition, but it was impossible to imagine him *making* the argument; the role of leadership in world affairs was not one which he had ever approached with this sort of dedication. And in this basic sense, isolationism and re-examinism were cousins. This at least was Acheson's conclusion, and in the last paragraphs of his remarks he pointed the course he believed in:

In the light of what I said earlier, in the light of all these things, does it make sense to say, "I want to re-examine our programs? I want to look at this all over again to see whether we should have started on it?" Is that the role that a leader in these troublesome times, these dangerous times, wishes to take in the world today? I think your answer is that it is not.

We are in for a period of great struggle. We are in for a period of sacrifice. We are in for a time which will take all the courage we have. Anyone who offers you easy answers, anyone who says that your life can go on undisturbed in this time is not telling you the truth. It is not worthy of your courage because you will respond to leadership. But there is hope. This is not a long dismal road with no hope at the end. It is the only road with hope. A road which requires determination and courage is not one from which you will shrink.

[5] Same source, p. 841.

Again, in the Book of First Corinthians it is written "that he that ploweth should plow in hope; and that he that thresheth in hope should be partaker of his hope."

We must look forward both with hope, with courage, and with determination to the future. We are not looking back. We are not pulling up our roots. We have put our hand to the plow and, having done it, there is only one way to look — that way is forward.[6]

This argument did not appeal to Mr. Taft and those of his general view, and the re-examination proceeded. Mr. Hoover spoke about the Rock of Gibraltar, and Acheson responded with a general denunciation of the extreme form of isolationism implied by that phrase (though not, perhaps, by the whole of Mr. Hoover's speech). "We are rejecting any policy of sitting quivering in a storm cellar waiting for whatever fate others may wish to prepare for us."[7] And if basically the debate was on attitudes, not issues, it gradually narrowed, at least in form. In the end it shaped itself around the question of the ways and means of sending ground troops to Europe. Senator Wherry of Nebraska introduced a resolution stating that "no ground forces of the United States should be assigned to duty in the European area for the purpose of the North Atlantic Treaty pending the formulation of a policy with respect thereto by the Congress." After some debate and modification, the resolution was referred to the joint Foreign Relations and Armed Forces committees, and there, on February 1, the hearings on the Great Debate began.

The first witness was General Eisenhower, who had meanwhile made a quick but extraordinarily comprehensive inspection trip to Europe. The basic theme of his address to Congress and his response to questions in Committee was one the reader will by now find familiar: "We must make sure that the heart and soul of Europe is right. . . . But we must not watch that so closely that we fail to get out in front to provide the leadership that will make this thing a complete success. So this faith in America is one that lies at the bottom of this whole thing. Faith that the leadership she can provide will inspire the same kind of feeling, the same kind of effort in our friends abroad."[8]

[6] Same source, p. 841.

[7] Remarks to a press conference, December 22, 1950 (*Bulletin*, XXIV, p. 6).

[8] Hearings, *Assignment of Ground Forces of the United States to Duty in the European Area*, Senate, Committee on Foreign Relations and Committee on Armed Services, 82d Congress, 1st Session. February 16, 1951, p. 6.

After General Eisenhower came Secretary of Defense Marshall. The highlight of his testimony was the statement that the troops the President planned to send to Europe were four divisions, and supporting troops to a total of about one hundred thousand men; [9] to advertise this decision to the Russians was a most unusual action, and General Marshall indicated that he had done so only because a great national debate should not be based on uncertainties as to what was being discussed. The remainder of his testimony closely paralleled that given by Acheson, who was the next witness, and to whose statements we now turn.

Much of his argument rehearsed matters which have already been treated in previous sections, and may be omitted here. Certain sections, however, were addressed particularly to issues which had arisen in the public debate. It had been argued that there was no way to defend Europe if indeed aggression should come; this argument had been made with particular force by Mr. Hoover. Acheson had two answers to this claim:

> Some have approached this problem as though the chief, if not the sole, question is: "How do we repel the attack after it is launched?"
>
> The trouble with talking about this part of the problem as if it were the main question, or even the question of primary concern to our own security, is that it increases the risk of losing Europe in other ways. It is not only the threat of direct military attack which must be considered, but also that of conquest by default, by pressure, by persuasion, by subversion, by "neutralism," by all the paraphernalia of indirect aggression which the Communist movement has used.
>
> If we approached this problem as though our sole concern were how we were going to act after Europe had been attacked, regardless of the human cost, whatever the devastation, then we can scarcely expect our European allies to show much enthusiasm for the prospects of the future. This kind of strategy drives our friends in Europe into a mood of nonresistance, a mood of "neutralism," which is, for them and for all of us, a short cut to suicide.
>
> So our first purpose — and this is something we need to make absolutely clear to our friends in Europe — is to deter the aggressors from attacking Europe. Our primary concern is not how to win a war after it gets started, but how to prevent it, and how to help Europe stay free in the meantime. [10]

[9] The figures on troops (but not the number of divisions) were later revised upward, and it is hard to avoid the conclusion that they should not have been stated, even with the reservations the Secretary attached.   [10] Same hearings, p. 78.

The argument that Europe could not be defended was not only destructive to European morale; it was false:

> The argument is sometimes advanced that the Western European defense forces cannot be made large enough to equal the forces available to the potential aggressor, man for man, and therefore would be useless. The difficulty with this argument is that it considers the European defense forces in isolation, as a sole weapon, instead of considering these forces as a vital adjunct to the other deterrent forces available. It is not the case that ground forces would or could be sufficient by themselves, or that air or sea power by themselves could or would be sufficient, but that the three elements of our deterrent forces, taken together, are the best means of preventing an attack from taking place.
>
> However overwhelming our available air-striking power is likely to be in the period ahead of us, the presence of defense forces in being in Western Europe is a vital part of the effectiveness of our air power as a deterrent to attack. Not only do air forces require bases from which to operate, which must be held on the ground by defense forces, but air power alone is not a sufficient deterrent against the risk of a quick all-out effort to seize the Continent. . . .[11]

One of the opposition arguments Acheson was willing to accept; it was true that the policy of building strength had its risks. But he also believed any other course held worse dangers; the point comes out clearly in a speech delivered some weeks later:

> It is one of the inescapable features of this situation that, as we eliminate the weaknesses which invite aggression, the tensions and the dangers of the immediate period may increase.
>
> Since the only alternative to this course would be to remain at a disadvantage and ultimately lose all, we have no choice but to plug ahead, building our combined strength as steadily and as rapidly as we can. That is the only way to work our way through this period of danger.[12]

And in the hearings he paid his respects to those who drew opposite conclusions from the fact that building strength was dangerous:

[11] Same hearings, p. 80.
[12] Address to the U.S. Chamber of Commerce, April 30, 1951 (*Bulletin*, XXIV, p. 767).

A number of questions have been raised about this effort to build up the forces in being, in Western Europe. Some have asked why we need to do this — why we can't continue to rely on deterrent force of our retaliatory air power, and our reserve power elsewhere. Some have argued that this European defense force cannot possibly be made large enough to be effective, while others have argued that this European defense force would be so great a threat to the Soviet Union that it would be provocative. These concerns, although contradictory of each other, have led to a common line of reasoning — that we should not move ahead with our European allies in building a defense force in Western Europe.

Apart from the helpless and defenseless predicament in which this course of action — or more accurately, this course of inaction — would leave us, there are a number of powerful considerations which point to the conclusion that our own security, as well as the security of our allies in Europe, requires vigorous efforts to build an effective defense force in Europe at the earliest possible moment.

One reason why we cannot continue to rely on retaliatory air power as a sufficient deterrent is the effect of time. We have a substantial lead in air power and in atomic weapons. At the present moment, this may be the most powerful deterrent against aggression. But with the passage of time, even though we continue our advances in this field, the value of our lead diminishes.

In other words, the best use we can make of our present advantage in retaliatory air power, is to move ahead under this protective shield to build the balanced collective forces in Western Europe that will continue to deter aggression after our atomic advantage has been diminished.[13]

In these sentences Acheson touched carefully on a point of the greatest significance in the whole discussion, and later that morning he expanded his comment. The following exchange further clarifies a vital truth which the Administration has not sufficiently emphasized.

SENATOR GREEN. You say, "But with the passage of time, even though we continue our advances in this field, the value of our lead diminishes."

[13] Hearings, *Assignment of Ground Forces of the United States to Duty in the European Area*, Senate, Committee on Foreign Relations and Committee on Armed Services, 82d Congress, 1st Session, February 16, 1951, pp. 78–79.

Now will you explain a little more why that necessarily follows?

SECRETARY ACHESON.   I find it difficult, but perhaps I can do it by an illustration.

If you and I are standing close together and I am pointing a .38 at you and you are pointing a BB gun at me, I have a considerable advantage. But if we are standing very close together and I am pointing a .45 at you and you are pointing a .38 at me, the advantage has declined. . . . I do not think I should go into this any more.[14]

Another point overlooked by the advocates of air power was the fact that open aggression by the armed forces of the Soviet Union was by no means the only danger faced by Western Europe.

Another reason why the availability of defense forces in being in Western Europe is necessary is that it enables the free nations to deal more effectively with, and thus to prevent, the various forms of aggression that threaten them.   So far, we have been talking about the possibility of bold, naked aggression by the Soviet Union itself.   But we have seen recent examples of another form of Communist aggression — disguised aggression through a satellite.

We see at the present time the build-up of forces in East Germany and the satellite states.   This build-up contains the possibility of overt moves which could be disclaimed by the real center of aggression.   In the absence of defense forces in being, satellites might be used for such disguised aggression in the hope that they could get away with it, since the free nations could respond only with the weapons of all-out general war, or not at all.   The presence of adequate defense forces would remove this temptation.

We have also become familiar with the Communist use of indirect aggression, in which the Communists employ the weapons of fear and threats to undermine confidence and paralyze the will to resist.   We saw this happen in Czechoslovakia.   The presence of adequate defense forces in being is also a bulwark against this kind of aggression.[15]

Having thus stated his opposition to the views of the re-examiners, Acheson continued with a direct discussion of the thinking and action which had led to the President's decision to send troops to Europe.   He pointed out

[14] Same hearings, pp. 106–7.   [15] Same hearings, p. 79.

that this decision, based on the advice of the Defense and State Departments, had been publicly announced by Mr. Truman as far back as September. He reviewed the development of the concept of "balanced collective forces"; he reviewed the events leading to the appointment of General Eisenhower to command these forces in Europe; he emphasized, as General Eisenhower had before him, that great efforts were under way in Europe — "roughly speaking, the combat forces of our European allies may be expected to double in the next year." Then he turned to the remarkable fact that the debate of December and January had led to a large measure of general support for five basic propositions, and from these he went on to state the issue as it remained, and his basic view of it:

First, there is general acceptance of the vital importance of a free Western Europe to our own existence.

Second, there is no dispute concerning the basic principles underlying the North Atlantic Treaty.

Third, there is general agreement on the necessity of increasing the strength of our own land, sea and air forces.

Fourth, it is generally agreed that the primary purpose of these policies is not just to keep us out of a land war in the North Atlantic area, but to prevent there being any war in that area.

Fifth, there also seems to be general agreement that we should send some additional troops to Europe to do our part in helping to build an integrated force, as one of the necessary deterrents to war.

What, then, is the issue? Fortunately it is a very narrow one. It involves the amount, the manner, and timing of the build-up of our Ground Forces now in Europe in the interests of the security of this country.

General Marshall has told you the size of the force which we have had in mind contributing under present conditions. Of course, the contribution of this country on the sea and in the air is understandably greater.

But it is not only the size of our contribution which is important, but the manner of it. The spirit of our participation is, in the final analysis, directly related to the morale of this entire operation, and morale, as General Marshall emphasized yesterday, is the vital ingredient of our security system.

We are bound to our allies by ties of common interest, and a clear appreciation of these ties is the fundamental basis of the actions we are here discussing. . . .

The thing that really holds the integrated force together is the continuing conviction that the national interest of each party is most effectively served by working together through the integrated force.

Finally, I should like to speak to the suggestion that we await the full development of Europe's own defensive force before making our contribution. The need for the strength to deter aggression is immediate, and we have already learned how swiftly events may move in the modern world. Our allies are building their forces now; the time for our own contribution is now. If each of the North Atlantic nations should wait to appraise its partners' efforts before determining its own, the result would be as disastrous as it would be obvious. Whatever risks we may run by following the policies which our country has pursued thus far, the greatest risk of all is that we might once again hear the bitter refrain: "Too little and too late." And this time there may be no opportunity to remedy the mistake.[16]

Always the debate came back to leadership; should the United States take the lead, or wait and see? This was where it had begun, really, and Acheson's argument was addressed to the fundamental disagreement which underlay the five agreed propositions. He and the majority with him believed that the United States must provide leadership, and however they might qualify their attack, the opposition did not. In his December speech Mr. Hoover had said that the Europeans must create an invincible barrier to Soviet aggression "before we land another man or another dollar on their shores." This was the basic issue, and on this issue there could be no compromise.

There were other issues in the debate, however. Of these the most important, and the most discussed, was whether or not the Chief Executive had the right to send additional troops to Europe, to serve as members of the defense force of the North Atlantic Treaty nations, without Congressional approval. Acheson was involved in this question from two angles, first, as one of the President's chief advisers, and second, as one of those who had interpreted and defended the Treaty when it was first considered by the Senate.

As a Presidential adviser Acheson, not surprisingly, held that the powers of the Chief Executive were clear and abundant. He had filed "a very substantial brief in that regard" on earlier occasions, and in response to questions from Senator Wiley it was inserted in the record. In essence it held as follows:

[16] Same hearings, pp. 84–5.

A. That the President's power to send the Armed Forces outside the country is not dependent on congressional authority has been repeatedly emphasized by numerous publicists and constitutional authorities. . . .

B. It is important to examine some of the purposes for which the President as Commander in Chief has dispatched American troops abroad. In many instances, of course, the Armed Forces have been used to protect specific American lives and property. In other cases, however, United States forces have been used in the broad interests of American foreign policy. . . .

C. In other cases United States forces have been used to implement provisions of treaties to which the United States was a party. It is the President's duty under the Constitution to take care that the laws are faithfully executed. That this applies to treaties (which are a part of the supreme law of the land) as well as to statutes is unquestioned. As stated by ex-President William H. Taft: "The duty that the President has to take care that the laws be faithfully executed applies not only to the statutory enactments of Congress but also to treaties. . . ."

D. Not only has the President the authority to use the Armed Forces in carrying out the broad foreign policy of the United States and implementing treaties, but it is equally clear that this authority may not be interfered with by the Congress in the exercise of powers which it has under the Constitution. . . . [17]

This was the constitutional position, as he saw it, but it was not really the central matter:

It seems to me that perhaps a little more is involved here, and that we are in a position in the world today where the argument as to who has the power to do this, that, or the other thing, is not exactly what is called for from America in this very critical hour, and if we could all agree on the fact that something should be done, we will perform a much greater role in the world, than by quarreling about who ought to do it. . . .

I think that regardless of the question of power or a division of power or responsibility, it is . . . vitally necessary to the complete unity of the American people behind this most important program that the Ameri-

[17] Same hearings, pp. 89–92.

can people feel that the Congress itself has certain responsibility and certain powers. I should think that the executive branch itself would be most anxious that they feel that Congress will at all times exercise that power. I can't visualize the unity of action in support of a long-term program such as this involves unless those conditions do exist, and do exist in such way as to convince the American people that the Congress can speak.

Now, of course, the mere power to make appropriations or to raise armies, which does reside in the Congress, would be in effect a participation and a joint participation along with the Executive in carrying out the treaty. But to my mind it seems to me that this particular treaty should be interpreted especially in the light of the admitted meaning of its terms and its conditions by the Executive when the Executive submitted the treaty to the Congress for ratification. . . .

We do not really solve this question by trying to split legal hairs as to what is the authority of the Executive, what is the authority of the Congress. They must act together and no strong policy which will carry out what is so necessary here can be done without the full unity of the Executive and the Congress in pursuing it. . . . [18]

There were great advantages to be obtained from cooperation, but this was a very different thing from any Congressional effort to limit by law the President's power to send troops; on this point Acheson's answer had been given earlier in the morning to his first questioner:

No one can foresee what the needs of the situation may produce and to attempt rigidly to tell our military authorities the strength of this, that, or other branch of the force which they can employ in advance of any particular military operation would be, I think, most unwise.[19]

Thus the objective was cooperation, but not in a straightjacket, and the problem, as friendly Senators saw it, was to frame a resolution which would make clear the support of the Congress, and in some sense its sharing in the policy, without at the same time limiting the clear-cut powers of the President. And of course the further, and perhaps controlling consideration, was to get a solid majority for whatever resolution might be agreed. This was primarily a problem for Senators, not Secretaries of State, and Acheson re-

[18] Same hearings, pp. 93, 99.   [19] Same hearings, p. 88.

fused to be drawn into public discussion on the detailed points involved. He contented himself with emphasizing that it was not a case in which Senators need fear that the American decision was guided or controlled by some un-American force; the President's decision was an American decision, not the product of some sort of command from the North Atlantic Council.

There remained one further point. When the North Atlantic Treaty was debated in the Senate, it had been the general understanding that there was no plan to send American ground forces to Europe as part of the new defense effort; moreover it had been made entirely clear that there was no legal commitment to send such troops under Article 3. Acheson himself had testified on this point in absolutely definite terms, and now a question arose as to whether the President's decision of September was not a violation of previous understandings between the Executive and Legislative branches. This point had particular importance for Acheson because some Senators interpreted his assurance that there was absolutely no legal commitment as an assurance that no troops would ever be sent under the treaty. He was able to show in testimony that this interpretation was quite unjustified. He admitted that in 1949 he would not have thought it would so soon become essential to send American troops to Europe. He pointed out that this change was the result of great changes in the international scene. It was typical of the division of the Republican side that this explanation was entirely satisfactory to Senator Morse and quite unsatisfactory to Senator Hickenlooper. Yet the record was entirely plain; there was no legal obligation to send troops, and there had been no promise that troops would never be sent.[20]

So the detour on what had been said two years before came back in the end to the basic question; under the Treaty it was our obligation to help, but under the Treaty it was our privilege to decide for ourselves what sort of help was needed. Now, in 1951, the President and his advisers believed, as they had not believed in 1949, that we should help with four additional divisions of ground troops. Would the Congress support them?

It turned out, in the end, that the Congress would. The Senate, after long debate, adopted on April 4, resolutions approving the despatch of four additional divisions "for the joint defense of the North Atlantic area." These resolutions also called for further Congressional approval of any further

---

[20] The discussion on this point can be found in the same hearings we have been quoting, pp. 122–23.

ground reinforcements, and the Constitutional question thus remained somewhat unsettled, the more so as these resolutions were advisory, not legal, in form. Both sides of the great debate claimed victory, and the issue need not be settled here.

With the debate on Troops to Europe we come to the end of the history of Acheson's position on the basis of policy toward free Europe, as it had unfolded by the summer of 1951. Since history does not stop for printers, the story continues after the point where we must stop. In May the President submitted to Congress a foreign aid program for the following year in which he asked for something over seven billion dollars for Europe, most of it for military aid. The task of building and defending the North Atlantic Community was certain to continue for many years. Yet for our purposes, the history so far considered is perhaps enough; Acheson's basic position contained a consistency and clarity not likely to be disturbed in the framing of additional undertakings. So we may leave the broad question of policy toward Europe with one last statement of his view:

There can be no real question as to America's willingness to contribute its fair share of manpower and equipment to the defense of the North Atlantic area. But we have another contribution to make which is equally vital — the spark of leadership. Since World War II, the Congress and the executive branch have recognized this fact and have cooperated fully in performing the many tasks which the role of leadership involves. From the formation of the United Nations to the recent designation of General Eisenhower as Supreme Commander of the North Atlantic Treaty forces, this country has remained continuously in the front ranks of the struggle to assure peace, freedom, and security throughout the world.

We sometimes forget the historic nature of the steps through which we have passed in the past 5 years in our efforts to establish peace and security in the world.

We sometimes lose sight of the profound advance which is represented by the close association which has grown up among the nations of the North Atlantic area, and the significance of this association for the entire world.

We have passed through the period of organization; we have passed through the phase of planning; we have passed through a time of the awakening of people to the nature of the true danger in the world. We are now deep in the period of action.

We must carry forward the construction of the forces upon which the hopes of peace of the entire civilized world are founded.[21]

[21] Same hearings, p. 85.

CHAPTER FIVE

Germany

THE GERMAN PROBLEM *cannot be disassociated from the general problem of assuring security for the free nations.*[1]

From 1941 through 1951 the policy of the United States in Europe has inescapably revolved around or near the problem of Germany; from nonbelligerent Lend-Lease to non-belligerent leadership in the Atlantic Community is a long course, and at each stage the German problem has been focal. Since January, 1949, the German policy of the American Government and its Secretary of State has been constantly and intimately connected with the broader policy of containing the Soviet Union and building the free world. German problems are thus of particular interest in that they show how a specific set of difficulties have been treated in the larger context. It is easier to talk of containment and community than to make them effective, and the case of Germany shows it.

The German problem also has a natural and large-scale interest of its own. Western Germany includes the bulk of the mines and factories from which the Germans twice constructed military strength that almost broke the life line of freedom in European history. This is the part of Germany that lies next to France — the geography is obvious, but the geographic fact has a political and emotional significance no American statesman can safely forget. Germany is next to France as no nation has ever been next to the United States.

For both containment and community, success in Germany is vital. In

[1] Address to the American Society of Newspaper Publishers, New York, N.Y., April 28, 1949 (*Bulletin*, XX, p. 585).

strategic terms, Germany is the grand prize of the struggle for power in Europe. Acheson has stated the matter simply: "Germany occupies a place of particular significance . . . because Soviet control over the Ruhr would put the Soviet rulers in a strong position to reach out for the rest of Europe. The Soviet rulers have long understood this simple strategic fact." [2] So a first charge upon American policy is to prevent Soviet control of the Ruhr.

Yet the negative task is only part of it. Germany must not merely be saved from the Soviet Union; she must be saved *for* the Atlantic Community, and for two reasons. Until she is a member of the community, in good standing with a full future, Germany, by geography and history, remains a grave danger to the West. And, conversely, without the strength and partnership of Germany, the Atlantic Community itself is gravely weakened. Acheson has made both of these points, at somewhat different times, and they are both now a part of American policy.

The objectives are thus simple and clear. If in foreign policy one could have one's goal by stating it, the German problem would now be solved. Unfortunately the same history and geography which dictate the goal of policy have dictated enormous difficulties, with the result that American foreign policy has no more complex task than the pursuit of its German objectives. Above and beyond the "normal" problems of the postwar life of Western Europe, the people of Germany have faced three special difficulties, each of which has had a major impact on their relationship to the world. They have been defeated, divided, and distrusted.

The defeat of Germany, and her unconditional surrender in May, 1945, can be viewed from two perspectives — that of the six years that followed, or that of the six years that went before. The standard perspective at the time was the latter. The first thought of the occupying Powers — and in particular of the United States — was to punish the worst offenders of the Nazi régime and to eliminate the military power and menace of Germany. So far from stimulating or assisting in German recovery, the occupying Powers looked upon the assets of Germany as a hunting ground for reparations which might assist the recovery of the victor nations, and if the United States refused any reparations for herself, she nevertheless approved the principle of reparations for others. Her own commander was specifically instructed not to concern himself with the economic recovery of the American zone of occupied Germany. Even those who vigorously opposed the preposterous Morgenthau Plan were not at first ready to argue that the

---

[2] Address to the U.S. Chamber of Commerce, April 30, 1951 (*Bulletin*, XXIV, p. 767).

United States should *help* the Germans. It is only in retrospect that this policy seems hard to understand; seen from the standpoint of V–E Day, from the standpoint of Hitler as a fact and not a memory, it becomes so natural as to be almost inevitable. The total defeat of a terrible aggressor carries penalties.

Yet the defeat of Germany has probably had less to do with her troubles than her division. The original hope of the Western Allies was that the defeated nation might be governed as a unit under a Four-Power Allied Control Authority. This proved impossible. The Soviet Union resisted any attempt to include its eastern zone in a unified administration — except on its own totalitarian terms; it also made impossible the negotiation of any German settlement; so the supposedly temporary arrangements for military occupation gradually hardened, and the division of Germany between East and West became constantly sharper. Economically this was gravely damaging; politically it was a constant source of tension, for Germans found the division of Germany was as unreal, and necessarily abhorrent, as Americans would find a division of the United States at the Mississippi.

Defeat and division, in combination, had produced by the end of 1947 an economic and political distress in Germany even more acute than those which prevailed in Western Europe as a whole, and this distress in turn imposed upon the American Government a special burden, for as Acheson has pointed out, "disaster was avoided primarily by American economic aid." In December, 1947, in London, Secretary of State Marshall made one further effort, along with his Western colleagues, to get some reasonable agreement on Germany with the Soviet Union. When this effort failed, the whole pattern of American policy toward Germany rapidly altered. Acheson described what happened in a major address on German policy shortly after he became Secretary of State, and we may take the following passage as a clear description of what was going on when he took the reins:

> This government made earnest efforts for two and a half years after the war to resolve the major issues arising from the defeat of Germany and to achieve a general settlement. During that period we participated in the four-power machinery for control of Germany established by international agreement in 1945.
>
> By the end of 1947 it appeared that the Soviet Union was seeking to thwart any settlement which did not concede virtual Soviet control over German economic and political life. This was confirmed in two

futile meetings of the Council of Foreign Ministers in Moscow and London. It was emphasized in the Allied Control Authority in Berlin, where the Soviet veto power was exercised three times as often as by the three Western Powers combined.

The resultant paralysis of inter-Allied policy and control created an intolerable situation. Germany became divided into disconnected administrative areas and was rapidly being reduced to a state of economic chaos, distress and despair. . . .

The German stalemate heightened the general European crisis. The European Recovery Program could not succeed without the raw materials and finished products which only a revived German economy could contribute.

By 1948 it became clear that the Western Powers could no longer tolerate an impasse which made it impossible for them to discharge their responsibilities for the organization of German administration and for the degree of German economic recovery that was essential for the welfare of Europe as a whole. These powers determined to concert their policies for the area of Germany under their control, which embraced about two-thirds of the territory and three-fourths of the population of occupied Germany.

These common policies were embodied in the London agreements, announced on June 1, 1948. . . .

The London agreements established a basic pattern for future action in the West. . . . The western zones were to participate fully in the European Recovery Program. An International Authority for the Ruhr was to be created to regulate the allocation of coal, coke and steel between home and foreign consumption, to insure equitable international access to Ruhr resources, and safeguard against remilitarization of Ruhr industry.

The Germans were authorized to establish a provisional government, democratic and federal in character, based upon a constitution of German inception. It would be subject, in accordance with an occupation statute, to minimum supervision by the occupation authorities in the interest of the general security and of broad Allied purposes for Germany. Coordinated Three-Power control was to be established, with the virtual abolition of the zonal boundaries.[3]

[3] Address before the American Newspaper Publishers' Association, New York, N.Y. April 28, 1949 (*Bulletin*, XX, p. 586).

Thus the punitive period after defeat came to a clear and complete ending, and thus also the Western Powers began to deal with the fact of a divided Germany. The London agreements held out to Western Germany a real prospect of increasing membership in the growing partnership of the free nations. Marshall Plan goods began to arrive in Germany, and a real recovery began.

The price of this recovery and this growing partnership was a sharpening of the existing division of Germany; dramatic evidence of this connection was given in the last week of June, 1948, when the Western Powers introduced, for their zones of Germany, a sweeping and extraordinarily beneficial reform of the German currency. This independent action, taken outside of the Four-Power authority in which the Russian veto had hamstrung all plans for recovery, was a clear token of the Western determination to proceed to make Western Germany live again. The Russians then blockaded Berlin. For the next ten months the Western zones of Berlin were kept free by the Anglo-American airlift, while the West retaliated by imposing its own blockade on trade between East and West Germany. Meanwhile the London agreements were carried forward, and plans for a new West German Republic were actively developed.

The decision to hold in Berlin was made while Acheson was a private citizen, but we may pause over it for a moment, because he has constantly referred to it, since he became Secretary of State, as an example of the method and the advantage of a policy of "situations of strength." The Soviet blockade aimed at a disruption of the Western effort to rebuild West Germany as a going concern. The West refused to pay blackmail, and refused to quit Berlin; it held on. Another point is worth noting: the West could not have held on if it had not been for the extraordinary will and courage displayed by the people of Western Berlin.

When Acheson took office, the blockade and the airlift were still in action and there was no immediate prospect of a solution to the problem. Meanwhile the economic recovery of Western Germany was proceeding at a great rate. The political planning among the Western countries was in less satisfactory shape. The London agreements called for a new occupation statute; negotiations to that end, however, were at an impasse. And this brings us to the third of the special problems of Germany — the problem of distrust.

The defeat of Germany, as we have seen, carried penalties. A much greater burden was imposed, however, by the original German aggression; to those Germans who indulge in self-pity, it may seem that they have suffered mainly because they were beaten, but to the Western victors, at least, and particularly to the Western *European* victors, the central point is that Germany has twice been the major cause of major wars. It has therefore been a constant part of Western policy to work against any development which might make it possible, ever again, for Germany to open an aggressive war. In the years after 1945 this policy took the shape of a complete demilitarization, accompanied by stringent limitations on the industrial facilities which might support a war machine. Even in 1948 and 1949, when economic reconstruction and political friendliness were in the air, the absolute opposition to military revival continued, and Acheson emphasized that the military safeguards were, in a way, the necessary condition of the economic and political concessions:

> Of exceptional importance [in the London agreements] were the guarantees of security against a German military revival, a point sometimes overlooked in present-day talk about the hazards inherent in rebuilding German economic and political life. The London agreements provide that there is to be consultation among the three occupying powers in the event of any threat of German military resurgence; that their armed forces are to remain in Germany until the peace of Europe is secure; that a joint Military Security Board should be created with powers of inspection to insure against both military and industrial rearmament; that all agreed disarmament and demilitarization measures should be maintained in force; and that long-term demilitarization measures should be agreed upon prior to the end of the occupation. It should be observed that these far-reaching safeguards are to accompany the more constructive aspects of the program and assure that the new powers and responsibilities assumed by the Germans may not be abused.[4]

Thus in early 1949 the United States stood firm in its view that there must be no military future for Western Germany. With this exception, however, it was ready to grant to the Germans a steadily increasing measure of self-government, and to remove most, if not all, of the restrictions upon German industry. The French were not so eager. Frenchmen could remember that purely military restrictions had been imposed after 1918, and that these restrictions, at the beginning, had had English and American support. When the chips were down, fifteen years later, the English and the Americans

[4] Same source, p. 586.

were no longer concerned. So in the months after the London agreements there was a constant and grinding divergence between French and American policy toward the future of Germany, with the British in between; specific agreements on specific points were slowly worked out, but there was no real meeting of minds.

Then suddenly, early in April, 1949, a complete, general, and extremely friendly agreement was reached at Washington in the space of a few days, by Acheson, Foreign Minister Schuman of France, and Foreign Minister Bevin of Great Britain. This agreement of course did not grow from thin air; it rested on months of complex and effective negotiation, in which a notable role was played by the American Ambassador in London, Lewis Douglas, and the American Military Governor in Germany, General Clay. Still, in essence, the agreement at Washington was a personal achievement by the three men who met there; and if it was a triumph for one more than another, the victory must be awarded to Acheson, for the agreements, in the main, followed the American position. They provided for a new and simpler Occupation Statute, under which the coming West German government would have wide powers except in foreign affairs and matters affecting military security. They provided for a gradual end to the wasteful and deeply resented practice of dismantling and removing German plants; they laid the groundwork for a complete fusion of the three Western zones under a new Allied High Commission headed by civilians. They formally approved an earlier agreement for the control of the Ruhr.

Yet what is most important about these agreements is not their specific content, but the fact that it proved possible to bring the three countries together on a policy so generous to the deeply mistrusted Germans. Let us leave aside the question of personal credit, and turn to the explanation given by Acheson himself:

Early this month I met with the foreign ministers of France and the United Kingdom for talks on Germany, the outcome of which we all regarded as momentous. It was not by mere coincidence that these agreements were initialed during the week the North Atlantic Treaty was signed. That historic instrument marks a decisive step toward the creation of a community of democratic nations dedicated to the attainment of peace and determined to insure its preservation by all the material and moral means at their disposal.[5]

[5] Same source, p. 585.

In other words, the new harmony of the Washington agreements was part and parcel of a new confidence in the mutual loyalty of the members of the Atlantic Community. Specifically, the French were willing to take chances on Germany, after the signing of the Treaty, that they were not ready to take before. This is surely part of what Acheson had in mind as he continued:

> The German problem cannot be disassociated from the general problem of assuring security for the free nations. No approach to German problems can be adequate which deals only with Germany itself and ignores the question of its relationship to the other nations of Europe. The objectives of United States policy toward the German people are interwoven with our interest in, and our policies toward, the other peoples of Europe. Here the basic considerations are the same whether they can extend to all of Germany or must be limited to Western Germany.[6]

And in the American view, the Washington agreements were a long step toward the rebuilding of a united Europe; Acheson continued with a general discussion of this task. Once again he emphasized that the German problem is a European problem, and that American policy depends in the end on the attitudes and purposes of the Europeans and the Germans:

> We have made clear our desire to aid the free peoples of Europe in their efforts toward recovery and reconstruction. We have made clear our policy to aid them in their efforts to establish a common structure of new economic and political relationships. . . .
> In this setting, it is the ultimate objective of the United States that the German people, or as large a part of them as possible, be integrated into a new common structure of the free peoples of Europe. We hope that the Germans will share in due time as equals in the obligations, the economic benefits, and the security of the structure which has been begun by the free peoples of Europe.
> We recognize that the form and pace of this development are predominantly matters for determination by the Europeans themselves.

[6] Same source, p. 585.

We also recognize that effective integration of the German people will depend upon reciprocal willingness and upon their belief in the long-range economic benefits and the greater security for all which will accrue from a joint effort.

The maintenance of restrictions and controls over the German economy and a German state, even for a protracted period, cannot alone guarantee the West against the possible revival of a German threat to the peace. In the long run, security can be insured only if there are set in motion in Germany those forces which will create a governmental system dedicated to upholding the basic human freedoms through democratic procedures.

These constructive forces can derive their strength only from the renewed vitality of the finer elements of the German cultural tradition. They can flourish only if the German economy can provide sustenance and hope for the German people. They can attain their greatest effectiveness only through a radically new reciprocal approach by the German people and the other peoples of Europe. This approach must be based on common understanding of the mutual benefits to be derived from the voluntary cooperative effort of the European community as a whole.

Through all of this effort, our basic aim with respect to the Germans themselves has been to help them make the indispensable adjustments to which I have just referred. We have tried to help them to find the way toward a reorganization of their national life which would permit them to make the great contribution to world progress which they are unquestionably capable of making. But it is important for us all to remember that no one but the Germans themselves can make this adjustment. Even the wisest occupation policy could not make it for them. It must stem from them. It must be a product of their own will and their own spirit. All that others can do is to help to provide the framework in which it may be made.

These are the conditions we consider essential for the long-term solution of the German problem. The purpose of the Washington agreements, and of the other decisions taken by the Western Powers, is to bring about these required conditions at the earliest practicable time. This has been the consistent purpose of the United States Government.[7]

[7] Same source, pp. 585–86.

The Washington agreements on Germany were less than a month old when, on May 5, 1949, it was announced that the Berlin blockade would be lifted. For some time it had been apparent that this particular Soviet move had been a backfire, and negotiations had been conducted by American and Soviet diplomats looking toward a restoration of the *status quo ante.*

The initial hint that the Soviet Union might be ready for genuine negotiation came in January, 1949, when Stalin answered some questions posed by an American journalist.[8] Following up this hint, Ambassador Jessup at the United Nations inquired of the Russian Malik whether Stalin meant what he said, and in particular whether his omission of the currency problem meant that the Soviet Union was prepared to abandon its stand on this issue, which had thus far been a bar to any settlement in Berlin. After a while Malik replied that the omission was deliberate, and it began to appear that a real chance for settlement existed. There followed a series of discussions (held at the Soviet consulate on Park Avenue, in New York), and in May agreement was reached. The agreement was a very simple one — both sides were to lift the restrictions imposed "on communications, transportation and trade" in the previous year, and afterwards the four Powers were to meet in Paris to discuss the German question generally, and Berlin specifically.

Here again one is tempted to speak of successful diplomacy, but it is better to take Acheson's own comment. First he placed credit where credit was due, and second he warned against supposing that the end of the blockade meant the end of the German problem:

> At six o'clock tonight, as you know, the blockade will be lifted in Berlin. . . . I thought it would be appropriate to draw your attention to two things. . . .
>
> In the first place, we are where we are in regard to the lifting of the blockade because of the superb performance of the pilots and their supporting crews, ground crews and so forth, who have been for ten months conducting this air lift. . . .

[8] Stalin's answers to the Kingsbury Smith questions were the beginning of the Soviet backdown in Berlin. They also provided the occasion for a series of comments at a press conference by Acheson in which it was demonstrated that the new Secretary of State was quite able to match the Soviet ruler in debate. Acheson's observations on this occasion have only a topical interest and are not included here, but any reader who thinks him a tool of Marshal Stalin would do well to consult the *State Department Bulletin* of February 13, 1949.

The second thing that I should like to mention is that while we are delighted that their efforts have brought the end of the blockade, we must not regard that fact alone as having solved the German problem. It has contributed greatly toward our being in a position where perhaps over a long period of time we can move forward to a solution. The lifting of the blockade puts us again in the situation in which we were before the blockade was imposed. It was an arbitrary and, in our view, an illegal measure. It has failed because they have indicated it was unsuccessful and because the countermeasures produced their effect. . . .[9]

The next step was the Four-Power meeting of Foreign Ministers. Acheson was in Paris for four weeks, and it is doubtful whether any other four weeks in his term as Secretary of State have seen him working harder for a smaller result. It turned out that the Soviet Union had no intention of relaxing its demand for a return to the chaotic and wholly unworkable Four-Power arrangements of 1945 and 1946, while the Western Powers were equally determined not to lose the progress they had made. The best the West could offer was to let Eastern Germany join in the new federal republic with its guarantees of free speech and secret elections, and it is hardly likely that Acheson and his colleagues were surprised when Vishinsky did not accept this proposal. Toward the end of the meeting the Russian proposed the preparation of a peace treaty looking toward the withdrawal of troops within a year, and when this long-expected bid for German favor was made, the Western ministers rejected it at once, pointing out that if the four ministers could not agree on a dozen lesser matters in Germany, it was fanciful to suppose they could agree on a peace treaty. Acheson refused, for America, to play ducks and drakes with human hopes in this fashion, and he added that the Soviet proposal was as "full of propaganda as a dog is of fleas; in fact it is all fleas and no dog." [10] When the conference finally adjourned, it could show only a limited tactical agreement on Berlin and some signs of progress toward an Austrian peace treaty — and in 1951 a final agreement on the Austrian treaty was still nowhere in sight.

To the present writing, the Paris meeting of the four foreign ministers is the last that has been held, although the spring of 1951 saw a prolonged session of their deputies in an effort to reach agreement on the agenda of a new meeting. It is now more than six years since the end of the European war, and the prospect of an agreed German peace treaty is as far away as ever.

[9] Remarks to a press conference, May 11, 1949 (*Bulletin*, XX, p. 662).
[10] Quoted in the *New York Times*, June 13, 1949.

Yet this does not mean that the conference of Paris was a failure; by 1949 the United States and the American people had long passed the stage where it seemed useful to pursue agreement merely for the sake of agreement. The significance of Paris was in what did *not* happen there. The West did not give ground, and the Soviet attitude on Germany was exposed for what it was, without concessions. Reporters covering the conference made much of the skill with which the Western ministers had dealt with the prosecutor Vishinsky, but to Acheson this was not the point; the point was that the situation, the facts, the realities, were more important than the conference. He took some trouble to explain this view in a press conference just after his return.

In the first place, I think it is important that everybody understands, and I am sure you do, although I doubt whether people throughout the country do, that these meetings of the Council of Foreign Ministers are not battles of individual champions where particularly bright ideas are whet or sharp maneuvers count for very much. It is not the personalities involved, it is not the ability of the individuals who represent countries, which makes a great deal of difference. I think the heart of the matter is somewhere else. . . .

It is in the progress that has been achieved in the restoration of Western Europe that you should look for the explanation of what happened at Paris. It has been the success of the cooperative efforts in Western Europe to which the United States has so greatly contributed in the last two years that made this meeting of the Council of Foreign Ministers different from its predecessors. . . . In other words, these conferences from now on seem to me to be like the steam gauge on a boiler. . . . They indicate the pressure which has been built up. They indicate the various gains or losses in position which have taken place between the meetings, and I think that the recording of this conference is that the position of the West has grown greatly in strength, and that the position of the Soviet Union in regard to the struggle for the soul of Europe has changed from the offensive to the defensive.

The significance of this is very important in explaining why no agreement was possible about Germany. Being on the defensive, the Soviet Union was forced to take, or did take at any rate, the attitude that it would not relax its hold in any way whatever upon any area which it controlled in Germany. . . . The whole program of the Western Powers has been to return as quickly as was safe responsibility to the Germans, responsibility for conducting their own affairs and for conducting their own affairs under a system which guaranteed the basic human freedoms and contained the safeguards necessary for the security of Europe and of the world.

That was a program from which we could not retreat one single solitary inch. We did not. We never could consider it, and no agreement was possible on the basis of our retreating from that position.

The Soviet Union was totally unable to accept that position because that meant relaxing their hold upon what they had. It meant that they could no longer carry on this Sovietization, this domination of the life of Germany which they controlled. . . .

That, I think, is the heart of the whole conference so far as Germany is concerned and it is a very significant fact. It indicated that in the West we are not on the defensive. . . . We are going forward with our program without any hesitation of any sort. Not the slightest delay has been introduced into our program in any way whatever, and the program is in better shape today than it ever was before. Now, that is a negative result from Paris but it is an important one.[11]

For just over a year after the Paris Conference, the German policy of the United States proceeded without essential change. General Clay retired as Military Governor, to be succeeded by John J. McCloy in the new and different job of High Commissioner. Under the terms of the Washington agreement the West Germans worked out the basis for their Federal German Republic, established with its capital at Bonn on June 15, 1949. The elections held later that year showed striking successes for the democratic parties of the center, and an equally striking reverse for the Communists, who polled less than 6 percent of the total vote. Acheson expressed his gratification at these results, and allowed himself also to comment with approval on the victory of those who believed in an economic system like the American. Both the comment and the limitation on it are significant:

We naturally welcome the results of this election insofar as they indicate a decision by the Germans to seek a solution of their economic difficulties through a system of free enterprise. But I wish to make it clear that the Germans remain entirely free, so far as we are concerned, to

[11] Remarks to a news conference, June 23, 1949 (*Bulletin*, XXI, pp. 860–61).

deal with this matter in their own fashion, providing always there is no contravention of democratic principles or of international obligations.[12]

As the Bonn Republic began its work in a task that was bound to be long and painful, even with the best of effort and luck, the Soviet Government hardened still further its grip on Eastern Germany. In October there was established in the Eastern Zone a Communist-controlled "German Democratic Republic," and almost at once there were held what the Communists were pleased to call elections — a plebiscite with ready-marked ballots handed out for open casting by the voter, under the watchful eye of loyal Communists. Acheson formally denounced the "Democratic Republic." The government, unlike Bonn, "is without any legal validity or foundation in the popular will." As for the "election fraud staged in the Soviet zone, our sympathy goes out to the East German people who have been treated in such a contemptuous and humiliating fashion by their oppressors."[13]

The Bonn government, though formed under a basic law and democratically elected, could hardly be called sovereign, since it lacked authority in foreign or military affairs. Inevitably and naturally, the establishment of so much whetted the German appetite for more, and in the spring of 1950 it seemed for a while as if German demands had outrun Western readiness to trust and cooperate. In the task of creating a community in which the Germans could be full members, unbalances of this sort were hardly avoidable — too many human emotions were involved to make the whole pattern smooth and simple. On May 14 Acheson and Foreign Ministers Bevin and Schuman restated their German policy in a fashion which gave particular emphasis to the burden which necessarily rested on the Germans:

> The Allies are resolved to pursue their aim laid down in the Washington agreement of April, 1949, . . . that Germany shall reenter progressively the community of free peoples of Europe. When that situation has been fully reached she would be liberated from controls to which she is still subject and accorded her sovereignty to the maximum extent compatible with the basis of the occupation régime. . . .
>
> The Western Powers desire to see the pace of progress toward this end as rapid as possible. Progress will depend upon the degree of confident and frank cooperation displayed by the government and the people of

[12] Remarks to a news conference, August 17, 1949 (*Bulletin*, XXI, p. 303).
[13] These remarks can be found in Department Press Releases No. 790 and No. 1085 of 1949.

the Federal Republic. In the first place the pace will be determined by the extent to which the Allies can be satisfied that their own security is safeguarded by the development in Germany of a desire for peace and friendly association with themselves. In the second place the pace will be set by the rate at which Germany advances toward a condition in which true democracy governs and the just liberties of the individual are assured. Therefore, the Western Powers wish to emphasize most strongly that the natural desire of the German people to secure relaxation of controls and the restoration of the sovereignty of their country depends for its satisfaction only upon the efforts of the German people themselves and of their government.[14]

These words of admonition were coupled, in the same month, by a quite extraordinary initiative from the government which was most concerned with German dangers and the German future. On May 9 the French Foreign Minister, Schuman, proposed that the steel and coal industries of Germany and France, and of any others in Europe who would join, should be unified under a single authority. Under this authority all nations would have equal rights, and the authority would work not for any one nation but for the general welfare. To this striking proposal the American Government and its Secretary of State at once gave hearty support. In Acheson's view this was precisely the kind of forward step which might lead to a wholly new pattern of European relations; it was also precisely the kind of step the Europeans could take only on their own initiative. Finally, and this point he emphasized to a Senate committee: "The Schuman proposal . . . could only have been made against a background of increased confidence in the economic and military security which has resulted from our economic and military assistance and the efforts of the European nations themselves." [15]

Taken together, the mild warning of May 14 and the Schuman proposal of May 9 give a fair pattern of the state of Western policy toward Germany as it stood in the late spring of 1950. There was to be a constant effort to establish mutual trust and confidence with Western Germany, and in that effort concessions and patience would be required on both sides. There was no thought of "remilitarizing" Germany, and no intention that Germans should bear arms; though voices had been raised in many quarters calling

[14] Joint Declaration on Germany, May 14, 1950 (*Bulletin*, XXII, p. 787).

[15] Hearings, *Mutual Defense Assistance Program, 1950*, Senate, Committee on Foreign Relations and Committee on Armed Services, 81st Congress, 2d Session, June 2, 1950, p. 5.

for German rearmament to help meet the Soviet menace, Acheson's was not one of them, and as late as June 5 he specifically and emphatically reiterated his opposition to German rearmament:

MR. JAVITS.   In your conferences with Mr. Schuman and Mr. Bevin was there any discussion about using West Germany in a military way or not using it, either way?

SECRETARY ACHESON.   We did not discuss that at all.   Our policies are fixed in that matter and I think there is no usefulness in going into that.

MR. JAVITS.   Then what was the presupposition of the conference on the question of that policy?   What did you all agree upon in advance with respect to that policy?

SECRETARY ACHESON.   Our discussions on the defense of Western Europe had to do with the fact that we have a very long way to go before we have any adequate defense and therefore we have to start on the fundamentals and work that out.

MR. JAVITS.   What was the presupposition in the conference with respect to the remilitarization of West Germany?

SECRETARY ACHESON.   The policy of all the governments, the Russian, our own, France, and Britain, is that Germany is to be demilitarized.

MR. JAVITS.   And not remilitarized?

SECRETARY ACHESON.   We are proceeding on that basis.   There is no discussion of doing anything else.   That is our policy and we have not raised it or revalued it.[16]

Then came Korea.

One of the most obscure and difficult areas in Acheson's record as Secretary of State is his exact role and purpose in the positions taken by the American Government on the question of German rearmament in the summer and fall of 1950.   The obscurity is in part quite natural, for the matter is necessarily one which is subject to the most private negotiations with America's allies.   The difficulty of the problem arises partly from the fact that so many

[16] Hearings, *To Amend the Mutual Defense Assistance Act of 1949*, House, Committee on Foreign Affairs, 81st Congress, 2d Session, June 5, 1950, p. 22.

different things can be meant by the word rearmament, and partly from the fact that there has been no lucid exposition of the change in American policy by Acheson or anyone else. Another complication arises from the vigorous feelings aroused by the issue, which is one on which Acheson's regular admirers and critics do not take their normal positions. In these circumstances, the fair course here seems to be to let the record speak, even more than usual, for itself.

Whatever else may be in doubt, it seems reasonably plain that it was the shock of Korea which shifted the position Acheson was ready to take publicly; compare the statement made above with the following discussion, which took place on August 30, during testimony before a Senate sub-committee on the four-billion dollar addition to military assistance funds:

> SENATOR WHERRY. . . . In view of the German situation — because this [bill] does not call for the arming of Germany at all — how effective do you think rearming of France and Western European countries will be if Germany remains unarmed? With all of this equipment and all of this manpower, how effective will it be? . . .
>
> SECRETARY ACHESON. . . . A program for Western Europe which does not include the productive resources of all the countries of Western Europe . . . Western Germany as well as France, and . . . the military manpower of all of Western Europe . . . Western Germany as well as France, will not be effective in the long-range political sense. Therefore we must include them both. . . . How you do it is a matter which has to be worked out in such a way that you get the enthusiastic cooperation of all the countries.
>
> SENATOR WHERRY. May I ask this question, then: You say it will not be effective, is that correct?
>
> SECRETARY ACHESON. That is what I said.
>
> SENATOR WHERRY. Now, are the military staffs, the general staffs of Great Britain and France and the United States of America in agreement that Germany should be rearmed under allied supervision?
>
> SECRETARY ACHESON. I think nobody can answer that at the present time.
>
> SENATOR WHERRY. Can the Secretary of Defense answer it?
>
> SECRETARY JOHNSON. It is not answerable today.
>
> SENATOR WHERRY. Therefore there is no agreement?

SECRETARY ACHESON. At the present time it has not reached that stage. It is in the stage of discussion.[17]

Acheson explained later in his testimony that he did not intend these statements to mean that there could be no useful defense plan without German participation — that was a matter for the military. His point was a little different:

> Over a period of time if you do not solve the proper need of the German people for security and for participation in the Western European scheme you will have a situation which will then cause so much trouble that your whole plan will not be effective.[18]

Caution in his public statements was inevitable, a point which Senator McKellar brought out very clearly a little later; the matter was under negotiation, and Acheson heartily agreed when McKellar suggested that it would be "exceedingly unwise and probably exceedingly hurtful if you gave out parts of it at a time at the request of gentlemen who would like to know."

Still, it was plain from this discussion that Acheson's policy had shifted. Of course Korea was not the only factor; a highly significant addition to the problem was the appearance of remilitarization in the Soviet zone. This remilitarization had been protested by the Western Powers back in May. Now, with the Korean fighting as proof that satellite troops were dangerous, this East German force took on a new meaning. The month of August saw a number of statements by Western leaders looking toward a revision of the policy of a totally disarmed and demilitarized Germany; High Commissioner McCloy, in particular, said that defense of Europe "will include Germany and require of the German people and their representatives straightforward and cooperative action." For Germany, Chancellor Adenauer made it clear that if there was to be German rearmament, there must be a full restoration of German sovereignty. This was where matters stood, in public at least, when the three Western foreign ministers met in New York on September 12.

By American initiative, the main subject of this meeting was the ways and means of adding German strength to the Western European defenses.

---

[17] Hearings, *Supplemental Appropriations for 1951*, Senate, Committee on Appropriations, 81st Congress, 2d Session, August 30, 1951, pp. 284–85.

[18] Same hearings, p. 287.

In the first sessions the American proposals, which apparently were both broad and sudden, did not win support, and a similar opposition developed in the meetings of the North Atlantic Council held a few days later. But after a breathing spell it proved possible to reach a certain level of agreement in both groups. The communiqué issued by the three foreign ministers on September 19 showed how far agreement had proceeded; without fixing the Allied position on German rearmament, it excluded certain extreme solutions at either end. "The re-creation of a German national army would not serve the best interests of Germany or Europe"; on the other hand, it was necessary to deal with the threat of subversion supported by the new forces of the Soviet zone, so "the Foreign Ministers have agreed to permit the establishment of mobile police formations." As for the area between a national army and mobile police formations, this was "at present the subject of study and exchange of views."

Although rearmament was the subject that filled the headlines, the September communiqué contained other important points. The general belief that the West would defend Western Germany if she were attacked was spelled out bluntly in terms reminiscent of the Atlantic Pact. "The Allied Governments will increase and reinforce their forces in Germany.[19] They will treat any attack against the Federal Republic or Berlin from any quarter as an attack upon themselves." At the same time the foreign ministers held out to the Germans a promise of further modification of the Occupation Statute — to allow Germany to conduct her own foreign affairs, particularly — and of a termination of the state of war technically existing between Germany and the Allies.[20]

As negotiations proceeded in the autumn of 1950, it gradually became plain that any American hopes for a rapid development of German armed forces would be disappointed. There was a wide gap between the form of rearmament satisfactory to the French and that which appealed to the Germans. Faced with this situation, the American Government settled down to a protracted period of negotiations. The next successful step in these negotiations came at Brussels in December when the North Atlantic Treaty Council announced that it had "reached unanimous agreement regarding the part which Germany might assume in the common defense." The Council turned over detailed negotiations with the Germans to the three Western occupying Powers, and since then talks have been proceeding. In early

---

[19] This of course was a part of the larger effort discussed in the last chapter.
[20] The full communiqué may be found in *Bulletin*, XXIII, p. 530.

January the French Foreign Minister announced in Washington that the
Brussels agreement included a decision that German troops should not be
more than one part in five of the Eisenhower defense force. What remained
for negotiation were such questions as the organization and control of these
prospective German forces. It would not be easy to find a solution in which
the Allied objection to "a German National Army" could be reconciled
with the German demand for full sovereignty. A special complexity arose
from the fact that German public opinion seemed still unready for remilitarization of any sort.

Acheson's view of these negotiations has not been fully stated, but in reporting on the Brussels meeting he remarked:

> We cleared away the obstacles which had been in front of German
> participation. We made it perfectly clear to the Germans that their
> participation is a matter to be discussed with them. Their will and their
> enthusiastic cooperation is an essential part of anything which is to be
> done. We made it clear that, if they take part in this effort, then clearly
> their relationships with the nations of Western Europe and with us in
> the United States will be and can be on a different basis from what they
> are now. [21]

This statement covered American objectives; it also covered a multitude
of policy difficulties still to be settled. In the summer of 1951 negotiations
for a German defense force were still proceeding in the North Atlantic
Treaty Organization and between the Allied High Commissioners and Chancellor Adenauer, and it appeared that the rebuilding of European defenses, at
least in its early stages, must proceed without German participation. The
reason for the delay was explained by General Eisenhower in his testimony
before the Senate Committees concerning the four-division movement of
American troops: "There is no hope as of today to start arming the Germans. There is a tremendous political platform to be established before this
could come about." [22]

American policy was obviously trying to establish this political platform,
and it seemed likely that by 1952 the job might be far enough along to permit the beginning of German participation in the Eisenhower army. It
remained a question whether the sudden démarche of September, 1950, had

[21] Remarks to a news conference, December 22, 1950 (*Bulletin*, XXIV, p. 4).
[22] Hearings, *Assignment of Ground Forces of the United States to Duty in the European
Area*, Senate, Committee on Foreign Relations and Committee on Armed Forces, 82d Congress, 1st Session, February 1, 1951, p. 21.

helped or hindered in this long-range task. But at least it could be said that by the end of 1950 the three Western governments were once more working together on the problem; there was general agreement on an eventual rearmament of Germans, if not Germany, as a part of free Europe.

One further point was clear. The American Government proposed to pursue its German objectives without being dismayed or distracted by violent Soviet protests. From October, 1950, to June, 1951, the Soviet Union and the Western Powers exchanged a long series of notes on the subject of a possible meeting of all four occupying Powers to consider the German problem once again. Steadily maintaining their continuing readiness to work for a united and truly democratic Germany, the Western Powers have as steadily refused to allow their own constructive efforts to be delayed by false hopes of a solution so often sought and never achieved. American policy on this matter, like American policy on Germany in general, could still be defined by terms which Acheson had used as early as April, 1949, and with this early statement of basic German policy we may properly conclude this chapter:

When this Government embarked, together with its Western allies, on the discussion of new arrangements for Western Germany, it did not mean that we had abandoned hope of a solution which would be applicable to Germany as a whole or that we were barring a resumption of discussions looking toward such a solution whenever it might appear that there was any chance of success. It did mean that this Government was not prepared to wait indefinitely for Four-Power agreement before endeavoring to restore healthy and hopeful conditions in those areas of Germany in which its influence could be exerted.

Should it prove possible to arrange for renewed Four-Power discussions, this Government will do its utmost, as it has in the past, to arrive at a settlement of what is plainly one of the most crucial problems in world affairs.

There are certain principles, however, the observance of which is essential, in our view, to any satisfactory solution of the German problem and which we shall have to keep firmly in mind in whatever the future may bring.

The people of Western Germany may rest assured that this Government will agree to no general solution for Germany into which the basic safeguards and benefits of the existing Western German arrangements would not be absorbed. They may rest assured that until such a solution can be achieved, this Government will continue to lend vigorous support to the development of the Western German program.

The people of Europe may rest assured that this Government will agree to no arrangements concerning Germany which do not protect the security interests of the European community.

The people of the United States may rest assured that in any discussions relating to the future of Germany, this Government will have foremost in mind their deep desire for a peaceful and orderly solution of these weighty problems which have been the heart of so many of our difficulties in the postwar period.[23]

[23] Address to the American Society of Newspaper Publishers, New York, N.Y., April 28, 1949 (*Bulletin*, **XX**, p. 588).

CHAPTER SIX

Spain

SPAIN *is a part of Western Europe which should not be permanently isolated from normal relations with that area. There are, however, certain obstacles to the achievement of this.*[1]

"The Spanish question," Acheson has said, "has been magnified by controversy to a position among our present day foreign policy problems which is disproportionate to its intrinsic importance."[2] Not because Spain is unimportant, but because so many matters are vastly more important, this judgment seems reasonable. Yet the Spanish problem shows with great clarity, in a relatively simple case, some of the pressures which bear upon American statesmen.

The issue in Spanish policy during Acheson's first two years as Secretary of State was this: Should the United States take the lead in reestablishing close and cordial relations with the Franco government? To this question some said emphatically yes, and some said angrily no, and the State Department, almost without heat, said yes-and-no. Perhaps the easiest way into this question is to take a look at Acheson in dialogue with a great friend of Franco Spain. He and Senator McCarran are having a talk about whether or not the United States, in 1949, should disregard the recommendation of the United Nations General Assembly and send an ambassador to Spain. This is not a question of recognition or non-recognition, although Senator McCarran persists in treating it as if it were; at the time of this discussion the United States had long granted full diplomatic recognition to the Franco

[1] Letter to Senator Connally, January 18, 1950 (Department Press Release No. 54, 1950).
[2] Same source.

régime, and was represented there by a full mission of diplomats, headed by a chargé d'affaires. Only the ambassador was missing, and this by a UN recommendation.

SENATOR McCARRAN. I want to say to you, Mr. Secretary, and I think I speak for the majority of this committee and I speak for a strong segment of the Congress, that we believe Spain should be recognized fully, diplomatically. Her ambassador should be recognized here and ours should be sent over there. I should like to have you state why that should not be carried out.

SECRETARY ACHESON. Senator, I tried to state a moment ago that, acting under this recommendation of the General Assembly, we have not appointed an ambassador. . . .

SENATOR McCARRAN. Are we to be enslaved to the United Nations? I never voted with that in mind.

SENATOR McKELLAR. Neither did I.

SECRETARY ACHESON. I do not think we are enslaved. I think we are doing our best to support it. I think our relations with Spain are friendly. There has been no effort on our part to have them otherwise. We have felt that the end aim of the United States policy and all democratic policy should be to reintegrate Spain into the family of freedom.

SENATOR McCARRAN. What is to prevent her now? What has she done except to fight communism? What has she done that makes her an offspring to whom the door is shut? You say we have had friendly relations. Yes, I might have friendly relations with you but you might slam the door in my face. Would that be a very friendly gesture?

SECRETARY ACHESON. Senator, I said that I thought the object of our policy was to reintegrate Spain.

SENATOR McCARRAN. What do you mean by the word "reintegrate" as regards to Spain?

SECRETARY ACHESON. I mean just that, to reintegrate Spain. You are familiar with the history of the origin and the conduct of the present Spanish régime and with the fact that the governments in Western Europe have felt that there are political differences between the democratic nations and the Government of Spain.

SENATOR McCARRAN. My impression of the present régime in charge of Spain was that they were fighting communism when we were sitting by blindly, and they are one nation that has fought communism where we are now spending $5,000,000,000 a year to try to curb communism. If that be their lack of position for integration, why it seems to me your position is exceedingly weak, Mr. Secretary. I think that Congress is of the same turn of mind, if I may express it.

SECRETARY ACHESON. I regret that you feel that way and that the Congress feels that way. I think that we are doing all we can do to bring about a solution.

SENATOR McCARRAN. Would you mind telling us what you are doing to bring about a solution and when we may look for it?

SECRETARY ACHESON. I do not know [when]. I think a great deal depends on the actions of the Spanish Government and the Spanish people. I do not think anybody expects or looks forward to the time in the immediate future when Spain has the same kind of government that some of the Western democracies have.

SENATOR McCARRAN. Do you mean by that she must change her present form of government before you will recognize her?

SECRETARY ACHESON. I said the opposite. I said we did not look forward to the time that Spain would have exactly the same form of government as they have in the West. I think that it is possible for the Spanish Government to make considerable progress in doing away with some of the more oppressive practices which they have. I think they can go quite a distance toward coming closer to the views of some of their neighbors. Our great effort in Europe is to bring about a unification of Europe. This is primarily a European problem. American policy toward Spain would have little usefulness if it did not go along with and bring along with it the same kind of policies on the part of France, Great Britain, Belgium, Holland, Italy, and the other countries of Western Europe. . . .

SENATOR McCARRAN. Let me say to you, Mr. Secretary, that so far as I am personally concerned as chairman of this subcommittee, I am not in favor of your policy with reference to Spain and until that policy is changed I am going to examine your appropriations with a fine tooth comb.[3]

Only those who have not faced the fine-toothed comb of Senator McCarran should smile at this exchange. But the hearing also produced a different

[3] Hearings, *State, Commerce, Justice, Judiciary Appropriations, 1950*, Senate, Subcommittee on Appropriations, 81st Congress, 1st Session, May 5, 1949, pp. 92–4.

set of questions, from a different senator, of a different party. Republican Senator Saltonstall asked a question which gave Acheson a chance to clarify both the exact issue at stake, and the broader problem of policy involved, on which he saw eye to eye with Saltonstall.

SENATOR SALTONSTALL. I would just like to add on the question of Spain, Mr. Secretary, you did not mention one thing that seems to me very vital. That is our own security. Your policy over in Spain and all through Europe is based on what is best for our security, I hope. If non-recognition of Spain is the policy of the Department of State now, I assume it is based on our security because of the attitude of other nations in Europe toward Spain and our wanting to work along with them. Is that a fair statement?

SECRETARY ACHESON. Senator, I think we ought to be very clear that there is no policy of nonrecognition of Spain.

SENATOR SALTONSTALL. I emphasized the word "security."

SECRETARY ACHESON. I want to emphasize it, but I do want to be clear on this question: Whether or not we have an ambassador has nothing to do with whether you recognize the country or whether you do not. It also seems to me to be a quite unimportant thing, unimportant both from the point of view of the United Nations and from the point of view of those who believe it is so wrong. When the United Nations made this recommendation, they thought it would have some effect. I think it has none. I have no argument to make in favor of the view that this has accomplished it. I do not think it has accomplished it.

So far as security is concerned, you are entirely right. Spain is a very important element in the security of the United States, and that is why it is so important and why we have been doing our best to bring about what I call a reintegration of Spain in the West.

In order to bring Spain into a system of collective security in the West, it must be by common agreement. You cannot get Spain into a thing such as the North Atlantic Treaty without some resolution of these difficulties with the other countries. There has to be a common desire and common understanding.

Now, some progress has recently been made in connection with economic relations with Spain. At a press conference yesterday, I pointed out to the press that any objection that existed with regard to Spain's applying to the Export-Import Bank for loans has been withdrawn. I pointed out that at the present time Spain is a very bad credit risk. The difficulty is not a political one but an economic one. For months and months we have been pointing out to the Spanish Government certain obvious things which it ought to do in order to correct its balance-of-payments problem which make it almost impossible to lend dollars. If those things can be done, then the way can be opened up.

SENATOR SALTONSTALL. The point of my question, as I see it, is the question of the North Atlantic Pact, the question of United Nations, the question of all these things from the point of view of just one person sitting in Congress or as a citizen; our foreign policy is looking toward our greater security?

SECRETARY ACHESON. It is.

SENATOR SALTONSTALL. What we have to do is not try to work by ourselves but to work with other nations to try to get our security, and I assume your whole policy with relation to Spain, working up the bad credit risk and everything else, is an effort to get greater security in this country by working with other countries in Europe toward a common policy?

SECRETARY ACHESON. That is it exactly.[4]

So, while Acheson held no brief for the notion that the withdrawal of ambassadors was useful, it was not just quixotry that led the State Department to go slow on its dealings with Franco Spain. It was Europe. But why should the European governments and so many of their people be hostile to Franco Spain? A week after this hearing Acheson addressed himself to the problem in some detail, and the argument says a good deal, both of Spain and of the man who made it.

As I have said, the important matter is not whether we send an ambassador instead of a chargé d'affaires; the important thing is what can be done to bring Spain into the community of free nations in Europe in both the economic and the defense fields. When you think about that you discover at once that the Western European Governments are opposed, and have publicly stated their opposition, to this collaboration with Spain in the economic and military fields.

Now why is that so? I say we get nowhere by using such words as "Fascism," but if we look at the situation in Spain, we will see some

[4] Same hearings, pp. 95–97.

perfectly simple fundamental facts which cannot be obscured. I presume that the foundation of liberty — individual liberty — is not in great phrases at all but in certain simple procedures and simple beliefs, and I should put first on the list of essentials for individual liberty the writ of habeas corpus and an independent judiciary. One of the things that all dictators do — from the time of the French Revolution and before the French Revolution down to the present time — is to take anyone that they do not like and throw him in the oubliette and there he stays until he dies or until they shoot him or until they take him out. The fundamental protection against that in free countries is the writ of habeas corpus.

Now what does that mean? That means that anybody who is detained against his will may at any time get an order from the court that he shall be produced in person before the court and that those who held him must justify the fact that they are holding him under the provisions of law. There is nothing more fundamental in the preservation of human liberty than that ancient British tradition which is now incorporated in most of the procedures in the free world. That right does not exist in Spain.

I suppose a second fundamental right, which is useful only if you have the first, is that if you are tried — and, of course, it follows from the writ of habeas corpus that you cannot be sentenced to prison unless you are convicted of some crime — the second right is that in being convicted of a crime you are convicted not by employees of the state but by your own fellow citizens. That is the right of trial by jury. It means that no judge, even though he be independent, certainly no administrative official, can order you put in jail. The only people who can do that are ten in some parts of the world, twelve in others — citizens just like yourself — and if they listen to the testimony and say Joe Doakes goes to jail, then he goes to jail. If they say he does not go to jail, then he does not go to jail. That is fundamental. That right does not exist in Spain.

Then there is the question of religious liberty, which is fundamental to a free exercise of the human personality. That right does not exist in Spain.

Then there is the right of association — association in political activities, association in trade union activities, association in benevolent activities — that right does not exist in Spain.

I could go on, but what I want to draw to your attention is that these certain fundamental basic rights of the individual which make the difference between what we call free Europe and the Iron Curtain countries — these rights do not exist in Spain, and the Spanish people are prevented from enjoying them by action of the Spanish Government.

It seems perfectly clear to the Western European countries that you cannot have an intimate working partnership with such a régime in the economic field and in the defense field. There must be some move to liberalize that. None of them say, nor do we say, that Spain, which has never been a full-flowered democracy, must become so. But they all say that there must be some move toward that situation because if there isn't, what is the use of having ambassadors? We have someone with a different title. It may raise the prestige of the individual a little bit, but what is the use of it all?

It is important only if it becomes a symbol, and if it becomes a symbol of the fact that after all we don't care much about these rights, then it is a bad symbol.[5]

Thus fundamentally it was the position of the Europeans, and Acheson's position too, that there could be no real partnership with a government actively hostile to freedom. The State Department therefore would not accept the arguments of Senator McCarran. But, for good or ill, the character of the Spanish régime was not the only element in the problem. Spain was important to Europe, and to the United States, and it was important to find some way of working with her. The American Government therefore remained willing to conduct normal economic relations with Spain, although these were made very difficult by the inefficiency of the Franco régime. And in the larger sense, the Government looked for a gradual understanding with Franco, and not for his overthrow. And if the reader wants to find a man who was angrier about this policy than Senator McCarran, he should consult the writings of Mr. Harold L. Ickes, in whose view all temporizing with Franco was spineless wickedness.[6]

Acheson was prepared to accept this dual opposition and walk a middle course:

The policy of the American Government is one which I am quite sure is calculated to please neither group of extremists in the United States

[5] Remarks to a press conference, May 11, 1949 (*Bulletin*, XX, pp. 660–61).
[6] For Ickes' views, see *The New Republic*, May 30, and December 12, 1949; February 6 and November 27, 1950.

— either those who say that we must immediately embrace Franco, or those who say that we must cast him into the outermost darkness. But it is a policy directed toward working with the Spaniards and with the Western Europeans, bringing about a situation where these fundamental liberties do exist in Spain and where the Western Europeans can bring Spain into the community.[7]

At the 1949 meeting of the General Assembly, the question of rescinding the recommendation on ambassadors was put to a test, and lost by a few votes, the United States abstaining. In 1949, the State Department and its Secretary believed that to vote affirmatively would give ammunition to those who claimed that the United States was indifferent to basic civil liberties. A year later the Department and the Secretary had a different view. By 1950 there was widespread acceptance, even in Western Europe, of Acheson's long-held view that the gesture of removing ambassadors had done more harm than good. The only reason for standing on the original resolution had been its symbolic meaning, and this was worn out. It had been a mistake in the first place, and it was time to end it. These points and some others were made by Acheson in a letter to Senator Connally in January, 1950:

In our view, the withdrawal of Ambassadors from Spain as a means of political pressure was a mistaken departure from established principle. It is traditional practice, once a state has been formally recognized, to exchange Ambassadors or Ministers and is usually without political significance. . . . However, the withdrawal of Ambassadors from Spain disregarded this principle. By attaching moral significance to the *refusal* to maintain full diplomatic relations with Spain, this action has also implied moral significance to the *maintenance* of full diplomatic relations through the return of Ambassadors. This situation inevitably led to confusion in public opinion both here and abroad. On the one hand, the question of returning Ambassadors to Spain has tended to become identified with the larger issue of whether it is desirable to have closer relations with the present Spanish Government. On the other hand, public bewilderment has been increased over the inconsistency of accrediting Ambassadors to such countries as those in Eastern Europe whose régimes we do not condone while, at the same time, refusing to appoint an Ambassador to Spain. . . .

It is the opinion of this Government that the anomalous situation

[7] Remarks to a press conference, May 11, 1949 (*Bulletin*, XX, p. 661).

with respect to Spain should be resolved. The United States is therefore prepared to vote for a resolution in the General Assembly which will leave members free to send an Ambassador or Minister to Spain if they choose. We would do this for the reasons I have already stated and in the hope that this aspect of the Spanish issue would no longer be available to be used by hostile propaganda to create unnecessary divisions within the United Nations and among our own people. Our vote would in no sense signify approval of the régime in Spain. It would merely indicate our desire, in the interests of orderly international intercourse, to return to normal practice in exchanging diplomatic representation.[8]

At the General Assembly meeting in September, 1950, the resolution of 1946 was rescinded, and the President, at the end of the year, appointed an American Ambassador to Spain. Mr. Truman's comments indicated a certain reluctance to take this step and a very considerable personal coolness toward the Franco régime, but the problem of policy was not a problem of personal feelings.

It was one thing, however, to renew the exchange of ambassadors, and quite another to get on intimate and cordial terms with the Franco régime. The authoritarianism which led to the withdrawal of ambassadors remained as a bar to intimate contact in a struggle for freedom. And the economic inefficiency which made Spain a bad credit risk in 1949 had not noticeably altered in 1951; indeed in the summer of 1950 the Administration only reluctantly accepted the Congressional authorization of a $62,500,000 loan to Spain. Acheson's position, at least in this most recent full policy statement, was still mixed:

These conclusions by the United States Government do not imply any change in the basic attitude of this Government toward Spain.

The policy of the United States toward Spain is based on the recognition of certain essential facts. First, there is no sign of an alternative to the present Government.

Second, the internal position of the present régime is strong and enjoys the support of many who, although they might prefer another form of government or chief of state, fear that chaos and civil strife would follow a move to overthrow the Government.

Third, Spain is a part of Western Europe which should not be permanently isolated from normal relations with that area. There are, how-

[8] Letter to Senator Connally, January 18, 1950 (Department Press Release No. 54, 1950).

ever, certain obstacles to the achievement of this. Spain, for reasons associated with the nature, origins and history of the present Spanish Government, is still unacceptable to many of the Western European nations as an associate in such cooperative projects as the European Recovery Program and the Council of Europe. We believe that this is a matter in which the Western European nations must have a leading voice. These programs, which require for their success the closest possible cooperation between the participants, are directed to the strengthening and development of the democratic way of life as opposed to the threats to it posed by Communist expansion. This is a policy which we and the Western European nations have agreed upon. It is not merely a negative reaction to communism. It is, rather, a positive program to support and strengthen democratic freedoms, politically, economically and militarily. In that context the participation of the present Spanish Government, unless and until there has been some indication of evolution toward more democratic government in Spain, would weaken rather than strengthen the collective effort to safeguard and strengthen democracy.

We are therefore continuing our efforts in a frank and friendly manner to persuade the Spanish Government that its own interest in participating in the international community, and particularly in the Western European community, requires steps toward democratic government, which offers the best hope for the growth of basic human rights and fundamental freedoms in Spain. It requires cooperation on the part of all parties and, as must be evident, it is not fundamentally a matter which can be successfully brought about by American action. The decision as to what steps can and should be taken is obviously one for Spaniards alone.[9]

This statement was made in January, 1950, and probably its emphasis is not correct for 1951. For the Spanish problem, like nearly everything else, was affected by time — and in particular by the new urgency of defensive preparations after Korea. Cooperation in defense was in some ways more practicable than economic aid; it was certainly more urgent, from the point of view of American strategists. Thus the summer of 1951 saw an effort by the United States to work out a bilateral agreement under which Franco would permit American air and naval bases in Spain. Even in 1951 this departure caused much dismay in Western Europe; undertaken any earlier, it

[9] Same source.

might have had very serious effects. Yet there was still no thought of partnership with Franco; there was still American pressure for a change in his régime.

So the dilemma remained; Spain was a most important part of Europe, and yet *Franco* Spain, for basic reasons, could hardly be a partner unless she changed her ways. In a problem of this sort only time, patience, and skill could produce useful results. The answer was not yes, and it was not no. It was yes *and* no. Acheson proposed to work on the problem, but he made no promises, and the following exchange is perhaps a fitting end to this summary sketch of his views on Spain:

SENATOR RUSSELL. Mr. Secretary, there are millions of people who are very much concerned about the part, if any, that Spain might or could play in the defense of Western Europe. Do you object to stating whether or not negotiations are being pursued to see whether or not the forces of Spain can be fitted into the defense of Western Europe?

SECRETARY ACHESON. May I answer that question a little less directly than you have asked it?

The importance of the association of Spain in the defense of Western Europe I think is clear. I think it is also clear that the relations of this country, and I hope of the other countries, with Spain, are now entering a new phase. We are sending a most able Ambassador to Spain, who is on his way at the present time. I am very hopeful that the objectives which you have in mind, and I am sure I have in mind, can be accomplished. That depends upon the actions of many nations, our own, our partners in the North Atlantic Treaty, and also on the actions of Spain. At the present time we have only intimations from statements made by the Spanish Government as to what their attitude would be. We hope before long that we will know more about that, and we hope that the development will be along the line of the close association of Spain and the Spanish contribution and mutual undertakings in regard to the defense of Western Europe.

SENATOR RUSSELL. I understand your answer then to be that you are hopeful that progress may be made?

SECRETARY ACHESON. Yes, sir.

SENATOR RUSSELL. It boils down to that.[10]

[10] Hearings, *Assignment of Ground Forces of the United States to Duty in the European Area*, Senate, Committee on Foreign Relations and Committee on Armed Services, 82d Congress, 1st Session, February 16, 1951, pp. 86–7. This same basic position was restated to a press conference when Admiral Sherman visited Franco in the following July; see *Bulletin*, XXV, p. 170.

CHAPTER SEVEN

The Southern Flank

FROM WESTERN EUROPE to Central Asia is a long way — about three thousand miles, if we take Italy as the end of Western Europe and India as the beginning of Central Asia. Along this path are many countries, and as many problems for the American Government. Moreover many of these problems are at least potentially explosive, and no man can say certainly that a few months will not bring urgent crisis. Who, in 1945, would have said that the urgent years for Iran would be 1946 and 1951, or that crisis would come for Greece in 1947 and for Yugoslavia in 1948, or that Turkey would remain calm, or that Israel would fight and win a war in 1948-49? Against the struggle for Europe and the struggle for Asia, these crises may seem small, but there is no law which says that they will never expand; world wars have started in this area before.

It is no simple matter to disentangle and discuss fairly the extraordinary complexities of American diplomacy in this part of the world. In Western Europe there is a sense of community, and it is proper to treat the area as a whole; east of the Adriatic that is no longer true. The area has in common hardly more than the single great fact that it lies in the path of Soviet ambition; the ways and means of meeting that fact are as different as the countries, and we cannot stop to trace in detail a diplomacy shaped in each case to special and peculiar difficulties. It is not accidental that we can find general speeches by Acheson on Western Europe and on Asia, but none on the southern flank. Moreover, in some parts of this area, the problems are of a sort which are not helped by open discussion, and Acheson's public record is surprisingly short. We shall find ourselves relying heavily on brief statements, sometimes coming from the White House or an ambassador, and not from the Secretary himself.

With this introduction, let us consider, as examples only, some of the problems that have arisen in four countries: Yugoslavia, Greece, Turkey, and Iran.

Yugoslavia

Since 1945 Yugoslavia has been governed by the Communist Tito. From the time of his rise to power until the middle of 1948, Tito seemed to be a devoted follower of the great Stalin, little father to all normal Communists. During this period his relations with the United States followed the standard Stalinist pattern of the time — they got steadily worse. Indeed during this period the Yugoslavs were particularly energetic in their anti-Western pronouncements and actions. In the religious and political persecution which did so much to alienate democratic opinion, they were well in the van, and the one really incendiary incident of these years, in Europe at least, was the shooting down of two American planes by Yugoslav gunners in 1946.[1] Because of her position as a fighting ally during the war, Yugoslavia was a member of the UN, and diplomatic relations with the Western Powers had been continuously maintained. But they could hardly have been less cordial than they were in the spring of 1948.

Then came Tito's break with the Kremlin, a great event, and one which gives the clearest kind of demonstration of the limitations upon American power to influence the world. This defection, almost the most important single setback the Kremlin has suffered in recent years, was not produced by the United States in any way, and it seems likely that if American policy had been more actively anti-Communist in Yugoslavia — if for instance there had still been a Mihailovitch remnant with Western support at the time — the split between the Kremlin and Tito would have been indefinitely delayed, and perhaps averted. As it was, when the pressure from Moscow became too heavy, Tito felt strong enough to declare his independence.

The first sudden rift, announced to an astonished world in June, 1948, widened steadily in the next two years, and as it did so, a series of delicate problems were posed for American diplomacy. The central difficulty was

[1] During the exchange of notes on this subject, the United States took an extremely strong line, and Acheson, as Acting Secretary, dispatched a virtual ultimatum which secured the release of the surviving airmen; later an indemnity of $400,000 was paid by the Tito Government.

that open support of Tito, at least at first, could only hurt his cause, since it would lend color to the Soviet charge that he was an imperialist lackey. It was only as Tito himself asked for help that it could be given. Another difficulty arose from the fact that the strictures Acheson applied to Spain applied also to Yugoslavia. At the same time the Yugoslav problem was considerably more important and more immediately dangerous than that of Spain, for Yugoslavia was at once the symbol of cleavage in international communism and the object of concerted pressure, first economic and then increasingly military, from the Soviet Union and its remaining satellites. The Yugoslavs needed help, but they had to get it unobtrusively, and they could hardly become partners, even if they wished to do so, unless they were ready to move some distance toward democracy.

In these circumstances it is not surprising that American policy toward Tito, in the last three years, has been sparing in publicity. For about a year the United States watched and waited, while Tito tried first to assert a continuing Stalinist loyalty in foreign affairs and then to maintain a posture of pure and virtuous independence from both Moscow and the West.

The Yugoslavs were not fools, however, and as early as July, 1948, they began to unblock the road to Western help by undertaking to compensate Western owners for property that had been nationalized. By 1949, when Yugoslavia began to suffer severely from a Soviet economic blockade, the West, under American leadership, was ready to respond with limited credit and other helpful steps at specific critical points. At the end of 1949, when the Soviet Union began to rumble about the necessity of crushing "the treacherous Tito gang," the United States went still further in its support of Tito. No announcement was made by Acheson, but as Ambassador-designate George V. Allen was leaving the White House on December 22 he made the following statement, which the President at once endorsed: "The President confirmed that the United States is unalterably opposed to aggression wherever it occurs or threatens to occur. Furthermore, the United States supports the principle of the sovereignty of independent nations. As regards Yugoslavia, we are just as opposed to aggression against that country as against any other, and just as favorable to the retention of Yugoslavia's sovereignty." At the very least, this statement was a warning that attack on Yugoslavia would not find the United States standing idly by; at most, as a declaration that Yugoslavia would get the same help as any other nation dealing with aggression, it was a most-favored-nation statement, and it meant that America would fight if Tito was attacked. A more binding statement was hardly justified, in view of the character of the Tito régime; what was said was enough to put the Kremlin on notice. Early in 1951, at a news conference, Acheson renewed this warning, applying directly to Yugoslavia a general warning issued by Mr. Truman the preceding July: "Those who have it in their power to unleash or withhold acts of armed aggression must realize that new recourse to aggression in the world today might well strain to the breaking point the fabric of world peace." [2]

Economic assistance to Yugoslavia continued in 1950; in particular, in the last months of the year, the United States responded to a plea for help in averting grave unrest after a crop failure caused by drought; a grant of $38,000,000 was approved by the Congress. This was supplemented by a credit and by food grants under the Mutual Defense Assistance Program.

There remained only military help, and early in 1951 that too was begun by the President, who acted under the discretionary authority granted to him in the Mutual Defense Assistance Act of 1950. On April 16 he announced the decision in letters to the chairmen of the Congressional committees concerned:

"I have found that Yugoslavia is a nation whose strategic location makes it of direct importance to the defense of the North Atlantic area, and that an immediate increase in its ability to defend itself over that which exists if no assistance is supplied will contribute to the preservation of the peace and security of the North Atlantic area." [3] This was the formal language required for the use of mutual defense funds, and it was also a statement of fact, for Yugoslavia lay directly on the right flank of the whole Eisenhower enterprise. So, Mr. Truman continued, he was granting up to $29,000,000, for the shipment of essential supplies to strengthen Yugoslavian defense. In the same month the Yugoslav government requested further help, in the form of weapons, and it seemed likely that the United States stood at the beginning, and not the end, of an increasing connection with the preservation of anti-Stalinist Yugoslavia.

Compared to the open and active leadership which the United States had given in Western Europe, and her direct role of advice and support in Greece and Turkey, this story of policy toward Yugoslavia proceeds in a minor key. Yet the essentials of the tune are not so different — economic support, a political assurance, and finally military aid. In the three years after 1948

[2] *New York Times*, February 15, 1951.   [3] *Bulletin*, XXIV, p. 719.

Tito survived, which was the first great object; he also fulfilled the terms of his agreements, and these terms were always clear-cut and cool; moreover there were signs and portents of some relaxation of the sterner aspects of his dictatorship, although Yugoslavia remained a clearly authoritarian state. In a time of danger and tension he had been helped, not hindered, and his régime had softened, not hardened. All in all, this was one of the quietest, but not the least successful of American undertakings while Acheson was Secretary, and it is not surprising that it was also one of the least criticized.

Yet though the policy itself has aroused little complaint, American help for Yugoslavia has frequently been used by critics as a proof that there must be something queer about the Administration's coolness toward such régimes as those in Franco Spain and Chiang Kai-shek's China. If we can deal with a Communist dictator, why not with men who are at least Christians? This question, so persuasive on the surface, overlooks two great facts. First, American policy toward Yugoslavia was in fact extremely cool; there was no effort or desire to achieve the sort of partnership that the critics wished to get with Chiang and Franco. As an example, the Administration was criticized because it did not in effect take over the direction of Chiang's armies during the Civil War; no American military advisers were to be found in the Yugoslav armies, though increased military aid would probably lead to military missions of a more restricted sort, and it seemed highly unlikely even in the event of war that Americans would or could take over the tactical direction of Yugoslav forces.

And this leads to the second and still more significant fact. A fundamental difference between Tito, on the one hand, and Franco and Chiang, on the other, was that Tito was the head of a far abler, less corrupt, more effective government. This fact might not be palatable or pleasant, but it meant that limited, arm's-length help to Tito was likely to have a value that could not be expected with such confidence from help to Franco and Chiang.

In combination, these two facts made it evident that it was not the American purpose, but the basic situation, which was different in the three cases here considered. This distinction occurs with great frequency in foreign affairs; it simply is not true that what works in one place will work everywhere; even a shrinking globe is much too big for that. Yet it is one of the traditions of American thinking to suppose that somehow a given policy can always be applied in the same way everywhere at once.

Greece and Turkey

The thrust that the Soviet Union was making in this case was directed at domination of the entire Near East, and, then, at all of Europe.[4]

From Yugoslavia to Iran the borders of the Soviet world touch on only two countries, Greece and Turkey. These two nations form, in the larger strategic sense, the roof of the Eastern Mediterranean and the Near East. If Turkey is the more important strategically, Greece has been the more vulnerable to infiltration and subversion, and Greece, furthermore, is of vital importance to Turkey. As Acheson had said in 1947, "The inexorable facts of geography link the future of Greece and Turkey. Should the integrity and independence of Greece be lost or compromised, the effect upon Turkey is inevitable." [5]

When Acheson became Secretary of State, the Greek-Turkish policy of the United States had been fixed for nearly two years. The decision to support the Greek government in its struggle against armed Communist rebellion, and to support Turkey in maintaining her will and capacity to resist Soviet pressure, was made in early 1947, at a time when Acheson was Acting Secretary of State; the issue was forced by Great Britain's decision that she could no longer carry the main burden in this area. The need for help to Greece and Turkey produced the Truman Doctrine, that "it must be the policy of the United States to support free peoples who are resisting attempted subjugation by armed minorities or by outside pressures."

It was hoped at first that the struggle in Greece could be brought to a quick end; Acheson, in sharing these hopes, had expressed himself as believing that the need for aid might decline after a year or so. It did not work out that way; the program of 1947 was continued and expanded in 1948, and when Acheson became Secretary the campaign against the Soviet-supported Communists in Greece was just beginning to show definite and considerable progress, under the advice and guidance of the same General Van Fleet who was later to add to his fame in Korea. The hopes of the new year were increased by the widening rift between Tito and Moscow, for Yugoslavia had

[4] Remarks to the Advertising Council, February 16, 1950 (*Bulletin*, XXII, p. 428).
[5] Hearings, *Assistance to Greece and Turkey*, Senate, Committee on Foreign Relations, 80th Congress, 1st Session, March 24, 1947, p. 11.

been a major source of supplies and a sanctuary for the Greek communists. And in due course the Yugoslav border was closed to the guerrillas.

In 1949 the war in Greece was won. In October the guerrilla forces announced a "cease fire," which, as Acheson remarked at the time, was a practical recognition of their defeat. Gradually the fighting came to a close, and Greece, for the first time since 1940, had a sort of peace. But she continued to need help, first in the reconstruction of her battered economy, and second in the maintenance of continued internal stability. And although the Turks made extremely good use of the military and economic help they received, Turkey too remained in the firing line. So each time Acheson went to the Congress to speak for a defense aid program, he found himself arguing for a substantial appropriation for Greek-Turkish aid. It was an expensive connection. By 1950 aid to Greece alone, since 1945, totaled more than a billion dollars, and the end was not in sight a year later.

In these circumstances, it is perhaps remarkable that in all of Acheson's appearances before Congressional committees, he was never questioned about the wisdom or even the magnitude of the Greek-Turkish aid program. In each appearance he would explain the need for the program, and each time the explanation, so far as the record shows, was accepted. We may content ourselves, then, with the following example, drawn from a statement to the Senate in June, 1950. It shows the general pattern of his thinking on both Greece and Turkey.

The success which has been achieved by the peoples of Greece is clear proof that the forces of aggression can be halted by invoking the proper measures at the proper time. For the first time since 1940, and as a result of American aid, the Government of Greece is now exercising full control over its territories and is in a position to concentrate its energies on the restoration of its civilian economy.

The importance of this achievement can only be fully understood when it is measured against what might have occurred if American assistance had not been provided. A Communist Greece . . . would have been a threat to the entire western world.

The immediate problem before the Greek people is to complete the recovery of their economy in order that their country may take its rightful and hard-earned place as a self-sufficient member of the community of free nations.

The provision of further military assistance to Greece is essential to the success of this effort. It is required in order to insure a continuance of internal stability and to make certain that Greece will not again become an easy target for Communist guerrilla activities. However, because of the substantial progress which has already been made in these directions, the requirements for such assistance in 1951 are considerably below those for previous years. Anything less would place in jeopardy the large investment we have already made in this undertaking.

Continued assistance to Turkey is also necessary. The record in Turkey is a good record and previous military assistance has been extremely effective. Although there has been a substantial reduction in the numerical size of Turkey's armed forces, to the benefit of Turkey's economic recovery, the combat effectiveness of these forces has been greatly increased through the provision of modern equipment and extensive training. At the same time, further modernization of these forces is still required and Turkey, which is spending between 35 and 40 percent of its revenues for military purposes, cannot increase its own expenditures for defense. Consequently, without our continued assistance this modernization cannot go forward.

It is of the greatest importance to us that Turkey, within the limits of its economic ability, should develop the maximum capacity to resist aggression. We are well on the road toward this objective, and it is in our national interest to pursue this objective to the end. The program proposed for 1951 will bring us a long way toward this goal.[6]

The broad approval given to the Greek-Turkish aid program was turned into active enthusiasm by the action of Turkish and Greek troops as a part of the United Nations force in Korea; both detachments distinguished themselves. And on the other side of the world, the development of a unified command in Europe under Eisenhower led to a new sense of urgency about the southern flank. So in early 1951 it began to appear that the American Government was hoping to extend the North Atlantic Treaty Organization to include Greece and Turkey. They might not be perfect democracies, but both of them were governed with a considerable respect to the opinions of their own people, and they occupied a focal area. For admission to the North Atlantic Pact the consent of all its members is necessary, and the

[6] Hearings, *Mutual Defense Assistance Program, 1950*, Senate, Committee on Foreign Relations and Committee on Armed Services, 81st Congress, 2d Session, June 2, 1950, pp. 6–7.

American initiative was not successful until after much negotiation; it was natural that the countries on the Western Front should be fearful of contracting connections that might lead to the diversion of strength from the center, and equally natural that small northern states should be hesitant to contract a binding commitment to defend Turkey. Necessarily the negotiations on this subject were private — but the American attitude is shown sufficiently by the following exchange:

SENATOR RUSSELL. . . . There are a great many people who feel, and I share that feeling, that the best investment we have made in all of the billions we have spent in undertaking to stay the advance of communism has been in Turkey. Are any efforts being made, or any negotiations being had, to tie Turkey more closely into the defense of Western Europe and into the mutual assistance and mutual defense efforts to which you refer repeatedly in your splendid statement?

SECRETARY ACHESON. Yes; I think efforts are being made, Senator Russell, and I think that we could also include Greece with the favorable things you said about Turkey. We are very much alive to the importance of bringing even closer than they have been in the past the co-operative planning and the relationship between Greece and Turkey and the North Atlantic defense.[7]

The general success of the Greek-Turkish program was the main reason for its popularity in Congress. Another element, however, was probably the fact that this program, more than any other in which Acheson was involved, except perhaps his policy in Spain, brought him criticism from liberals and the anti-Communist left. Especially at the beginning, in 1947, the program was condemned by many as a form of imperialistic interventionism in support of reactionaries, un-American in its reliance upon force, and unwise in its open opposition to the Soviet Union. As the years passed and Soviet intentions became ever more clear, the last part of this indictment was dropped, but there remained many who felt that the Greeks and Turks were doubtful comrades. Acheson did not agree, and in the following passage he undertook

[7] Hearings, *Assignment of Ground Forces of the United States to Duty in the European Area,* Senate, Committee on Foreign Relations and Committee on Armed Services, 82d Congress, 1st Session, February 16, 1951, p. 87. Formal agreement to bring Greece and Turkey into the North Atlantic Treaty was reached in September, 1951, at Ottawa. Actual membership would have to wait on the Senate's consent and similar constitutional processes in other countries.

at once to explain the success of the program and to pay his compliments to those whose sentiments were offended by Greek and Turkish imperfections. He might have added, and did on other occasions, that both the Greeks and the Turks were in the habit of holding elections and tolerating opposition, a fact somewhat more remarkable, given their historical background, than any particular failings.

We must be prepared to meet wherever possible all thrusts of the Soviet Union. It will not always be possible to anticipate where these thrusts will take place, and we will not always be able to deal with them with equal effectiveness. In the case of Greece and Turkey we were able to meet that thrust effectively because the Greeks and the Turks were determined to maintain their independence. There were a lot of Greeks and Turks that did not like their government. There were a lot that did. But they were united in a common belief that they preferred it to any form of government that might be imposed upon them from outside. The Greeks were able, with our assistance, to meet military force with military force. The Turks have successfully resisted the powerful Soviet pressure brought against them. It should be borne in mind that in this case we were not dealing with threats to Greece and Turkey alone. The thrust that the Soviet Union was making in this case was directed at domination of the entire Near East and, then, at all of Europe.

It has been suggested by some people that the Greek and Turkish Governments were not our kind of democracy and therefore we should not have given them our aid. Of course, they do not have exactly the same kind of institutions that we do. But we are not dealing here with the kind of situation where we can go from one country to another with a piece of litmus paper and see whether everything is true blue, whether the political, economic, and social climate is exactly, in all its details, the kind that we would like to have either for them or for us. The only question that we should ask is whether they are determined to protect their independence against Communist aggression, and if they are, we should recognize our basic unity with them on this point.[8]

Like Yugoslavia, Greece provided an opportunity for comparisons. Acheson's critics were particularly fond of the notion that what had been done in Greece could have been done in China. Because this suggestion assumed a

[8] Remarks to the Advertising Council, February 16, 1950 (*Bulletin*, XXII, p. 428).

similarity between two countries differing in size and population alone by a factor of 50, Walter Lippmann once remarked that on this theory one might as well use one and the same plan for dealing with a kitten and a tiger. Yet between 1949 and 1951 Acheson seldom went before any committee of the Congress without encountering this line of argument. His own mind and temperament are intensely practical, so that this farfetched comparison has never struck him as attractive; probably this attitude owes something to his long experience of the dangers of generalization in international politics, and something to his lawyer's sense of the case, not the theory. In any event he has not always been patient with those who think that what works in one place must necessarily work in another. The following comment on the attempt to compare Greece and China shows both his thought and his impatience on the subject.

May I say ... something that I have long wanted to get off my chest, and since you are helpless victims, you must listen to it. It seems to me that a great deal of the discussion of our foreign affairs loses in helpfulness because it is misdirected in aim. There seems to be a great interest in many quarters in trying to point out a logical inconsistency. They say if you do so and so in Greece, why don't you do so and so in China? The idea is that we must always act exactly the same way in every country in the world, and if you don't somebody rings up score one on the cash register. That, I think, is not a helpful way of discussing foreign policy and it is a very false trend.

The United States in my judgment acts in regard to a foreign nation strictly in regard to American interests or those wider interests which affect American interest. And if it is to American interests or those wider interests which affect it to do one thing in one country and another thing in another country, then that is the consistency upon which I propose to advise the President, and I am not in the slightest bit worried at all because somebody can say, "Well, you said so and so about Greece, why isn't all of this true about China?" I will be polite. I will be patient and I will try to explain why Greece is not China, but my heart will not be in that battle.

Therefore, what I think we should all do is to look at the problem before us. Don't bounce it off another problem somewhere else, but hit it directly and say, "What is the common sense thing from the point of view of American interest to do here?"

Once we can solve that, we can have little side humorous debates about how different it is from something else but we are on the main track there and we will pursue American interests which it is my duty to pursue and which it is the wish of all of us to pursue.[9]

Iran

In 1945–46 and again in 1951 Iran came to the center of the stage. In both cases the American purpose and policy was fundamentally the same, arising from what Acheson has called "our interest in and concern for the independence and security of Iran." [10] In 1945–46 the danger arose from Soviet pressure in northern Iran; it appeared that the Soviet Union was not prepared to honor its agreement to withdraw its troops, hoping that with a little more time it could leave behind a firmly established satellite government at least in the area of Azerbaijan. This design was frustrated by the energetic mobilization of world opinion through the United Nations, and as it occurred before Acheson's appointment as Secretary we need not discuss it further.

The danger of 1951 was more complex. It was that a dispute between the Iranian and British governments might grow into a sharp split, in which both sides would lose the benefit of the enormous and productive oil fields and refineries operated by the Anglo-Iranian Oil Company. The background to this dispute included many of the elements which complicate the making of policy in Asia — there was the long and growing resentment of Iranians against foreign capital and foreign companies; there was passionate nationalism; there was, at least at first, a certain insensitivity in the British reaction, though it is only fair to note that the British case rested on an agreement freely and formally accepted by Iran; there was the evident fact that only foreign technicians could make the oil resources of Iran productive; there was the ever-present threat of Soviet intervention, either by armed force or by internal subversion. For the United States it could not be a matter of backing one side or the other. The British were our closest allies; the Iranians must not be lost, and the oil was important to everyone.

---

[9] Extemporaneous remarks to the National Press Club, January 12, 1950 (Department Press Release No. 21, 1950, p. 14).

[10] Hearings, *The Mutual Security Program*, House, Committee on Foreign Affairs, 82d Congress, 1st Session, June 26, 1951, p. 16.

In this situation the State Department adopted a policy of mediation and caution.

We have stressed to the governments of both countries the need to solve the dispute in a friendly way through negotiation, and have urged them to avoid intimidation and threats of unilateral action. In our talks with the British Government, we have expressed the opinion that arrangements should be worked out with the Iranians which give recognition to Iran's expressed desire for greater control over and benefits from the development of its petroleum resources. . . . In talks with the Iranian Government, we have pointed out the serious effects of any unilateral cancellation of clear contractual relationships . . . We have stressed the importance of the Iranians achieving their legitimate objectives through friendly negotiation with the other party, consistent with their international responsibilities. This would have the advantage of maintaining confidence in future commercial investments in Iran and, indeed, in the validity of contractual arrangements all over the world.[11]

Thus by urging moderation on both sides the United States tried to help find a way through an explosive situation. Its urgings were bound to carry some weight with both sides — with the British because British intransigeance could be met by an American decision to help the Iranians to run their oil fields and refineries, and with the Iranians because it was also possible to refuse this help, and even to organize a boycott of Iranian oil, though this would be a painful and expensive course. Yet there was no assurance that this influence could be controlling. The British, at least in the later stages of the dispute, showed real flexibility and readiness to negotiate; it was not certain that the Iranians would do the same. In its effort to help, the United States in early July sent Mr. Averell Harriman to Iran as a special envoy, but two months later the eventual result was unknown. And even if this particular crisis should be resolved, it was certain that it would not be the last of its kind in the Middle East.

Meanwhile the American interest in Iran remained, and it was the policy of the Administration to continue and expand the economic and military help which had been given to Iran since the end of the war. Inflamed Ira-

[11] Statement of U.S. position on Iranian Oil Situation, May 18, 1950 (*Bulletin*, XXIV, p. 815). This is a departmental statement, not a first-person comment by Acheson himself.

nian nationalism made it far from easy to establish a good basis for economic development, but the American Government was not prepared to let the situation go by default.

The problems of all these countries were different, and there were still further complexities in other parts of the Near East. If this brief survey has given some hint of the variety and difficulty of the task faced by the American government, it will have served its purpose. Yet the whole area, for American policy, was held together by two general similarities, and to balance our emphasis on its many special complexities, we may conclude with a general statement made by Acheson on June 26, 1951:

> Russian ambitions in this area are centuries old; so too are the internal problems which threaten the stability and security of this area. Our policy toward this vital area of the Near East is to help the governments and peoples of this area to build the kinds of military, political and economic strength that will discourage aggression from without, protect them against subversion from within, strengthen their will to achieve stability and progress, and help to remove some of the causes of unrest. It is our aim to provide aid programs of an impartial character, that will enable the governments and peoples of this area to work out their own solutions to their problems.[12]

[12] Hearings, *The Mutual Security Program,* House, Committee on Foreign Affairs, 82d Congress, 1st Session, June 26, 1951, p. 15.

CHAPTER EIGHT

The Far East Before Korea

THE ASIAN PEOPLES *are on their own and know it and intend to continue on their own. . . . We can help only where we are wanted and only where the conditions of help are really sensible and possible.*[1]

American Far Eastern policy under Acheson has two great phases — before and after Korea; in this chapter we shall be concerned with the Far Eastern problem as it was before the North Korean aggression. And of course the greatest single problem of Far Eastern policy, in this period, was the problem of China. China stands at the focus of interest and debate on the quality of Acheson's policy. So let us first consider the Chinese question and then summarize briefly the main elements of Acheson's policy in Asia as a whole, as it was before Korea.

1. China, 1945–1949

Two characteristics differentiate the problem of China from any other we shall have to consider. It has aroused more feeling, and it has been more thoroughly discussed. Even the question of the relief of General MacArthur has not been so exhaustively and repetitiously discussed, and even the question of Alger Hiss has not produced so much sentiment. The fact that the problem has been so much debated is for us a real advantage, in that Acheson has made exhaustive public statements on nearly every aspect of the problem. The matter of high feeling is less helpful, for foreign policy is not

[1] Remarks to the National Press Club, January 12, 1950 (*Bulletin*, XXII, p. 118).

good material for a lawsuit, and as people become committed to fixed positions, they often cease to think in moderate terms. I have tried, in the discussion that follows, to limit myself to a direct presentation of the views and policies which have guided Acheson, and to his own explanations; while I find his position a good deal more persuasive than that of his ardent opponents, I have no desire to interpose myself as judge in a matter which will remain under debate for a long time. It should be fully understood, then, that in what follows the reader is getting one side of a hotly debated question. This does not make it the wrong side.

The real root of the bitterness in discussion of American policy toward China is the great and tragic fact that between the middle of 1945 and the middle of 1949 China was won by Communists who openly proclaimed their loyalty to Stalin. One side says that this was the fault of the American Government, and the other says that it happened in spite of the best efforts of the United States, and that no American can properly be held responsible for it. In this discussion, of course, everything turns on the facts of these four eventful years, and therefore we must first consider this period, although when Acheson became Secretary of State the outcome of the struggle for China was already painfully clear.

Acheson has stated his opinion of the events leading to the great Communist victory on a number of occasions, but never more clearly than in a long prepared statement made on June 4, 1951, before the Senate Committees considering the relief of General MacArthur. Since even his political opponents congratulated him on the clarity and interest of this exposition, it seems best to let it speak for itself, almost uncondensed and only briefly annotated:

Now gentlemen, I will take advantage of the kindness of the Committee in permitting me to make a somewhat extended statement on United States policy in regard to China.

I should like to state at the outset what I am going to try to do, and that is I want to present to the Committee the problem which confronted the United States and China in 1945, and in doing that I shall have to give some of its roots in history.

I should like to point out what the times of decision were. There were moments in this period from 1945 on, moments of decision, and I should like to point out those moments. I should like to point out the considerations which were taken under advisement when decisions were made, and I should like to say what the decisions were and how they were made.

One further preliminary observation I think is important, and that is that American aid cannot in itself insure the survival of a recipient government or the survival of a people that this government is trying to help against aggression.

What our aid must do and can do is to supplement the efforts of that recipient government and of that people itself. It cannot be a substitute for those efforts. It can only be an aid and a supplement to them.

The United States Government, in aiding another government, does not have power of decision within that country or within that government. That power of decision remains with the government, the people in it. Those are thoughts I think we should have in mind.

With those preliminary statements, we come to the problem which faced the Chinese and American Governments in 1945.

The Japanese had been defeated. The Chinese Government was in the extreme southwestern part of China. The task which had to be solved by the Chinese Government was, in effect, how to create a nation, and how to have the authority of the Chinese Government exercised throughout that nation.

Now, I do not say re-create a nation; I say, advisedly, create a nation; because for almost an indefinite period in the past there had not been in our sense a nation in the territory which we call China, and I will come to and explain to you why that is so, a nation in the sense of a government in control throughout that area.

Therefore, the question which had to be faced was how to create that nation and how to create the authority of the nation in that area. . . .

The Chinese Government that we are talking about — the Nationalist Government — had not had authority — indeed, no Chinese Government had had authority, by which I mean substantial authority — throughout China since the period of the Manchus.

Here is the picture which confronted everybody at the time I am talking about. The great northern area of China, Manchuria, was occupied by the Soviet Union, with its own armed forces. In the second place, the north central and southeast parts of China were in the control of the Communists and the Japanese.

I say both the Communists and the Japanese because the Japanese held the cities and the major lines of communication; whereas, the surrounding areas were occupied by the Communists.

That part of China included what we call North China, swinging down through central China, on to the southeast and coming quite far south and southeast in China.

The south central and southern part of China was occupied by the Japanese, who had troops along the coast and for considerable areas inland and the government itself was, as I said before, in the extreme southwestern part of China.

Another important fact, which must never be lost sight of in our consideration, is that in addition to these facts as to who actually occupied and exercised authority in certain parts of China, all of China was in the grip of a very profound social revolution. . . .

General MacArthur has spoken to you about the depth and strength of this social revolution.

It grew out of a similar experience in almost all wars, that as the governments concerned have to make tremendous efforts, as, in some areas, the controls of government become weakened, and promises are made, people move forward in social economic ways, at least they move forward in acquiring new social and economic rights; and this was going on in China, in the age-long battle between the peasants and the landlords.

The peasants had made advances and there was a new idea of profound importance.

If I may speak briefly, on the general area of Communist control:

The Communists controlled an area containing one hundred and sixteen million people, which was one-fourth of the population of China. The geographical area was fifteen percent of the country we call China, exclusive of Manchuria.

This area included in it some of the most heavily populated areas of China, the area which had most of the railway communications, important industrial developments, and important cities.

Now, let us take a look at Manchuria.

Manchuria, except in a wholly nominal way, and then only for a period of two or three years, part of 1928, 1929, 1930 and part of 1931, had never been in any way under the control of the present Nationalist Government of China; and, until his death in 1927 or 1928, the old marshal [2] had been the war lord of Manchuria, and controlled it absolutely.

Upon his death, the young marshal [3] took over his authority, and in

[2] Chang Tso-lin, the "old marshal," actually declared his formal independence in July, 1922, and gave no allegiance to any outside power from then until his death in 1928.
[3] Chang Hsueh-liang, son of the "old marshal."

1928 after Chiang Kai-shek had taken Peking and defeated the Communists and the northern war lords, the young marshal announced his adherence to the National Government. That was a pretty nominal adherence.

It meant that he recognized the government of Chiang Kai-shek as the National Government of China, but the administration in Manchuria did not change, and he continued to exercise the authority.

However, that authority continued for a very short period of time, and in 1931 the Japanese invaded Manchuria and set up their puppet state, and all Chinese authority disappeared from Manchuria. I mention this to point out to you that the National Government had no roots of any sort in Manchuria, a very important thing for us to remember.

When we come to North China, we find that in 1927 the struggle between the left wing of the Kuomintang Party, which was established at Hangkow, and the right wing of the party under Chiang Kai-shek came to a head. The Chiang Kai-shek forces won; the Russian, Borodin, who was then advising the Government, had to flee from China, and in 1928 Chiang Kai-shek moved into Peking and there announced the official unification of China. That was in 1928.

The battle with the Communists which began in 1927 in open warfare continued until 1936, and in the period of 1934 and 1935 the Communists were forced to make their long march from the southeastern portion of China to the northwestern portion of China. There they established themselves in the period 1934–35.

In the meantime, however, the Japanese who were in Manchuria were moving into North China, and in 1935 the Japanese undertook to set up another puppet state in North China which would comprise the five northern provinces of China; and at that time they had sufficient physical control of the area to do that.

I point all of this out to make clear to you again that in North China the authority of Chiang Kai-shek's government, which was established in 1928, had been in very large part eliminated by 1935, and instead of his government having power in North China, that was in part controlled through Japanese puppets, Japanese, and in part was controlled by the Communists in the northwest.

With this review then, let us just mention once more the principal problems which confronted the Chinese Government and confronted the American Government in its efforts to help the Chinese Government.

These were: The Soviets in Manchuria, the Japanese and the Communists struggling against one another to control a vast area in northwestern, north central and southeastern China — the Communists I have already mentioned — and at the same time this great problem of the revolution in thought and in social relationships which was going on throughout all China.

So the first period of decision, the first time after the war when important decisions were made and had to be made, was the period 1945 and 1946. Now, I do not mean for a moment that important decisions were not made before and after, but that was the first great moment of decision.

The situation was stated in a nutshell by General Wedemeyer in November 1945 very shortly after VJ-Day, and I should like to read, not very much, but I should like to read from General Wedemeyer's report in November 1945.

He says:

"Chinese Communist guerrillas and saboteurs can, and probably will, if present activities are a reliable indication, restrict and harass the movements of National Government forces to such an extent that the result will be a costly and extended campaign. Logistical support for the National Government forces, and measures for their security in the heart of Manchuria have not been fully appreciated by the Generalissimo or his Chinese staff. These facts, plus the lack of appropriate forces and transport, have caused me to advise the Generalissimo that he should concentrate his efforts on the recovery of North China and the consolidation of his military and political position there, prior to any attempt to occupy Manchuria. I received the impression that he agreed with this concept."

Now, General Wedemeyer has five conclusions to this report of 1945:

First, that the Generalissimo will be able to stabilize the situation in South China, provided he accepts the assistance of foreign administrators and technicians, and engages in political, economic and social reforms through honest, competent civilian officials.

Second. He will be unable to stabilize the situation in North China for months, and perhaps, even years, unless a satisfactory settlement with the Chinese Communists is achieved, and followed up realistically by the kind of action suggested in paragraph one — that is the paragraph which has just been talked about, the political, economic and social reforms.

Third. He will be unable to occupy Manchuria for many years unless satisfactory agreements are reached with Russia and the Chinese Communists.

Fourth. Russia is in effect creating favorable conditions for the realization of Chinese Communist and possibly their own plans in North China and Manchuria. These activities are violations of the recent Sino-Soviet Treaty and related agreements.

Fifth. It appears remote that a satisfactory understanding will be reached between Chinese Communists and the National Government.

Now, in short, what General Wedemeyer reported and advised was, first of all, that the Generalissimo must consolidate his own position in South China and to do that he must take into consideration this revolution that I have been talking about. And General Wedemeyer stressed then — and you will see over and over again he stresses — the same point, that there must be political, economic, and social reforms in order that the Chinese Government might put itself at the head of this great demand for improvement, which was existing in China, and not allow the Communists or anybody else to take that advantage away from them.

In the second place, he points out that to establish himself in North China he must come to agreement with the Communists.

In the third place, he points out the only way to establish himself in Manchuria is through agreement with the Russians.

He ends up by saying that the outlook on all of these fronts is dark, and he points out that force is not available to accomplish these efforts, partly because force cannot accomplish some of them, and secondly, because there is not enough force available to take on the problems which I have already mentioned.

Now, in that situation the United States Government had three choices open to it.

One choice was to pull out of China and say, "We have defeated the Japanese. The Chinese from now on must paddle their own canoe, and we have to wash our hands of it." That was an impossible choice to take because with the presence of 1,235,000 armed Japanese troops in China, exclusive of Manchuria, and of another 1,700,000 Japanese civilians — Government officials, economic people, clerks, and businessmen, one thing or another — there was a Japanese force and a Japanese influence so great in China that by throwing its weight to either side in this civil war it could have taken over the administration of the country, and Japan in defeat would have found itself in actual control of China, a result which we could not, of course, help to bring about.

The second choice was that the United States Government might have put into China unlimited resources and all the necessary military power to try and defeat the Communists, remove the Japanese, and remove the Russians from Manchuria.

That was a task so great and so repugnant to the American people that the Government could not undertake it, and it was one which was not in accord with American interests.

The third choice, and the one which was chosen, was to give important assistance of all sorts to the Chinese Government and to assist in every way in the preservation of peace in China and the working out of the agreements which were so necessary to enable the Chinese Government to re-establish itself in those parts of China where it had been before and to get, for the first time, into areas of China where it never had been.

Now, I should like briefly to talk about the Chinese Communist situation and the background of that as it existed in 1945 and then I will take up each of the other elements of this problem.

The relations between the Nationalist Government and the Communists have had a long history in China. I shall not take time to go through it all.

Prior to 1927 there was a period of collaboration. From 1927 to 1937 there was a period of war. From 1937 onward there was again a period in which the official attitude of both the Government and the Communists was that the differences between them were political in nature, had to be settled by political means; and beginning in 1937 they worked out arrangements for collaboration in fighting the Japanese, which never were very effective, but were agreements between them.

Later on, as you will see, they began working very vigorously at arrangements to bring about a settlement by negotiation in China. This official view was stated by the Generalissimo on September 13, 1943, where he said — and this is one of many times when he said this from 1937 on — "I am of the opinion that first of all we should clearly recognize that the Chinese Communist problem is a purely political problem and should be solved by political means."

As I said, there was an agreement reached between them in 1937 for their joint efforts against the Japanese. That agreement did not work, and reports were made over and over again that a very large part of the Communist armed forces and a very large part of the Nationalist armed forces were immobilized so far as the war against Japan was concerned because they stood facing one another and maneuvering against one another.

It was the effort of our government throughout the war period to try and reach some kind of an arrangement so that these two forces instead of watching one another would both fight the Japanese. If they did that, there was a very important contribution to the war.

I will not go into all the efforts that were made by General Stilwell and others in the early period.

In the spring of 1944 Vice-President Wallace went on a mission for President Roosevelt. Among other places, he went to China, and there he had talks with the Generalissimo, and they talked about two of the great important problems that I have been discussing. One was Manchuria and the other was the Communists.

The Generalissimo was most anxious to get help of the United States in improving relations, as he stated it, between [China] and the Soviet Union because without that improvement the prospects for China were very difficult indeed. They discussed what could be done along that line.

They also discussed the Communist problem, and the Generalissimo pointed out vigorously that the Communists were, as he stated it, not people of good faith, claimed that they were not Chinese, that they had their interests with an alien power. But, nevertheless, he said, "This is a political problem and we have got to settle it by political means."

He stated that he would not regard any help from the United States, in attempting that, to be meddling into the internal affairs of China, and he would be grateful for help.

And finally, before Vice-President Wallace left China, he [Chiang] reversed the position which he had taken earlier in which he had opposed any American military people having any relations with the Communists, and withdrew his objection to that.

Now, in the fall of 1944, and after these discussions, the President sent another personal representative to China, and that was General Hurley. General Hurley was not then Ambassador. He became Ambassador in the early part of 1945, but he went out as the personal representative of the President in order to try and unify this military effort, and there, with the consent and approval of the Generalissimo and of his Cabinet, he undertook to act as mediator between the Yenan Communist authorities and the Chungking Nationalist authorities, and they had meetings, some in Yenan at which General Hurley was present, some in Chungking in which they worked out a series of agreements.

Some of these agreements had to do with the conduct of the war, and then some of them went beyond that, and a very important and basic agreement was worked out.

The beginning of it was under the mediation of General Hurley. It was announced on October 11, 1945, and that was the agreement on the general principles of a peaceful settlement of the differences between the Chinese Communists and the Chinese Nationalists.

It was announced after General Hurley's departure from China and was made public, as I said, on October 11th. This called for the convening of the National Assembly and for a political consultative conference of all party and nonparty leaders.

It called for the inauguration of a constitutional government for all of China; for the formation of a committee of government and Communist representatives to discuss the reorganization of the armies and the reduction of all the armed forces in China.

Now, these agreements were of the greatest possible importance, and they established the basis for the efforts which General Marshall later took on.

May I just pause again for a moment to point out that the problem between the Chinese Government and the Chinese Communists differed in one important respect from the relations between — from the problems of governments, say, in Europe after the war with Communists in their country, because in China the Communists were not scattered through the population as an element of the population. They were people who had a defined area, with a large population subject to their control, 116 million.

They had a government of their own; they had an army of their own; and, in effect, they had a separate country within China, and the task was to put these two things together so that there would be one country and one government. Now, that was what they were working on. . . .

Now I have dealt with the background of this Communist business, and I am coming back to that, when we get to the mission of General Marshall.

I now want to go back and deal with a problem that has to do with another important aspect of this thing, and that is, Manchuria.

I want to talk about Yalta.

The Yalta agreements were made in the very early part of 1945. Later on, in August of 1945, treaties were signed between the Chinese Nationalist Government, and the Soviet Union, which grew out of and were based upon these Yalta agreements.

Now, first of all, the Yalta agreements, from the point of view of the wartime effort, and the interest of the United States and its major fighting allies — I think this has been referred to many times, and I shall make it brief — at the time these agreements were entered into at Yalta, we did not know whether we had an atomic bomb or not. That was not proved until some months later, that we had one, and it was not used until considerably later.

It was the then military opinion, concurred in by everyone, that the reduction of Japan would have to be brought about by a large-scale landing on the islands of Japan, and the forecast of that fighting, which came from the fighting on the other islands in the Pacific, indicated that it would be a very bloody and terrible battle.

It was of the utmost importance that the Russians should come into the war in the Far East, in time.

Now, there was very little doubt that they would come in, but the grave danger was that they would really wait until the war was over, and until we had expended our effort and blood to win the war, and they would come in and do what they wished.

It was very important, in the view of the military people, and the others, too, present, that they should come in in time, so that none of the 700,000 Japanese troops in Manchuria, and none, if possible, of the 1,235,000 Japanese troops in China, would come back to strengthen the troops of the main islands of Japan; but that they would be occupied with the Russian effort on the mainland.

That was the purpose, and in making the agreements, the price which was paid for the agreements was that three months after the end of the European war, the Russians would enter the Far East war; that they should have the southern half of Sakhalin, the Kuriles; that their former rights in Port Arthur and Dairen should be returned to them; and their former interest in the two railways in Manchuria.

The Russians took the same attitude toward these rights that the Chinese took toward their rights in Formosa.

The Russians had lost theirs to the Japanese by war in 1904; the Chinese had lost theirs to the Japanese by war in 1895.

Russia made its claim for those rights, and the claims were granted at this meeting at Yalta. . . .

One of the other things that I should like to point out about Yalta was that unquestionably the Russians had it in their power not only to take what was conceded to them, but much more, besides.

There was very little likelihood that anybody would have the will, and few people could have the power, to throw them out of any area on the mainland which they might occupy, and where they might wish to remain, so that this agreement gave them the basis for a legal claim to something considerably less than they might have taken without a legal claim.

I should also like to point out that at the time the Chinese entered into this treaty with the Russians, a few months after Yalta, that is, in August, 1945, they regarded the arrangements which they had made with the Russians on the basis of Yalta, as very satisfactory.

Such statements were expressed by the Generalissimo, Chiang Kai-shek, and by the Chinese foreign minister. In fact, in 1947 the Chinese foreign minister expressed grave apprehension that the Soviet Union might cancel the treaty with China of 1945, in which China had conferred these rights to the bases in Port Arthur, the interests in Dairen, and the interest in the railway.

They regarded that as a very valuable treaty because it also carried with it the obligation of the Russians to evacuate Manchuria, to recognize the Chinese Nationalist Government, and to aid in the reestablishment of Chinese sovereignty in Manchuria.

Now these agreements, as I shall point out later on, did have a very important effect and bearing when it came to the question of the reoccupation of Manchuria by the Chinese, because it was on the basis of these agreements that both the Chinese Communists and the Russians agreed to occupation by the National Government's forces.

Now may I speak briefly about the problem of the Japanese, and here I shall have to get a little bit out of the chronological thing and perhaps run this Japanese part through to its end.

I have pointed out to you the very great importance of the presence of the Japanese in China, the 1,235,000 troops, 1,700,000 civilians. It was decided very early in the game, between the Chinese Government, the

Nationalist Government and ourselves, that one of our major efforts must be to get these people out of China and back into Japan.

That wouldn't have been too hard a job to do if they were all just marching on to ships. The great difficulty about it was that these armed soldiers controlled most of the important cities in central China, in southeast China and east China, and also the main lines of communication.

If they had been told to drop their guns on the ground and march to the coast at once, those areas would have been occupied by the Communists, and the Nationalist Government forces would never have gotten in there without fighting.

Therefore the task was to have the Japanese evacuate the areas which they held at the time when the Government forces could be moved and were moved by us into those areas. That was the task to perform.

In order to do that we landed 50,000 Marines in China. The function of these Marines was to occupy the principal seaports, to guard the principal rail lines close to those seaports, and later to take over the areas along the eastern coast where coal was produced and guard the lines along which the coal came to the principal consuming centers. That was to allow the industrial life of China to continue, and those coal areas and the coal railroads were being constantly raided by the Communists.

So the Marines had to go in there, hold coal, which was the heart of the industrial life of China, hold the seaports so that they would not be captured by Communists, and then receive the Japanese as they were marched to the railheads and down their railroads, and put them on ships and take them back to Japan.

At the same time our Armed Forces airlifted Chinese armies, whole armies, from South China into the areas to be evacuated and which were being evacuated by the Japanese. Now that was a tremendous undertaking most skillfully carried out, and it was that undertaking which permitted the Chinese Government to really get back into areas of China which it would have had the utmost difficulty in even getting into without that colossal effort.

By the end of '46 we had removed 3,000,000 Japanese, just a few thousand under 3,000,000, from China to Japan — one of the great mass movements of people.

After the agreements between the Chinese Nationalists and the Chinese Communists that I have spoken of in 1945, October 11, 1945, armed clashes broke out again between the two parties; and both the government authorities, the Chinese Government authorities, and the American Government authorities, were gravely disturbed that civil war would break out.

If that happened, then the whole chance of dealing with any of the problems which you and I have been discussing this morning would disappear.

If there was civil war going on in China, fighting between the Government forces and the Communist forces, all possibility of removing the Japanese either disappeared or was gravely diminished.

The possibility of occupying North China became much dimmer; the possibility of moving into Manchuria became non-existent; and the possibility of really getting any reforms in southern China or any other part of China would be greatly diminished. So, the peace became a major objective of both the Chinese Government and the United States Government in its efforts to help the Chinese Government.

It was in that situation that General Marshall was asked by the President to go to China at the end of 1945. . . .

At the outset I will go into a matter of detail which really is quite out of place in the broad picture which I am trying to paint for you here; but since it has been talked about a great deal, I think it is important to clear it up, and that is the preparation of the instructions which were issued to General Marshall.

I think he was questioned about that, and there have been various charges and countercharges having to do with the preparation of those instructions. The story is very simple.

At the end of November, 1945, Secretary Byrnes and General Marshall met. This was after General Marshall had been asked to go to China.

Secretary Byrnes read him a memorandum suggesting the outline of instructions for him. General Marshall did not approve of it.

General Marshall said that he would wish to try his own hand, assisted by some of his associates, in drafting the instructions.

This he did; and a draft was prepared by him, in conjunction with four generals who were working very closely with General Marshall. This was submitted to Secretary Byrnes.

On the 8th of December Secretary Byrnes made his suggestions to General Marshall — that is, suggestions of changes or alterations or additions to the draft prepared by General Marshall.

General Marshall's draft, with Secretary Byrnes' suggestions, was discussed at a meeting in Secretary Byrnes' office on Sunday morning, December 9, 1945, by Secretary Byrnes, General Marshall, Mr. John Carter Vincent, General Hull, and myself. I was then Under Secretary of State.

Those of us went over the instructions. General Marshall approved the suggestions made by Secretary Byrnes, and we then had a completely agreed draft.

In the course of that meeting the outline of a letter from the President to General Marshall was discussed and directions were given for its preparation.

There was also approved at the meeting a memorandum from Secretary Byrnes to the Secretary of War, requesting certain help in connection with the removal of the Japanese and the movement of Chinese armies into the North and laying down certain restrictions on those movements.

There was also agreed upon the form of a press release, I believe — it was agreed that day or a few days later — but the important papers were agreed at that meeting.

They were taken up by Secretary Byrnes with the President, who went over them; and they were put in final shape, unchanged from the agreements of December 9.

The President then had a meeting with General Marshall, at which I was present — there were three of us at that meeting, the President, General Marshall, and myself — and at that point the signed letter and the enclosure were handed to General Marshall.

It was ascertained by the President at that meeting that these papers were unanimously approved and agreeable to all concerned, and to himself.

Now, that is the account of the preparation of these instructions.

All the papers concerned are printed in the white book,[4] with one exception. The press release, which I mentioned a moment ago, which was given out on the 15th of December — everything in the press re-

---

[4] Acheson refers to the Department of State publication commonly known as the Chinese White Paper, hereafter cited as *United States Relations with China*, Department of State Publication 3573, August, 1949.

lease was in General Marshall's instructions. In other words, the press release was a verbatim statement of what was in the instructions to General Marshall, except that certain paragraphs in the instructions were omitted from the press release.

One of those omissions had to do with what is printed in the White Paper and in the memorandum from Secretary Byrnes to the Secretary of War. That was the discretion and authority given to General Marshall in not moving Nationalist Government troops into areas in which there was fighting until he thought that that was a wise thing to do.

That was not to be stated and released because obviously it wouldn't work if it were.

Two other omissions had to do with things which we would do if the Chinese Government asked us to do it. Obviously you do not print in the newspapers that you will do something if somebody else asks you to. You leave it to the other person to ask you to do that if they wish. That is the story of the instructions.

General Marshall arrived in China at the very end of December, 1945. By February, 1946, three major agreements had been reached between the Chinese Government and the Communists. These agreements grew out of the earlier agreements of October 11, 1945, which discussed the general principles for working out peacefully the differences between the Communists and the Government.

The agreements of January and February, 1946, carried into considerable detail how this should be done. In regard to these three agreements which I shall describe, General Marshall had a part only in one, and that was in the first one. [Acheson later corrected this statement by noting that General Marshall also had a part in the third agreement.]

The first agreement was for the cessation of hostilities. It provided that all fighting should cease, and it provided for the setting up of an executive headquarters in which there would be American chairmanship and Nationalist and Communist representation, the purpose of this executive headquarters being to bring the fighting to an end, and these tripartite teams were set up which went to every area where there was any clashing between the troops, and together they brought that fighting to an end and tried to have that truce develop into a more substantial truce.

General Marshall played a very considerable part in working this out. The executive headquarters was the really great instrumentality which set up and worked very well until the two parties fell apart — then nothing worked.

The second agreement was an agreement for governmental reorganization and for a constitutional government, and the third agreement was for a military reorganization and the integration of the Communist forces into the National Government. . . .

The second agreement for working out a constitutional government recognized the preponderant strength of the Kuomintang position in the National Government. It provided that there was to be an interim state council, sort of a provisional government, which would govern until the new constitution was established and elections were held throughout China and a constitutional government was set up in which all the people of China would have their representatives, and which would function on a two-party or multiparty system.

The interim state council was to function in this interim period as the supreme organ of the state. The Kuomintang Party was given 20 of the 40 seats in this national council. The other 20 seats were distributed among the Communists and the other parties and to some nonparty people. It was provided that the Generalissimo, Chiang Kai-shek, as the President of China, should select all the members of the council, that is, he would select those from his own party and those from all the other parties. However, he would have to appoint a certain number from these other minority parties. That would leave him with 20 people whom he had selected from his own party, with 20 people whom he had selected from the other parties, including the Communists, and it would also leave him with a veto over any action of this council which could only be overridden by a three-fifths vote, which could not be done if his own party stayed with him.

Now, that, I say, was the temporary government. That was to continue until the constitution was to be agreed upon on May 4, through the National Assembly, May 4, 1946, and it was hoped that at an early date, sometime in 1946 or 1947, I believe it was, there could be an election, and they would then set up a regular constitutional government with legislative, judicial and executive branches, in which all parts of China would be represented, so that this country would have a government extending over all of the area.

The third agreement had to do with the amalgamation of the forces, and that was the most important one. It provided that there should be a great reduction in forces on both sides, because China could not support the tremendous military establishment which existed on the Nationalist side and on the Communist side together.

The army was to consist of 60 divisions. Of those 60 divisions 50 were to be National Government divisions and 10 were to be Communist divisions. These divisions were to be grouped together in armies, armies which would contain three divisions or whatever the Chinese military order of battle is. There would be several divisions in each army.

The divisions were to be stationed in certain numerical strengths in various parts of China.

The important thing here about the agreement, as we look back on it, was that so far as Manchuria was concerned, the agreement provided that in Manchuria there should be 15 divisions of the new government's troops. Of those 15 divisions, 14 should be national government divisions and one should be a Communist division. That was of the greatest possible importance. If that could have been carried out, the whole situation might have been very different.

In 1946 the situation of comparative peace which had been brought about as a result of the agreements in the early part of the year began to deteriorate. Fighting broke out in various places.

General Marshall, in trying to stop this fighting, through the executive headquarters, got drawn into greater detail in some of the political negotiations between the two parties, because this fighting rapidly took on political aspects.

One side or the other would believe that it could gain an advantage by capturing this or that city or area, and believed it could strengthen itself in the negotiations; and then would start an attack. Either the Communists would attack the Nationalists or the Nationalists would attack the Communists, and in that way this situation became worse and worse; and General Marshall's efforts were unable to deal with it.

Therefore, the whole discussions between the Communists and the Nationalists in the attempt to work out the interim government, and the long-term constitutional government, got into more and more and more confusion and trouble.

The Prime Minister of China, Doctor Sun Fo, has an interesting comment on this period. In a New Year's message which he delivered on January 1, 1949, speaking of the period which I have been discussing, he said:

"The Government had decided to call this conference because it was generally realized that the country and the people needed recuperation and peace, so that rehabilitation work could be started. Had these measures been carried out at that time all of us would have seen more prosperity and happiness in our midst. Unfortunately, all the parties concerned could not completely abandon their own selfish ends and the people in general did not exert sufficient influence in promoting this peace movement."

The result of the breakdown was that the situation developed into one of very considerable fighting by the end of 1946, and when General Marshall left China in January, 1947, to return to Washington, the American effort to mediate in this struggle between the Government and the Communists ended.

General Marshall issued a long statement, which I shall not bother to read to you now, but it sums up very clearly his understanding of the difficulties which brought failure to his mission, and his understanding of the difficulties in the Chinese Government, which could not really permit it to function unless they were removed.[5]

These difficulties, in some respects, had their roots in the fact that the liberal elements in the Kuomintang Party were the ones which were dealt with much more severely by the war and the inflation. Inflation and war tend to eliminate the middle class, and that is where the liberal elements came into the Kuomintang, and as the inflation and the war went forward, the power in the party shifted more to the extreme right wing; and General Marshall, in his farewell message, spoke of the importance of more liberal leadership in the Kuomintang Party itself.

But as I say, the effort to mediate came to an end with his departure. From then on we go into the military period of the struggle between the two governments.

The National Government reached a peak of its military holdings toward the end of 1946. In the middle of 1946 it had approximately 3,000,000 men under arms. These were opposed by something over 1,000,000 Communist troops of whom about 400,000 were not regulars but were guerrilla troops.

Until the end of 1946 and the early part of 1947, the gains, the military gains made by the Nationalist Government appeared to be impressive, but in fact they were not, and General Marshall repeatedly pointed out to the Government that what it was doing was over-extending itself militarily and politically, since it neither had sufficient troops to garrison this whole area nor did it have sufficient administrators to administer the areas that it was taking over.

[5] For General Marshall's statement see *Bulletin*, XVI, p. 83.

Therefore what it was doing by this military advance was weakening itself both militarily and through administrative ineptitude, because it didn't have the necessary administrators, it was not giving the people of the occupied areas what they had been led to expect when the National Government came in, so politically it was doing itself harm, and militarily it was doing itself harm.

General Barr points out it was during this period that what he calls the wall psychology [6] took possession of the Chinese Nationalist Army. He had pointed out over and over again that in modern warfare the most disastrous of all things to do is to retreat into a city behind walls and take a defensive position. Modern warfare must be a war of maneuver.

Therefore, time and time and time again these Nationalist lines got pushed way forward; finally, the troops at the end take up defensive positions behind some kind of walls, a long line of communication has to be guarded, which eventually is cut, and over and over again the troops at the end of the line either go over to the side of the enemy without firing a shot, or sufficient of them do so that those who want to fight can't fight.

That was the story of the war from 1946 on. At first, it looked very successful — lots of areas occupied, important cities taken — but the armies all go to garrison, they become immobilized, and maneuver and initiative is left with the Communists.

At the end of '46 the Government had 2,600,000 men under arms and the Communists had about 1,100,000 of regulars.

However, in firepower, in rifle firepower, the Government still enjoyed a superiority of three or four to one over the Communists.

In 1946, when this fighting started, General Marshall was acting as mediator. He called on both sides to stop the fighting. Both professed to want to do it, but did not do it.

Therefore, General Marshall asked for and obtained from this Government an embargo on the shipment of combat materiel into China.

---

[6] The Committee text reads "war psychology," but this is a stenographic misunderstanding. General Barr's discussion of the "wall psychology" may be found in *United States Relations with China*, Department of State Publication 3573, August, 1949, p. 337. General Barr, who later commanded the 7th Division in Korea, was the chief of the U.S. military Advisory Group in China in 1948. His own testimony on these matters is highly important. Hearings, *Military Situation in the Far East*, Senate, Committee on Foreign Relations and Committee on Armed Services, 82d Congress, 1st Session, June 4, 1951, pp. 2948–3053.

That embargo lasted from the time it was imposed in [August] 1946[7] . . . until May 1947. During that time the Nationalists were winning the battles, they won the fights they had, they occupied the cities, but they immobilized themselves.

We have talked from time to time here about the great necessity for reform in China. General Marshall, during his mission to China, stressed that over and over again with the Generalissimo, pointing out that the whole possibility of any kind of armed action against the Communists must at last rest upon a belief in the country and their own belief that they had something which was worth fighting for, and was progressive and good, and that if we did not have reform in China, we were never going to get this spirit which was necessary to fight and defeat the Communists.

After General Marshall returned, in the summer of 1947, the President, on the recommendation of General Marshall, sent General Wedemeyer to China on a fact-finding mission. General Wedemeyer, before he left, stressed again, as he had in 1945, the great importance and the necessity for reform.

He said before he left the United States:

"To regain and maintain the confidence of the people, the Central Government will have to effect immediately drastic and far-reaching political and economic reforms. Promises will no longer suffice. Performance is absolutely necessary   It should be accepted that military force in itself will not eliminate Communism."

General Wedemeyer went to China and returned. He made recommendations, which are printed in the White Paper, in which he recommended assistance of economic and military equipment for a five-year period, which would require Congressional authorization. Although his actual recommendations do not call for a grant of military aid, it is possible to read that in. He does talk about the desirability of that.

However, General Wedemeyer recognized the desirability and importance of avoiding direct United States involvement in the civil war in China by stating:

"Although advice indicated above" — that is, technical military advice — "does provide advice indirectly to tactical force, it should be carried on outside operational areas to prevent the criticism that American personnel are actively engaged in fratricidal warfare."

[7] This exact month was named later in Acheson's testimony, in response to a question from Senator Brewster.

There are other recommendations in the Wedemeyer Report which I shall not dwell upon at the present time. We are now directing our attention to the aid part of it.

The Secretary of State, General Marshall, then had prepared, and with the approval of the President, sent to Congress a recommendation for aid to China. He made before the Foreign Relations Committee a very frank statement of the problems facing the United States Government in considering aid to China.

He made it clear that there were steps which had to be taken and could only be taken by the Chinese Government, which were essential to meet the Communist threat.

And, he took the position strongly, that the United States Government had to be extremely careful that it did not commit itself to a policy involving the absorption of its resources to an unpredictable extent by assuming a direct responsibility for the civil war in China, and for the Chinese economy.

He also pointed out that we must be prepared to face the possibility that the Chinese Government might not be able to maintain itself against the Chinese Communist forces.

That was stated quite clearly by General Marshall. In fact, he said:

"An attempt to underwrite the Chinese economy and the Chinese Government's military efforts will result in a burden on the U.S. economy and a military responsibility which I cannot recommend as a course of action for this government."

Now, the program of aid which General Marshall presented was a program of $570,000,000 in economic assistance over a 15-month period. He pointed out that the experience gained in the program would throw light on the possibilities of future programs.

The program was sufficient in size, it was thought, to free the major portion of the Chinese Government's own foreign exchange assets for the purchase of such military supplies, from foreign sources, as it might need.

It was not recommended that we should have military advisors in combat areas.

It was not recommended that we should take measures of military aid which would lead to U.S. military intervention in China, or direct involvement in the civil war.

Now, this question was very carefully considered in the Executive Branch, at a meeting in June, 1948, attended by Secretary Marshall,

Secretary of the Army Royall, General Bradley, and General Wedemeyer, and the decision which I have just spoken of was taken.

There was already a United States military advisory group in China that had been established in 1946, and in 1947 the commanding officer of the group had been authorized to give advice on a confidential basis to the Generalissimo, advice of a strategic nature, but the United States was not willing to assume responsibility for the strategic direction of the war.

General Marshall in a message to General Barr pointed out one reason why. He said:

"I think you will agree that implications of our accepting that responsibility would be very far reaching and grave, and that such responsibility is in logic inseparable from the authority to make it effective. Whatever the Generalissimo may feel moved to say with respect to his willingness to delegate necessary powers to Americans, I know from my own experience that advice is always listened to very politely but not infrequently ignored when deemed unpalatable."

Therefore we did not take responsibility for the strategic direction of the war, nor did we recommend that American officers should be with troops in combat areas.

This recommendation was considered by the Eightieth Congress. The Eightieth Congress — and I shall not go through a whole long story — the Senate bill reduced the period of time from fifteen months to twelve months. It reduced, split the appropriations and recommended $338,000,000 for economic aid and $125,000,000 as a special grant to be used at the discretion of the Chinese Government.

The debate indicates that the Chinese Government would probably use this $125,000,000 for military aid. In the course of the legislative history, the House put in a provision authorizing military advice on the so-called Greek model, that is having officers with troops in combat areas and strategic advice. That was stricken out by the Senate, and in speaking about it Senator Vandenberg said:

"As in the case of Greece and Turkey, your Committee recognizes that military aid is necessary in order to make economic aid effective. It proposes to make military supplies available at China's option. Your Committee believes that as a matter of elementary prudence that this process must be completely clear of any implication that we are underwriting the military campaign of the Nationalist Government."

And, as I say, the House provision was stricken out.

That was agreed to in conference, and the bill was passed chiefly as written by the Senate.

I said that the bill authorized $338 million for economic aid. However, when it came to the appropriation process, Congress only appropriated $275,000,000 for economic aid and $125 million for military aid. So a total was actually made available by the Congress of $400,000,000 as against $570,000,000 requested.

I shall not go in detail through the campaigns of 1947 more than I have already done. The real collapse of the government in a military way began in the latter part of 1948. The first large-scale defection and collapse occurred in September 1948 with the fall of Tsinan, where government forces without any effort at all went over to the other side and surrendered with all their materiel.

The U.S. Army Intelligence Review of Military Developments in 1948, in January 1949, sums it up this way:

"The Nationalists entered 1948 with an estimated strength of 2,723,000 troops. Recruitment and replacement of combat losses kept this figure constant through mid-September. By February 1, 1949, however, heavy losses had reduced Nationalist strength to a million and a half, of which approximately 500,000 are service troops. This represents a reduction of 45 percent of the Nationalist Government's total strength in a four-and-a-half-month period.

"Communist strength, estimated at 1,150,000 a year ago, has mounted to 1,622,[000], virtually all combat effectives. Whereas the Nationalists began 1948 with almost a 3-to-1 numerical superiority, the Communist forces now outnumber the total Nationalist strength and have achieved better than 1½-to-1 superiority in combat effectives.

"The events of the last year, and more specifically those of the last four and a half months, have resulted in such overwhelming losses to the National Government that, acting alone, its military position has declined beyond possible recoupment.

"On the other hand, these same events have so enhanced the position and capabilities of the Communists that they are now capable of achieving a complete military victory over the [Nationalist] forces."

In mid-November, 1948, General Barr, who was the head of the military mission to China, reported to the Department of the Army:

"I am convinced that the military situation has deteriorated to the point where only the active participation of United States troops could effect a remedy. No battle has been lost since my arrival due to lack of ammunition or equipment. Their military debacles, in my opinion, can all be attributed to the world's worst leadership and many other morale-destroying factors that led to a complete loss of the will to fight."

In another report early in 1949, he explained some of the causes for the National Government defeats. He says:

"The Government committed its first politico-military blunder by concentrating on the purely military reoccupation of former Japanese-held areas. It gave very little realization to the regional areas or the creation of efficient local administrations. Its strategy was burdened by an unsound strategy conceived by a politically influenced and militarily inept high command.

"Throughout the structure and machinery of the National Government there are interlocking ties of interests, family, financial and political. No Chinese, no matter how efficient, can hope for a position of authority because he is the best qualified man. He must have other backing. In too many cases, such backing was the support and loyalty of the Generalissimo and his army comrades, which kept them in posts of responsibility regardless of their qualifications. The direct result has been the unsound strategy and faulty tactics of the Nationalists in their fight against the Communists."

By the end of 1948 the struggle in North China had virtually ended with the complete collapse of the Nationalist armies. Eighty percent of all the materiel which we had furnished, both during the war and after, to the National Government, was lost; and 75 percent of that is estimated to have been captured by the Communists.

One reason for this large capture, General Barr points out, when he says, "that the Chinese Nationalist government never destroyed any — the troops never destroyed any of the materiel, when they were about to surrender or run."

He says, "The Chinese seemed inherently unable to destroy anything of value."

Now, at the very end of my remarks here, I briefly sum up some of the things, material and otherwise, which the United States did in aid of its policy in China.

Speaking, first, of things on which it is impossible to put a dollar value, first, is the aid rendered by the United States forces in China in planning and in carrying out the movement of the Chinese Government forces into the areas occupied by the Japanese.

Second, is the evacuation of the Japanese troops from those areas.

Third, is the aid rendered by the United States Marines in North China; in occupying key areas and maintaining control for the government of essential railway lines until the Government was able to take over.

Fourth, the aid provided by the United States military advisory group.

Apart from this, the United States Government, in the period from VJ-Day until early 1949, authorized grants and credits to China totaling approximately $2,000,000,000, of which approximately $1,600,000,000 were grants; and $400,000,000 were on credit terms.

This total is divided almost equally between military and economic aid. The amounts do not include United States surplus property, except where the sales were on credit terms.

Surplus property, with a total estimated procurement cost of over a billion dollars, has been sold to China for the agreed realization to the United States of $230,000,000, of which $95,000,000 were on credit terms.

By the spring of 1949 the military position of the Chinese Government collapsed to the point where the Chinese Communists controlled the major centers of population, and railways from Manchuria south to the Yangtze.

The military collapse of the Chinese Government had, for the most part, been the consequence of inept political and military leadership, and a lack of the will to fight on the part of its armies, rather than inadequate military supplies.

It was at that time the considered judgment of responsible United States Government observers in China that only the extension of unlimited American economic and military aid involving the use of our own troops and operations which might require the extensive control of Chinese Government operations would enable the Nationalist Government to maintain a foothold in South China.

It was believed that United States involvement in Chinese civil war under the existing conditions would be clearly contrary to American interests.

As the last note of this tragic story, I should like to read you the message of the Acting President of China, General Li Tsung-jen.... May 5, 1949, in a letter which he addressed to President Truman....

He had described our help to China during the war, and then he had discussed our aid to China after the war as I have described it to you. He says:

"This policy of friendly assistance was continued when some years ago General Marshall under instructions from your good self took up the difficult task of mediation in our conflict with the Chinese Communists to which he devoted painstaking effort. All this work was unfortunately rendered fruitless by the lack of sincerity on the part of both the then government and the Chinese Communists.

"In spite of this your country continued to extend its aid to our Government. It is regrettable that owing to the failure of our then government to make judicious use of this aid and to bring about appropriate political, economic and military reforms, your assistance has not produced the desired effect. To this failure is attributable the present predicament in which our country finds itself." [8]

This is the end of the prepared statement, but the discussion immediately following is pertinent:

CHAIRMAN RUSSELL. That is a very clear, concise statement, Mr. Secretary.

I believe that I now have a better idea of what our policy had been, I might say, after World War II, than I had. I didn't keep myself informed of our policies in China as I should, perhaps. . . . Senator Wiley, I believe it is your time for questioning.

SENATOR WILEY. All right, Mr. Chairman.

Mr. Secretary, I think that you should be complimented on a pretty clear-cut statement as to the facts that heretofore were not brought to our attention [9] in relation to this Chinese situation, and a very clear-cut statement of the complex position that we occupied in seeking to find the way to combat the Communist influence.

What have you to say about the purported influence of Communist sympathizers in the Department during this period, whether you know of their having any influence in arriving at the determinations that you

[8] Hearings, *Military Situation in the Far East*, Senate, Committee on Armed Services and Committee on Foreign Relations, 82d Congress, 1st Session, June 4, 1951, pp. 1838-57.

[9] Senator Wiley's comment is somewhat surprising; almost all of Acheson's statement was a résumé of facts published two years before in the White Paper on China.

have described here as the various steps which were finally arrived at?

SECRETARY ACHESON. Senator Wiley, I think this whole matter has been discussed at very great length before the Foreign Relations Committee by Secretary Byrnes, when those charges were originally made in 1946.

I do not believe that the officers of the State Department who were either attached to the Military Establishment, first under General Stilwell, and then under General Wedemeyer, or the officers attached to our diplomatic and consular missions, had any other purpose in mind at any time than their service to the United States and serving American interests.

I think that during the war their great effort was the one which I have discussed here this morning, of trying to bring all forces in China together for the purpose of fighting the Japanese.

I think you will find that running throughout the voluminous documents in the White Paper, in which the reports of some of those officers are reprinted. I do not believe there was or is any Communist influence any way affecting the determination of Chinese policy, either then or now.[10]

In a week of questioning after his China statement, Acheson was repeatedly asked to cover and recover the ground which has just been discussed. None of the questions brought out any important modification of what he had said.

He stuck to his interpretation of the Yalta agreement. Although he granted that Senator Hickenlooper was "entitled to make the point" that this agreement was concluded behind the back of Chiang Kai-shek, he continued to believe that the reasons for the agreement were "valid reasons in the light of the military situation as it was then thought to be," and that "at that time these agreements were in the best interests of China and of the Allies." [11]

Under heavy questioning as to the amount and quality of arms and ammunition shipped to Chiang, especially after 1947, he stuck to his acceptance of General Barr's view that not a single battle had been lost since his arrival "due to lack of ammunition or equipment." He added that of course the detailed discussion of this problem was a matter for the military establishment (which had already filed extensive briefs with the Congress on the point).

[10] Same hearing, p. 1858. [11] Same hearing, p. 1885.

He repudiated entirely any notion that the American Government "tried to force any consolidation with Communists upon Chiang," and he emphasized over and over that Chiang himself had repeatedly stated that some sort of political solution was the necessary way out. He produced additional evidence of a general American support for this policy, at the time, in the form of a message signed by MacArthur, Wedemeyer, and Spruance, suggesting that "United States assistance to China . . . be made available as a basis for negotiation by the American Ambassador to bring together and effect a compromise between the major opposing groups in order to promote a united democratic China." [12]

There was one remark from his own past which Acheson's opponents undertook to use against him. On March 20, 1947, testifying on the Greek-Turkish Aid Program as Acting Secretary, he had said, "The Chinese government is not in the position at the present time that the Greek government is in. It is not approaching collapse; it is not threatened by defeat by the Communists." On the surface this sounded like a statement that the situation in China was not too serious. Acheson explained that he had been talking about the difference between a government on the verge of total collapse and one which was not; the Chinese collapse occurred over two years later, and the defeat by the Communists eighteen months later; in 1947 there had seemed no reason to conclude that collapse was even that near. "I have been over our military assistance and economic assistance to China, and I think I have described exactly and as fully as I possibly can why the courses were adopted which were taken." [13]

Acheson's statement to the Russell Committee did not include any summary judgment on the events of 1945–49, and the prolonged questioning dealt more with matters of detail than with general conclusions. In concluding this section, then, let us go back to earlier statements in which he under-

[12] Same hearing, p. 2047. General MacArthur denied that his message could reasonably be interpreted as consistent with the Marshall mission, but neither General Wedemeyer nor Admiral Spruance supported this view. It is also interesting to take Acheson's statement of the Chinese Communist position in 1945 and compare it with General MacArthur's contention that "the Communists, but a nebulous threat at the time, constituted only one of many factions which sought to secure the balance of power." (p. 2249.)

[13] Same hearing, p. 2198. It remained a fair conclusion from this 1947 comment that Acheson, among others, had not fully estimated the gravity of the peril in China. This was an error, it seems to me, which was made by both sides in the China controversy of 1947–49; those who wished to avoid excessive involvement in China tended to make statements like Acheson's, and those who wished to help Chiang tended to argue that relatively small amounts of aid would do the job. Both underestimated the strength and significance of the Communist power.

took to summarize the story of Chiang's collapse as he understood it. The first is from his Press Club speech of January 12, 1950:

The reasons for the fall of the Nationalist Government in China are preoccupying many people. All sorts of reasons have been attributed to it. Most commonly it is said in various speeches and publications that it is the result of American bungling, that we are incompetent, that we did not understand, that American aid was too little, that we did the wrong things at the wrong time. Other people go on and say: "No it is not quite that, but that an American general did not like Chiang Kai-shek and out of all that relationship grows the real trouble." And they say: "Well, you have to add to that there are a lot of women fooling around in politics in China."

Nobody, I think, says that the Nationalist Government fell because it was confronted by overwhelming military force which it could not resist. Certainly no one in his right mind suggests that. Now, what I ask you to do is to stop looking for a moment under the bed and under the chair and under the rug to find out these reasons, but rather to look at the broad picture and see whether something doesn't suggest itself.

The broad picture is that after the war, Chiang Kai-shek emerged as the undisputed leader of the Chinese people. Only one faction, the Communists, up in the hills, ill-equipped, ragged, a very small military force, was determinedly opposed to his position. He had overwhelming military power, greater military power than any ruler had ever had in the entire history of China. He had tremendous economic and military support and backing from the United States. He had the acceptance of all other foreign countries, whether sincerely or insincerely in the case of the Soviet Union is not really material to this matter. Here he was in this position and four years later what do we find? We find that his armies have melted away. His support in the country has melted away. His support largely outside the country has melted away and he is a refugee on a small island off the coast of China with the remnants of his forces.

As I said, no one says that vast armies moved out of the hills and defeated him. To attribute this to the inadequacy of American aid is only to point out the depth and power of the forces which were miscalculated or ignored. What has happened in my judgment is that the almost inexhaustible patience of the Chinese people in their misery ended. They did not bother to overthrow this government. There was really nothing to overthrow. They simply ignored it throughout the country. They took the solution of their immediate village problems into their own hands. If there was any trouble or interference with the representatives of the government, they simply brushed them aside. They completely withdrew their support from this government and when that support was withdrawn, the whole military establishment disintegrated. Added to the grossest incompetence ever experienced by any military command was this total lack of support both in the armies and in the country, and so the whole matter just simply disintegrated.

The Communists did not create this condition. They did not create this revolutionary spirit. They did not create a great force which moved out from under Chiang Kai-shek. But they were shrewd and cunning to mount it, to ride this thing into victory and into power.

That, I suggest to you, is an explanation which has certain roots and realism and which does not require all this examination of intricate and perhaps irrelevant details.[14]

And since the decision was caused by the situation in China itself, it followed that it should not be laid at the door of the United States:

It has been urged that relatively small amounts of additional aid — military and economic — to the National Government would have enabled it to destroy Communism in China. The most trustworthy military, economic, and political information available to our Government does not bear out this view.

A realistic appraisal of conditions in China, past and present, leads to the conclusion that the only alternative open to the United States was full-scale intervention in behalf of a Government which had lost the confidence of its own troops and its own people. Such intervention would have required the expenditure of even greater sums than have been fruitlessly spent thus far, the command of Nationalist armies by American officers, and the probable participation of American armed forces — land, sea, and air — in the resulting war. Intervention of such a scope and magnitude would have been resented by the mass of

[14] Remarks to the National Press Club, January 12, 1950, *Bulletin*, XXII, pp. 112–13. The estimate of the Chinese Communists in this passage is somewhat lower than that given in the later testimony quoted on p. 151 and p. 159 above.

the Chinese people, would have diametrically reversed our historic policy, and would have been condemned by the American people. . . .

The unfortunate but inescapable fact is that the ominous result of the civil war in China was beyond the control of the government of the United States. Nothing that this country did or could have done within the reasonable limits of its capabilities could have changed that result; nothing that was left undone by this country has contributed to it. It was the product of internal Chinese forces, forces which this country tried to influence but could not. A decision was arrived at within China, if only a decision by default.[15]

2. China, 1949–June 25, 1950

Although both critics and friends tend to forget it, the events we have been discussing occurred, in the main, before Acheson had the primary responsibility for the policy of the State Department; the great defeats of Chiang Kai-shek, indeed, occurred at a time when he was not in the State Department at all. It is only as we come into 1949 that we find Acheson — always under the President — directly responsible for China policy.

In early 1949 the big question was whether to make a last great effort to save Chiang. Pressure for such an effort was great, and the campaign speeches of Governor Dewey had made it seem that with a Republican victory such an attempt would be made. The Truman Administration decided against it, and its reasons were stated by Acheson in a letter to Senator Connally on March 15, 1949, opposing a bill to extend credits of a billion and a half for economic and military aid to Chiang. In essence the Administration view was that the proposed help would not do the job, that it would be sending good money after bad, that it would "embark this Government on an undertaking the eventual cost of which would be unpredictable but of great magnitude, and the outcome of which would almost surely be catastrophic." [16]

The Administration would not underwrite Chiang; what would it do?

[15] Letter of Transmittal, *United States Relations with China*, Department of State Publication 3573, August, 1949, pp. xv–xvi.
[16] Same source, pp. 1053–54.

To this question, through most of 1949, neither Acheson nor anyone else gave a clear answer. It was not a good time for making long-term decisions, in the Administration view, because "Future developments in China, including the outcome of political negotiations now being undertaken [between the Nationalists and the Communists], are uncertain." [17]

In these circumstances, the decision was to continue with a modest level of E.C.A. assistance to the Nationalists and to keep a free hand in other respects. The United States of course continued to recognize the Nationalist government, from which Chiang had temporarily withdrawn, as the official government of China. And in June Acheson indicated his support for a proposal, eventually accepted, to appropriate $75,000,000 for use in the "general area" of China; this fund, in the handling of which the President was given a completely free hand, was used largely to support anti-Communist activities in nearby countries like Indo-China. Meanwhile Acheson announced a comprehensive review of the problem of policy in the new situation of Asia, and in the summer and autumn this review proceeded under the general direction of Philip C. Jessup. The object of the review was stated by Acheson in a top-secret memorandum to Mr. Jessup on July 18, 1949:

> You will please take as your assumption that it is a fundamental decision of American policy that the United States does not intend to permit further extension of Communist domination on the continent of Asia or in the Southeast Asia area.
>
> Will you please draw up for me possible programs of action relating to various specific areas not now under Communist control in Asia under which the United States would have the best chance of achieving this purpose.
>
> These programs should contain proposed courses of action, steps to be taken in implementing such programs, estimate of cost to the United States, and the extent to which United States forces would or would not be involved.
>
> I fully realize that when these proposals are received it may be obvious that certain parts thereof would not be within our capabilities to put into effect, but what I desire is the examination of the problem on the general assumptions indicated above in order to make absolutely certain that we are neglecting no opportunity that would be within our capa-

[17] Same source, p. 1054.

bilities to achieve the purpose of halting the spread of totalitarian communism in Asia.[18]

This memorandum clearly foreshadowed significant developments in policy to meet the new situation in Asia. But before we move on to consider these changes, some attention must be given to two events that occurred earlier. One was Acheson's much quoted remark about waiting for the dust to settle, made in February, 1949. Once again his own explanation of it came out in the hearings of the Russell Committee, two years later:

> Let me dispose of this "dust" business.
> That phrase is a phrase which I believe I used at a private meeting with some members of the House of Representatives in 1949. . . .
> As I recall, what I was trying to say, at that time, was that I could not see clearly as to what the outcome in China was going to be until, as my phrase was, "until the dust settled," that is, until the situation had become more clear.
> And, it was not a policy which I was advocating, it was a phrase which I used to describe my own inability to see very far in this situation.[19]

The distinction here drawn is a narrow but important one; the State Department was waiting for an uncertain situation to become more clear; it was not committing itself to a policy of inaction. Yet necessarily, while it waited, there could not be much action.

One other major decision was taken before the memorandum of July 18— the decision to publish the White Paper on China. This document, issued in August, 1949, has been widely criticized and discounted, but it has nevertheless resisted most of the complaints launched against it. The policy it recounts may be rejected, but the facts and evidence — the essential accuracy of the document — have not been successfully challenged. Yet it is clear that the intent of the White Paper was to show that not the United States but the situation and government in China were responsible

[18] This memorandum was read into the record of a Senate Foreign Relations subcommittee by Ambassador Jessup on October 4, 1951. See the Committee print (not available at this writing). The text as given here is taken from the *New York Times*, October 5, 1951.
[19] Hearings, *Military Situation in the Far East*, Senate, Committee on Armed Services and Committee on Foreign Relations, 82d Congress, 1st Session, June 2, 1951, pp. 1765–66.

for what had happened there. To publish such a document was certainly a most unusual step; public criticism of a friendly government is always unusual, and for this decision too Acheson has been attacked. Again his explanation was given to the Russell Committee:

> I would like to say this about the reason for doing that. One of the very great and perplexing questions in the conduct of foreign affairs is the conflict that goes on in your mind between the harm you will do to some foreign nation in carrying out its policy by making a lot of material public, and the great harm that happens if the people of the United States do not understand the facts of the situation. That was very clear in this particular case.
>
> I think General Marshall was continually in the very perplexing situation of knowing that if he put out some full information it would make the course of the Nationalist Government in China much more difficult.
>
> If he did not put it out, the American people would not understand the situation, and then if a disaster occurred, it would occur as a great shock to them, they wouldn't have known anything about this.
>
> This was a problem. At the time this was finally put out, it seemed to me we were in the position where the American people had to know what had gone on, and I tried to have a document prepared which was as complete as possible to give the story of the preceding years.
>
> At that time the Nationalist Government had been driven out of all of China, and I think it was at that point in Canton, which was just about to fall and which did fall not long after that. . . . So I resolved that question in favor of giving as full a picture of events as possible because it seemed that the disasters had already overtaken the Nationalist Government.[20]

What is seldom noticed about the White Paper on China is that with its publication Acheson also announced, in outline, the new policy of the United States toward a China in Communist hands. This policy coupled a promise of help to any Chinese who remained loyal to China, and a warning of serious consequences for any government which attached itself to Soviet imperialism. This announcement is of major importance:

> And now it is abundantly clear that we must face the situation as it exists in fact. We will not help the Chinese or ourselves by basing our

[20] Same hearing, pp. 1769–70.

policy on wishful thinking. We continue to believe that, however tragic may be the immediate future of China and however ruthlessly a major portion of this great people may be exploited by a party in the interest of a foreign imperialism, ultimately the profound civilization and the democratic individualism of China will reassert themselves and she will throw off the foreign yoke. I consider that we should encourage all developments in China which now and in the future work toward this end.

In the immediate future, however, the implementation of our historic policy of friendship for China must be profoundly affected by current developments. It will necessarily be influenced by the degree to which the Chinese people come to recognize that the Communist régime serves not their interests but those of Soviet Russia and the manner in which, having become aware of the facts, they react to this foreign domination. One point, however, is clear. Should the Communist régime lend itself to the aims of Soviet Russian imperialism and attempt to engage in aggression against China's neighbors, we and the other members of the United Nations would be confronted by a situation violative of the principles of the United Nations Charter and threatening international peace and security.[21]

These sentences of this letter contain two points which became the basic elements of policy toward China as Acheson presented it six months later, in two major speeches of early 1950. His first point was that by the nature of the situation the real enemy of China was the Soviet Union. This point he spelled out in important detail:

The attitude and interest of the Russians in North China, and in these other areas as well, long antedates communism. . . . But the Communist régime has added new methods, new skills and new concepts to the thrust of Russian imperialism. This Communistic concept and techniques have armed Russian imperialism with a new and most insidious weapon of penetration. Armed with these new powers, what is happening in China is that the Soviet Union is detaching the northern provinces [areas] of China from China and is attaching them to the Soviet Union. This process is complete in outer Mongolia. It is nearly complete in Manchuria, and I am sure that in inner Mongolia and in Sinkiang, there

---

[21] Letter of Transmittal, *United States Relations with China*, Department of State Publication 3573, August, 1949, pp. xvi–xvii.

are very happy reports coming from Soviet agents to Moscow. This is what is going on. It is the detachment of these whole areas, vast areas — populated by Chinese — the detachment of these areas from China and their attachment to the Soviet Union. . . .

I should like to suggest . . . that this fact that the Soviet Union is taking the four northern provinces of China is the single most significant, most important fact, in the relation of any foreign power with Asia. . . .[22]

Two months later, after the terms of a new Sino-Soviet Treaty had been announced, Acheson amplified this point. He noted that the great Soviet aid which had been so much discussed by Soviet propagandists was a loan of between forty-five and sixty millions a year, as compared "with a grant — not a loan — of four hundred million dollars voted by the American Congress in the single year 1948." He went on to quote the London *Economist*, which had remarked that "The new rulers of China have deliberately cut off their country from the possibility of American economic assistance which would have been forthcoming for a United China on a far larger scale and with fewer strings attached than the loan now received with so much official gratitude from Moscow." Then he turned to the political side of the matter:

Can the Chinese people fail to observe that, whatever may be the promises for the future, under the terms of the treaty and agreements recently concluded at Moscow, the USSR has special rights in China which represent an infringement of China's sovereignty and which are held by no other foreign power? It is Soviet Russia which, despite all the tawdry pretense of the treaty terms, occupies the role of empire builder at China's expense.

These are the realities that must be faced by the Chinese people. In facing them, they can well consider what it means to brush aside an established friendship for new-found and voracious friends. Our friendship has been founded on the belief that anyone who violates the integrity of China is the enemy of China and is hostile to the interests of the United States. We have fifty years of history and a world war to prove that this belief is not a mere matter of words. This belief has been proved by deeds. We can and shall stand on the record.[23]

[22] Remarks to the National Press Club, January 12, 1950 (*Bulletin*, XXII, p. 115).
[23] Address to the Commonwealth Club, San Francisco, March 15, 1950 (*Bulletin*, XXII, p. 469).

Thus in Acheson's view the great fact of Asia was the conflict of interest between China and the Soviet Union. He summarized its meaning as follows:

> The consequences of this Russian attitude and this Russian action in China are perfectly enormous. They are saddling all those in China who are proclaiming their loyalty to Moscow, and who are allowing themselves to be used as puppets of Moscow, with the most awful responsibility which they must pay for. Furthermore, these actions of the Russians are making plainer than any speech, or any utterance, or any legislation can make throughout all of Asia, what the true purposes of the Soviet Union are and what the true function of Communism as an agent of Russian imperialism is. . . .
>
> What does that mean for us? It means something very, very significant. It means that nothing that we do and nothing that we say must be allowed to obscure the reality of this fact. All the efforts of propaganda will not be able to obscure it. The only thing that can obscure it is the folly of ill-conceived adventures on our part which easily could do so and I urge all who are thinking about these foolish adventures to remember that we must not seize the unenviable position which the Russians have carved out for themselves. We must not undertake to deflect from the Russians to ourselves the righteous anger, and the wrath, and the hatred of the Chinese people which must develop. It would be folly to deflect it to ourselves. We must take the position we have always taken that anyone who violates the integrity of China is the enemy of China and is acting contrary to our own interest. That, I suggest to you this afternoon, is the first and the greatest rule in regard to the formulation of American policy toward Asia. . . .
>
> I suggest that the second rule is very like the first. That is to keep our own purposes perfectly straight, perfectly pure and perfectly aboveboard and do not get them mixed up with legal quibbles or the attempt to do one thing and really achieve another.[24]

The implication of this rule was obvious: the United States must not undertake to intervene in Chinese affairs. To do so would be to provide a convenient lightning rod for resentments which would otherwise flow toward the Soviet Union. And in particular, in January, 1950, it meant that the

[24] Remarks to the National Press Club, January 12, 1950 (*Bulletin*, XXII, p. 115).

United States must not intervene by force in Formosa; so this is a good place to treat the Formosan problem as it stood before Korea.

Acheson's stand on Formosa, as he repeatedly explained to the Russell Committee, was clear and straightforward from the time he took office until June 25, 1950, when it was changed by the fact of war in Korea. Up to that time, his view, and the view of the Administration as a whole, was that the United States should not intervene by force in this area. In December, 1949, the Defense Department urged the sending of a military mission and some military equipment to Formosa, but the President accepted the State Department view that nothing short of American armed force would do the job, and all concerned were agreed that such intervention would be undesirable. This general position was publicly announced by President Truman on January 5, 1950, in answer to pressure from members of Congress supporting the opposite policy. And in commenting on the President's statement, the same day, Acheson very clearly defined the issue as he understood it. First he emphasized that military strategy was not the controlling consideration:

> The underlying factors in the decision are not in that area. They have to do with the fundamental integrity of the United States and with maintaining in the world the belief that when the United States takes a position it sticks to that position and does not change it by reason of transitory expediency or advantage on its part. . . . It is important that our position in regard to China should never be subject to the slightest doubt or the slightest question.[25]

The fundamental fact about Formosa, in this context, was that the United States had fully and firmly agreed that it "should go back to China." That position had been taken at Cairo and confirmed at Potsdam, and from the Japanese surrender onward Formosa had been administered by the Chinese. So Acheson rejected any notion that the United States should wriggle into Formosa by a trick argument about the absence of a formal treaty ending Japanese sovereignty; "The United States of America, as Mr. Truman said this morning, is not going to quibble on any lawyers' words about the integrity of its position." The United States would continue moderate economic assistance to Formosa; this was friendly help, not intervention. But military advice and equipment were not being sent because this was not the missing element in the defense of Formosa:

[25] Remarks to the press, January 5, 1950 (*Bulletin*, XXII, p. 80).

That is not the trouble. The trouble lies elsewhere, and it is not the function of the United States, nor will it or can it attempt to furnish a will to resist and a purpose for resistance to those who must provide for themselves.[26]

In other words, Formosa was essentially a Chinese question, and as long as the contending Chinese forces refrained from aggressive adventures, the United States would not intervene by force, nor would she give useless military help short of intervention.

Before we leave this matter of policy toward Formosa in 1949, there is a specific aspect of it which must be considered in detail because it aroused severe criticism later. Under the basic policy of non-intervention in Chinese matters, it seemed likely that Formosa would soon fall to the Reds. There was nothing enjoyable about this, for the Administration as a unit recognized that Formosa had strategic value, although it hardly shared the view later expressed by General MacArthur, that the loss of Formosa would drive the American defensive perimeter back to the West Coast. The loss of Formosa was bad, but it was preferable to an unprovoked intervention by American armed force. In this situation Acheson authorized the preparation and distribution of a paper giving guidance to information officers as to the American line on the anticipated fall of the island. This was not a policy paper, but a paper on information policy — a very different thing. It was not a paper *advocating* the fall of Formosa; it was a paper about what to say if Formosa fell. And in two places, as Acheson later acknowledged, this paper gave an emphasis different from that actually felt by the Administration; it suggested that information officers argue that "Formosa has no special military importance," and it urged them to counter the "false impression" that the loss of Formosa "would seriously damage the interests of either the United States or of other countries opposing communism." He explained this emphasis in the following passage:

The reason that we adopt this attitude, is that it is the only attitude which will have the desired effect, which is to minimize the damage to the prestige of the United States and to the morale of others should Formosa fall.

It is a very common attitude in dealing with all matters of information, whether in the public or foreign information field, or in any other field. It is familiar to members of this Committee that if a captain in

[26] Same source, p. 81.

command of a company finds that the companies on either side of him
are falling back and taking punishment, what he says to his men is,
"Don't give it a thought. It doesn't matter at all. You are doing fine.
Dig in. Hold it. It is all right."

You are all familiar with Mr. Churchill's great statement in 1940
that the British would fight on the beaches, fight in the streets, and fight
in the hills. I don't think any of you thought that that was a scientific
report on the military programs of the British General Staff.

This was an attitude and statement which had great effect.

In the field of politics we are quite familiar with statements which
are made about the Gallup Poll's report that this or that candidate or
party is behind, that candidate or party says, "Why, it doesn't mean
anything; I haven't started my campaign yet; wait until I get going."

Those are common attitudes. I don't know any other attitude
which would be sounder to take if you believed, as we did believe — and
rightly believed — that an event was going to happen which would be
damaging to our prestige, than to say keep your chin up, it doesn't
matter, this isn't important, we will go ahead and deal with it in some
other way.[27]

So Acheson's general policy of non-intervention in China was applied to
Formosa; less often noted, but equally important, was the fact that the
other aspect of American policy toward Red China was *also* applied to
Formosa. At the very end of his statement of January 5, Acheson made an
exceedingly important qualification: American restraint in Formosa was
necessarily conditional upon restraint by others. This passage is of the
highest importance:

I am informed . . . that some of you wish me to say what if any
significance is to be attached to the sentence in the next-to-last paragraph of the statement which says, "The United States has no desire to
obtain special rights or privileges or to establish military bases on
Formosa at this time." The question is, what does the phrase "at
this time" mean. That phrase does not qualify or modify or weaken the

[27] Hearings, *Military Situation in the Far East*, Senate, Committee on Armed Services
and Committee on Foreign Relations, 82d Congress, 1st Session, June 1, 1951, pp. 1673–74.
The hearings also contain the text of the policy information paper and some views very
different from Acheson's.

fundamental policies stated in this declaration by the President in any respect. It is a recognition of the fact that, in the unlikely and unhappy event that our forces might be attacked in the Far East, the United States must be completely free to take whatever action in whatever area is necessary for its own security.[28]

So the Communists were warned that a resort to war would change the situation in Formosa. And this was simply a specific application of a general warning which Acheson had already given in his letter of transmittal for the White Paper. This general warning was repeated still more emphatically in March, 1950:

> [The Chinese people] should understand that, whatever happens within their own country, they can only bring grave trouble on themselves and their friends, both in Asia and beyond, if they are led by their new rulers into aggressive or subversive adventures beyond their borders. Such adventures would violate not only every tradition and interest of the Chinese people; they would violate the United Nations Charter. They would violate the peace which the Charter was designed to preserve.
>
> I say this so that there may be no mistake about the attitude of the United States, no opportunity to distort or twist it, and so that all in China may know who would be responsible for all that such adventures might bring to pass.[29]

Act and speak so that the Chinese people will recognize their real enemy in Soviet Russia; at the same time make it clear that aggression will have grave consequences. This in essence was the policy adopted after the Communist victory on the mainland of China. It was not a policy that promised large short-term results, and it was bound to demand energetic American action if in fact the Red Chinese were determined upon aggressive adventures. It did, however, keep the record straight, and for democracies this is of transcendent importance.

Within this general policy the much-debated question of recognition of the Chinese régime, like that of its admission to the United Nations, was a relatively minor tactical problem, dependent on the attitudes and behavior

[28] Remarks to the press, January 5, 1950 (*Bulletin*, XXII, p. 81).

[29] Address to the Commonwealth Club, San Francisco, Cal., March 15, 1950 (*Bulletin*, XXII, p. 469).

of the Peiping régime, and not upon American prejudices. In his testimony before the Russell Committee Acheson repeatedly emphasized that the United States had constantly and successfully opposed recognition of Red China and its admission to the UN but it is important to observe that the ground for this position was simply that the Reds refused to accept and honor the normal practices and obligations of sovereign governments. Not only did they refuse to recognize the international obligations of the government they sought to supersede, but they persisted in treating American diplomatic personnel in provocative and even barbaric fashion. It was traditional American practice to give recognition as a matter of course to any effective régime, however unattractive, if it met basic standards of international behavior, but from the beginning the Red Chinese ignored these standards, and until they learned and applied the rudiments of international decency the United States would not recognize them. It was as simple as that. In the UN the same principle applied, and if Acheson rejected the use of a veto in opposing a seat for Red China, it was because the veto was a dangerous and only partly effective instrument, while persuasion had neither disadvantage.

It may be that the Red Chinese behaved as they did with the object of keeping the United States at arms' length; evidently it was in the interest of devoted Stalinists to keep alive and fan any anti-American feeling they could find. But Acheson and the Administration were not prepared to repay this treatment with diplomatic recognition, and Acheson repeatedly and emphatically denounced the Red Chinese for their abuse of Americans and American rights.[30] If the Peking government had changed its tactics, and behaved in a reasonable way, there might have developed a real and bitter issue between the Administration and its opponents, for in that case the proper course, under Acheson's basic policy, would have been to grant regular recognition to the effective government, and certainly the opposition at home would have found this outrageous; but this situation did not develop, and the battle over recognition in 1949 and early 1950 was in reality a sham battle.

In summary, American policy toward China in early 1950 was based on a determination to avoid, so far as possible, any entanglement that might give grounds for anti-American feeling in China. It aimed at pointing the finger of Chinese opposition toward the Soviet Union. It refused diplomatic

---

[30] See, for example, his personal message of November 18, 1949, calling upon all nations who had representatives in China to protest the treatment of American consular personnel in Mukden (*Bulletin*, XXI, pp. 799–800).

recognition to a régime which by normal standards was literally unrecognizable. It anticipated the collapse of the Chiang régime, and it would not fight to prevent it. It warned of the consequences of aggression. This policy may be subject to debate and difference, but it can hardly be claimed that it was either pro-Communist or meaningless.

3. The Rest of the Far East

The policy of the United States toward the vast area of Asia which is not China cannot be compressed into a few pages without manifest injustice; yet space compels it. Fortunately we have the advantage that in early 1950 Acheson undertook exactly this task, and we can in the main rely on his own words.[31]

The first great point which he emphasized in these statements was that Americans must deal with a quite extraordinary situation of change and unrest in the Far East. The following passage states the fundamental background of the problem as Acheson understands it:

There is in this vast area what we might call a developing Asian consciousness, and a developing pattern, and this, I think, is based upon two factors which are pretty nearly common to the entire experience of all these Asian people.

One of these factors is a revulsion against the acceptance of misery and poverty as the normal condition of life. Throughout all of this vast area, you have that fundamental revolutionary aspect in mind and belief. The other common aspect that they have is the revulsion against foreign domination. Whether that foreign domination takes the form of colonialism or whether it takes the form of imperialism, they are through with it. They have had enough of it, and they want no more.

These two basic ideas which are held so broadly and commonly in Asia tend to fuse in the minds of many Asian peoples and many of them tend to believe that if you could get rid of foreign domination, if you could gain independence, then the relief from poverty and misery would

[31] There were two speeches on Asia, one before the National Press Club on January 12, 1950, and one before the Commonwealth Club of San Francisco on March 15. All quotations in this section are from the Press Club speech, which is less formal and more detailed.

follow almost in course. It is easy to point out that that is not true and, of course, they are discovering that it is not true. But underneath that belief, there was a very profound understanding of a basic truth and it is the basic truth which underlies all our democratic belief and all our democratic concept. That truth is that just as no man and no government is wise enough or disinterested enough to direct the thinking and the action of another individual, so no nation and no people are wise enough and disinterested enough very long to assume the responsibility for another people or to control another people's opportunities.

That great truth they have sensed, and on that great truth they are acting. They say and they believe that from now on they are on their own. They will make their own decisions. They will attempt to better their own lot and on occasion they will make their own mistakes. But it will be their mistakes, and they are not going to have their mistakes dictated to them by anybody else.

The symbol of these concepts has become nationalism. National independence has become the symbol both of freedom from foreign domination and freedom from the tyranny of poverty and misery.

Since the end of the war in Asia, we have seen over 500 million people gain their independence and over seven new nations come into existence in this area.

We have the Philippines with 20,000,000 citizens. We have Pakistan, India, Ceylon and Burma with 400,000,000 citizens, southern Korea with 20,000,000, and the United States of Indonesia with 75,000,000.

This is the outward and visible sign of the internal ferment of Asia. But this ferment and change is not restricted to these countries which are just gaining their independence. It is the common idea and the common pattern of Asia, and as I tried to suggest a moment ago, it is not based on purely political conceptions. It is not based purely on ideological conceptions. It is based on a fundamental and an earthy and a deeply individual realization of the problems of their own daily lives. This new sense of nationalism means that they are going to deal with those daily problems — the problems of the relation of man to the soil, the problem of how much can be exacted from them by the tax collectors of the state. It is rooted in those ideas. With those ideas they are going forward. Resignation is no longer the typical emotion of Asia. It has given way to hope, to a sense of effort and in many cases, to a real sense of anger.[32]

[32] Remarks to the National Press Club, January 12, 1950 (*Bulletin*, XXII, p. 112).

The next fundamental element in the problem is the American attitude toward Asia.

Let's consider for a moment another important factor in this relationship. That is the attitude of our own people to Asia. What is that fundamental attitude out of which our policy has grown? What is the history of it? . . .

What has our attitude been toward the peoples of Asia? It has been . . . that Americans as individuals are interested in the peoples of Asia. We are not interested in them as pawns or as subjects for exploitation but just as people.

For one hundred years some Americans have gone to Asia to bring in what they thought was the most valuable thing they had — their faith. They wanted to tell them what they thought about the nature and relationship of man to God. Others went to them to bring to them what they knew of learning. Others went to them to bring them healing for their bodies. Others and perhaps fewer went to them to learn the depth and beauty of their own cultures, and some went to them to trade and they traded with them. But this trade was a very small part of American interest in the Far East and it was a very small part of American interest in trade. It was a valid interest; it was a good interest. There was nothing wrong about it, but out of the total sum of the interests of the American people in Asia, it was a comparatively small part.

Through all this period of time also, we had, and still have great interests in Asia. But let me point out to you one very important factor about our interests in Asia. That is that our interests have been parallel to the interests of the people of Asia. For fifty years, it has been the fundamental belief of the American people — and I am not talking about announcements of government but I mean a belief of people in little towns and villages and churches and missionary forces and labor unions throughout the United States — it has been their profound belief that the control of China by a foreign power was contrary to American interests. The interesting part about that is it was not contrary to the interests of the people of China. There was not conflict but parallelism in that interest. And so from the time of the announcement of the Open Door policy through the Nine-Power Treaty to the very latest resolution of the General Assembly of the United Nations, we have stated that principle and we believe it. And similarly in all the rest of

Asia — in the Philippines, in India, in Pakistan and Indonesia, and in Korea — for years and years and years, the interests of Americans throughout this country have been in favor of their independence. This is where their independence societies and their patriotic groups have come for funds and sympathy. The whole policy of our government insofar as we have responsibility in the Philippines was to bring about the accomplishment of this independence and our sympathy and help. The very real help which we have given other nations in Asia has been in that direction and it is still in that direction.[33]

This simple statement of a long American interest was of fundamental importance for reasons which are central to Acheson's thinking on the Far East:

Now, I stress this, which you may think is a platitude, because of a very important fact: I hear almost every day someone say that the real interest of the United States is to stop the spread of Communism. Nothing seems to me to put the cart before the horse more completely than that. Of course we are interested in stopping the spread of Communism. But we are interested for a far deeper reason than any conflict between the Soviet Union and the United States. . . .

People will do more damage and create more misrepresentation in the Far East by saying our interest is merely to stop the spread of Communism than any other way. Our real interest is in those people as people. It is because Communism is hostile to that interest that we want to stop it. But it happens that the best way of doing both things is to do just exactly what the peoples of Asia want to do and what we want to help them to do, which is to develop a soundness and administration of these new governments and to develop their resources and their technical skills so that they are not subject to penetration either through ignorance, or because they believe these false promises, or because there is real distress in their areas. If we can help that development, if we can go forward with it, then we have brought about the best way that anyone knows of stopping this spread of Communism.

It is important to take this attitude not as a mere negative reaction to Communism but as the most positive affirmation of the most affirmative truth that we hold, which is in the dignity and right of every nation,

[33] Same source, pp. 113–14.

of every people, and of every individual to develop in their own way, making their own mistakes, reaching their own triumphs but acting under their own responsibility. That is what we are pressing for in the Far East and that is what we must affirm and not get mixed up with purely negative and inconsequential statements.[34]

Thus the basic interest of the people of Asia, and the traditional basic interest of the people of the United States were the same, and it was because Communism was destructive of this joint interest that the United States was opposed to its spread. Acheson continued with a discussion of Soviet imperialism in China, and the problems of American policy in furthering the basic American interest. Then, pointing out that military problems, though important, were not the whole of the matter, he turned to problems of "subversion and penetration."

The susceptibility to penetration arises because in many areas there are new governments which have little experience in governmental administration and have not become firmly established or perhaps firmly accepted in their countries. They grow, in part, from very serious economic problems, some of them growing out directly from the last war, others growing indirectly out of the last war because of the disruptions of trade with other parts of the world, with the disruption of arrangements which furnished credit and management to these areas for many years. That has resulted in dislocation of economic effort and in a good deal of suffering among the peoples concerned. In part this susceptibility to penetration comes from the great social upheaval about which I have been speaking, an upheaval which was carried on and confused a great deal by the Japanese occupation and by the propaganda which has gone on from Soviet sources since the war.[35]

This general difficulty required a variety of activities. Those which concerned Japan and Korea can best be treated in the next chapter, for they are intimately connected with the issues which arose in the Korean war. They are set off from other areas, moreover, by the fact that they were the countries in which the United States had a particularly large direct responsibility. Further South, as Acheson pointed out, it was different:

[34] Same source, p. 114.
[35] Same source, p. 116.

In the southerly part of the area, we are one of many nations who can do no more than help. The direct responsibility lies with the peoples concerned. They are proud of their new national responsibility. You can not sit around in Washington or London or Paris or the Hague and determine what the policies are going to be in those areas. You can be willing to help, and you can help only when the conditions are right for help to be effective.

That leads me to the other thing that I wanted to point out, and that is the limitation of effective American assistance. American assistance can be effective when it is the missing component in a situation which might otherwise be solved. The United States cannot furnish all these components to solve the question. It can not furnish determination, it can not furnish the will, and it can not furnish the loyalty of a people to its government. But if the will and if the determination exists and if the people are behind their government, then, and not always then, is there a very good chance. In that situation American help can be effective and it can lead to an accomplishment which could not otherwise be achieved.[36]

The doctrine of the "missing component" is the heart of Acheson's policy toward the nations and people of the Far East. It remains to consider very briefly some instances of American action under this principle.

In the Philippines, we acted with vigor and speed to set up an independent sovereign nation which we have done. We have given the Philippines a billion dollars of direct economic aid since the war. We have spent another billion dollars in such matters as veterans benefits and other payments in the Philippines. Much of that money has not been used as wisely as we wish it had been used, but here again, we come up against the matter of responsibility. It is the Philippine Government which is responsible. It is the Philippine Government which must make its own mistakes. What we can do is advise and urge, and if help continues to be misused to stop giving the help. We cannot direct, we should not direct, we have not the slightest desire to direct. I believe that there are indications that the Philippines may be facing serious economic difficulties. With energetic, determined action, they can perhaps be avoided or certainly minimized. Whether that will be true or

[36] Same source, pp. 116-17.

not, I can not say, but it does not rest within the power of the American Government to determine that. We are always ready to help and to advise. That is all we can and all we should do. [Later in 1950 the United States, at Philippine request, sent to the Islands a special mission to make recommendations on financial and economic conditions. The mission recommended a bold combination of internal reform and American help. If it could be worked out, this would be a case in which both money and counsel were supplied as "missing components."]

Elsewhere in southeast Asia, the limits of what we can do are to help where we are wanted. We are organizing the machinery through which we can make effective help possible. The Western Powers are all interested. We all know the techniques. We have all had experiences which can be useful to those governments which are newly starting out if they want it. It cannot be useful if they don't want it. We know techniques of administration. We know techniques of organizing school districts, and road districts, and taxation districts. We know agricultural and industrial techniques, all of which can be helpful, and those we are preparing to make available if they are wanted, where they are wanted, and under circumstances where they have a fighting chance to be successful. We will not do these things for the mere purpose of being active. They will not be done for the mere purpose of running around and doing good, but for the purpose of moving in where we are wanted to a situation where we have the missing component which, if put into the rest of the picture, will spell success.

The situation in the different countries of southeast Asia is difficult. It is highly confused in Burma where five different factions have utterly disrupted the immediate government of the country. Progress is being made in Indochina where the French, although moving slowly, are moving. There are noticeable signs of progress in transferring responsibility to a local administration and getting the adherence of the population to this local administration. . . . [Already in early 1950 the United States was providing the missing component of arms and equipment to Indochina, and Acheson remarked a year later that this action was clearly a vital element in the French successes of 1951.]

In Malaya, the British have and are discharging their responsibility harmoniously with the people of Malaya and are making progress.

In Indonesia, a great success has been achieved within the last few weeks and over a period of months. The round table conferences at The

Hague in which great statesmanship and restraint were displayed, both on the Dutch and the Indonesian side, have resulted in this new government being formed. Relations of this government with the Dutch will be very good, and the Dutch can furnish them great help and advice, and we will be willing to stand by to give whatever help we can rightly and profitably give. That situation is one which is full of encouragement although it is full of difficulty also. [Among other things, the United States granted a loan of one hundred million dollars to the Indonesians, a month after this speech.]

As one goes to the end of this semi-circle and comes to India and Pakistan, we find really grave troubles facing the world and facing these two countries there, both with respect to Kashmir, and the difficulties — economic difficulties growing out of the differences in devaluation, settlement of monetary plans back and forth, et cetera. We know that they have assured one another and they have assured the world that as stubborn as these difficulties may be and difficult as they may be of solution, they are not going to resort to war to solve them. . . .

In India and in Pakistan we are willing to be of such help as we can be. Again, the responsibility is not ours. Again we can only be helpful friends. Again the responsibility lies with people who have won their freedom and who are very proud of it. [In 1950, and again in 1951 on a much larger scale, the United States sent wheat to India to meet the threat of famine. If the aid of 1951 was slow, and its terms less than realistic in view of India's capacity to pay, this was hardly the fault of the Executive Branch.]

So after this survey, what we conclude, I believe, is that there is a new day which has dawned in Asia. It is a day in which the Asian peoples are on their own and know it and intend to continue on their own. It is a day in which the old relationships between East and West are gone, relationships which at their worst were exploitation and which at their best were paternalism. That relationship is over and the relationship of East and West must now be in the Far East one of mutual respect and mutual helpfulness. We are their friends. Others are their friends. We and those others are willing to help but we can help only where we are wanted and only where the conditions of help are really sensible and possible. So what we can see is that this new day in Asia, this new day which is dawning, may go on to a glorious noon or it may darken and it may drizzle out. But that decision lies within the countries of Asia and within the power of the Asian people. It is not a decision which a friend or even an enemy from the outside can decide for them.[37]

Asia was returning, after a very long time, to Asian control. This was the central fact with which Acheson began and ended.

It remains to consider one last point — the matter of the military security of the area. This we have left to the last, because it is the proper point of connection with the later events in Korea. As Acheson stated it on January 12, 1950, the problem of security had two aspects, that of the American defensive perimeter, and that of the general defense of the independent countries of the Far East. The vital distinction between these two sides of the problem is often overlooked. Here is the statement:

What is the situation in regard to the military security of the Pacific area and what is our policy in regard to it?

In the first place the defeat and the disarmament of Japan has placed upon the United States the necessity of assuming the military defense of Japan so long as that is required, both in the interest of our security and in the interests of the security of the entire Pacific area and in all honor in the interest of Japanese security. We have American and there are Australian troops in Japan. I am not in a position to speak for the Australians but I can assure you that there is no intention of any sort of abandoning or weakening the defenses of Japan and that whatever arrangements are to be made either through permanent settlement or otherwise, that defense must and shall be maintained.

This defensive perimeter runs along the Aleutians to Japan and then goes to the Ryukyus. We hold important defense positions in the Ryukyu Islands and those we will continue to hold. In the interest of the population of the Ryukyu Islands, we will at an appropriate time offer to hold these islands under trusteeship of the United Nations. But they are essential parts of the defensive perimeter of the Pacific, and they must and will be held.

The defensive perimeter runs from the Ryukyus to the Philippine Islands. Our relations, our defensive relations with the Philippines are contained in agreements between us. Those agreements are being loyally carried out and will be loyally carried out. Both peoples have learned by bitter experience the vital connections between our mutual

[37] Same source, p. 118.

defense requirements. We are in no doubt about that, and it is hardly necessary for me to say an attack on the Philippines could not and would not be tolerated by the United States. But I hasten to add that no one perceives the imminence of any such attack.

So far as the military security of other areas in the Pacific is concerned, it must be clear that no person can guarantee these areas against military attack. But it must also be clear that such a guarantee is hardly sensible or necessary within the realm of practical relationship. Should such an attack occur — one hesitates to say where such an armed attack could come from — the initial reliance must be on the people attacked to resist it and then upon the commitments of the entire civilized world under the Charter of the United Nations which so far has not proved a weak reed to lean on by any people who are determined to protect their independence against outside aggression.[38]

After war broke out in Korea, Acheson's critics claimed that this statement was an invitation to aggression in that area. His reply was that the situation as it developed showed the accuracy of what he had said. Korea was not a part of the American military perimeter; it was a part of the "commitments of the entire civilized world under the Charter of the United Nations." And the question that was raised on June 25 was not a question of American military defense, but a question of world peace.

[38] Same source, pp. 115–16.

CHAPTER NINE

Security and Loyalty in the Department
of State

THE FIRST THING *that I should like to say is in the nature of a categorical affirmation. I should like to say that never in its long and honorable history has the Department of State ever been in better shape than it is today.*[1]

We have seen that one of the questions which was raised when Acheson was nominated as Secretary was that of the loyalty and security of employees of the Department of State. We have seen that at that time Acheson asserted that he proposed to continue the program of security protection that had been initiated under General Marshall, and that he agreed with Senators who hoped that the program would continue under the supervision of John E. Peurifoy. During 1949 and early 1950 this program continued; I pass over the details of its administration because we shall find them discussed by Acheson a little later. It is enough to say here that the Department of State continued a program which seemed somewhat harsh to many believers in civil liberties, but which had won the unstinted praise of many Republican leaders of the 80th Congress.

Then, in February, 1950, Senator Joseph R. McCarthy of Wisconsin touched off a noisy discussion of the political complexion of the Department of State, and there followed a prolonged inquiry into his charges, in hearings which run nearly two thousand pages. Toward the end of the hearings Senator Lodge of Massachusetts remarked that the general subject was vastly too extensive to be treated thoroughly even in such a protracted inquiry, and he was certainly right. For the notion that lay behind many of the charges was that unless every single random accusation, every single

---

[1] Extemporaneous remarks to the American Society of Newspaper Editors, April 22, 1950 (*Bulletin*, XXII, p. 711).

insinuation, could be traced to its source, and entirely demolished, the Department of State must be branded as a hotbed of Communism.

There may be a proper place somewhere for some such Augean inquiry, though I doubt it. In any case this book is not the place. It seems to me that we shall have given this matter somewhat more than the attention it deserves if we do three things: (1) Examine in some detail a typical specific charge made against the Department of State by its principal accuser; (2) consider the whole story of the relationship between Acheson and Alger Hiss; (3) present clearly the argument made by Acheson himself in defense of the Department. To this task we may now proceed, but we may begin with this simple statement: Nowhere in the entire discussion has anyone presented any persuasive evidence that the State Department under Acheson was anything but energetic and devoted in guarding against Communist infiltration.

The Method of Senator McCarthy — a case study

Whatever else may be said of him, it seems clear that in 1950 Senator McCarthy emerged as the chief spokesman of those who believed that the State Department was heavily infiltrated by Stalin's agents. It is therefore a necessary part of this discussion that we should consider his charges. To do this exhaustively is impossible; Senator McCarthy has never been at a loss for something to say and in the nature of the case it is possible to make in a single sentence an accusation which it may take thousands of words to answer.

One way out of this difficulty would be to ignore the Senator, or to reply to his accusations with a short and satisfying word. In cases of this kind, which occur often in American public life, this is the usual course of leading men; the tradition of silence in the face of scoundrels is one honored by Washington, Lincoln, and many more. For a busy public man, life is too short to track down and answer every charge that irresponsible men may make. This is the course which Acheson has usually taken with regard to charges made against him personally and I propose to follow his example.

Yet it does not seem right to follow this method with the whole body of Senator McCarthy's charges. Rightly or wrongly, he has become a significant figure, and he has won the ear of a very substantial number of Americans; many of them honestly believe that Senator McCarthy is more smeared than smearing.   To dismiss him with a few unkind words would hardly be persuasive to this large group, and I cannot believe that they are unwilling to consider more substantial evidence.

I have therefore undertaken to provide, in this section, a case study of one particular set of accusations — those made against Ambassador-at-Large Philip C. Jessup. Mr. Jessup's case is a useful one for this purpose, for a number of reasons.   First, he is the highest ranking officer against whom charges were made and heard before the Senate subcommittees which have inquired into the McCarthy charges; McCarthy has never called Acheson a Communist or Communist-fronter, although he has called him nearly everything else.   Second, because of Mr. Jessup's high position, the charges against him have a particular importance; he is Acheson's close associate and trusted friend, and if he were a Communist sympathizer he would indeed be in a position to damage American interests.   Third, because of the fact that Mr. Jessup was accused before Congressional committees, the Department of State and Mr. Jessup himself have undertaken the task of making a detailed reply to the McCarthy charges; we thus have both sides of the case.

In taking a single case for thorough treatment, we should be able to give an accurate picture of the method of Joe McCarthy.   Of course it is always possible for a man to be in error in one part of what he says, and in this respect a single set of charges may not be conclusive.   Yet the crucial question about Senator McCarthy is not his accuracy, but his purpose, and on this point a single case history can be persuasive.   I will ask the reader — especially if he is friendly to Senator McCarthy — to consider the following questions as he looks at the record which follows: Does this man tell the truth as he knows it?   Does he recognize corrections when they are made public?   Does he try to keep the record straight or crooked?   I shall reach my own conclusions on these points, but I hope the record may allow the reader to judge them for himself.

The procedure of this inquiry is a simple one — to state Senator Mc-Carthy's charges, to consider the unrefuted evidence offered by Mr. Jessup and the Department of State in reply, and then to restate the McCarthy position in the light of that evidence.   We shall also be concerned to see whether Senator McCarthy himself amended his charges.

Senator McCarthy first mentioned Mr. Jessup on March 8 in the following statement, "Although I shall discuss the unusual affinity of Mr. Philip C.

Jessup of the State Department for Communist causes later in this inquiry, I think it pertinent to note that this gentleman now formulating top-flight policy in the Far East affecting half the civilized world was also a sponsor of the American-Russian Institute." [2]

On March 20 Mr. Jessup had his chance to reply to this accusation. The first and sweeping charge he answered in a number of ways. The record was full of his clear and uncompromising statements of hostility to Communism, and he supplied this record to the committee. He had also proved his position by actions; he had worked in the United Nations for the American position and against the Russian position on the problems of Korea, Berlin, China, the Italian colonies, and Indonesia; the proceedings in which he had so worked were a matter of public record. Nor was this a matter of recent conversion; there was no pro-Communism anywhere in his past. The great teacher of his early maturity had been the Republican elder statesman Elihu Root, and he had been Mr. Root's authorized biographer. He was able to produce volunteer character witnesses who wrote in the strongest terms of his loyalty and character — the three most distinguished who spoke up in these days were Henry L. Stimson, George C. Marshall, and Dwight D. Eisenhower.

More specifically, Mr. Jessup stated that so far from having an "unusual affinity for Communist causes," his affinities were those normal to one of his profession and background. He was a member of such organizations as The American Philosophical Society, the Foreign Policy Association, The American Society of International Law, the Sigma Phi Society, the Carnegie Endowment for International Peace, the American Bar Association, and the American Legion.

But what about the American-Russian Institute? This was, in 1950, a declared Communist-front organization, and McCarthy had said he was a sponsor of it. This was the only specific claim, indeed, and the specific answer follows:

"Are these charges and insinuations true? Senator McCarthy asserts that I was a 'sponsor' of the American-Russian Institute. It is true that my name appears on a list of the sponsors of a dinner given by the American-Russian Institute, but not as a sponsor of the organization itself. The dinner in question was one given on May 7, 1946, on the occasion of the presentation of its first annual award to Franklin D. Roosevelt which was accepted on

[2] Hearings, *State Department Employee Loyalty Investigation*, Senate, Subcommittee of the Committee on Foreign Relations, 81st Congress, 2d Session, March 8, 1950, p. 28.

behalf of his family. Senator McCarthy pointed out that the names of Howard Fast, Saul Mills, Ella Winter, John Howard Lawson, and Langston Hughes also appear on the list.

"He did not point out that approximately 100 persons were named on this list of sponsors and that it also included the names of H. V. Kaltenborn, George Fielding Eliot, Dean Christian Gauss of Princeton, and Mary Emma Woolley, former president of Holyoke. The entire list is already in evidence as an exhibit of this committee, and the committee can make its own judgment as to the caliber and variety of the people who are on it. A search of my files has failed to reveal any information concerning this incident, nor do I remember attending the dinner. From approximately February to June of 1946 I was seriously ill in a hospital in New York City, so it is unlikely that I attended.

"I do recall, however, that I was asked by Mr. William Lancaster, a prominent New York lawyer, to permit my name to be used as a sponsor of a dinner which was to be held on October 19, 1944. I had met Mr. Lancaster through his activities on the Foreign Policy Association, at a time when General Frank McCoy was president and Senator Alexander Smith and I were members of the board. I accepted, but was unable to attend the dinner. I shall be glad to make the entire list of approximately 250 sponsors available to the committee.

"It is utterly irrelevant to the charges or insinuations that I or anyone else agreed to sponsor dinners of the American-Russian Institute of New York City in 1944 or 1946. There was no reason why a loyal American should not have done so. The Attorney General expressly excluded the American-Russian Institute of New York from the first lists of subversive publications which were published, and did not include it until April 21, 1949. The Committee may be interested in knowing that I turned down invitations to speak at dinners held by this organization in both 1948 and 1949." [3]

We are now in a position to rewrite Senator McCarthy's first accusation; it should read like this:

"Although men of the highest integrity strongly endorse Ambassador Jessup, although he has worked and spoken against Communism for years, and although he has shown the usual affinities of a professor of international law, I think it pertinent to note that this gentleman now formulating policy, etc., etc., was also a sponsor of two dinners given in 1944 and 1946 by an

[3] Same hearings, pp. 215–75.

organization declared subversive three years later, at a time when he was refusing its invitations."

The next question is whether Senator McCarthy did in fact rewrite his charges, and the answer is that he did, in three ways; he continued to charge "affiliation" with Communist fronts, still including the American-Russian Institute; he added the charge of a supposed connection with Owen Lattimore, and he claimed the whole defense would fall unless the government provided a clear look at all its personal files, not only on Mr. Jessup, but on Mr. Lattimore. We must consider each of these aspects of his method.

Let us take first the matter of Mr. Jessup's supposed connection with Communist fronts. Mr. Jessup had stated flatly that he had "never knowingly supported or promoted any movement or organization which I knew had as its objective the furtherance of Communist objectives," and he had dealt with the one specific accusation McCarthy had made. He had also listed several non-Communist and anti-Communist bodies to which he belonged. Yet one month later on April 20 Senator McCarthy made a speech in which he had the following to say about Mr. Jessup: "Why does he always join Communist fronts? Why not anti-Communist organizations?" [4] The disproved accusation is repeated. And the repetition of the general charge is accompanied with a new specific accusation, that Jessup had been a leader in the Institute of Pacific Relations, which McCarthy called a front organization. It happened that Jessup had already discussed his membership in this organization in terms to which McCarthy made no reference:

"From 1933 to 1946 I was closely associated with the Institute of Pacific Relations. I am proud of my association with that organization, which was founded by a group of leading businessmen and scholars in Honolulu sometime in the mid-twenties for the purpose of increasing knowledge and friendship among the peoples of the Pacific area. Despite the controversy which has occasionally surrounded it, it has continued to discharge the functions for which it was created. . . .

---

[4] *Bulletin*, XXII, p. 964.

These and subsequent quotations from Senator McCarthy are usually taken from the *Department of State Bulletin* and not from the *Congressional Record* because unfortunately Senator McCarthy has been known to insert in the *Congressional Record* versions of his speeches which differ significantly from what he has actually said. I have myself checked the *Bulletin's* quotations against the original press releases from Senator McCarthy's office or else, as in the case of his speech to the American Society of Newspaper Editors, against the official transcript of the proceedings.

"I first became associated with it in 1933 when the late Newton D. Baker was its chairman. . . .

"My first contact with the organization was to attend in 1933 one of the periodic international conferences which have been held by the organization. In those meetings leaders of business and banking, former high officials of government, journalists, labor leaders, researchers and teachers from all of the Pacific countries have met for a common study of the problems of the area.

"Many of the leading figures whom I have since met in the United Nations I first met through my connection with the Institute of Pacific Relations, including Mrs. Pandit, presently Indian Ambassador to the United States, and Dr. Hu Shih, the great Chinese philosopher who was former Chinese Ambassador in Washington. . . .

"I was a member of the Board of Trustees of the American Council [of the Institute] from about 1933 until my resignation because of health and the pressure of other work in 1946. I was Chairman of the Board of Trustees of the American Council during 1939 and 1940. . . . I was succeeded as Chairman of the American Council by the late Dr. Ray Lyman Wilbur, President of Stanford University, who was succeeded by Robert G. Sproul, President of the University of California, and now by Gerard Swope, honorary President of the General Electric Company. Throughout my connection with the Institute, the Board of Trustees has included leaders of American business, finance, and academic and public life." [5]   Against this recital, which I have considerably shortened, McCarthy's evidence of the Communist character of the Institute of Pacific Relations is interesting; first, he charged that its magazine, *Far Eastern Survey*, followed the Party line, and that Jessup had been in charge of it. The exact language is important:

"Dr. Jessup had control of the magazine, *Far Eastern Survey*, when the Communist campaign in 1943 was initiated therein to smear Chiang Kai-shek and deify all the Communists . . . I pointed out that he was head of the Research Advisory Board having complete control of the magazine during the height of the Communist Party line campaign." [6]

It happened that Mr. Jessup had already stated to the Senate committee that he became chairman of the Research Advisory Board in 1944, not 1943. [7] It also happened that the job of a research advisory board falls somewhat

---

[5] *Bulletin*, XXII, p. 518.   [6] *Bulletin*, XXII, p. 964.

[7] The date is important because the article which first enraged supporters of Chiang Kai-shek appeared in July, 1943. It is worth noting, incidentally, that a representative of Chiang was allowed space for a reply to this article.

short of "complete control." The question that remains is whether the magazine was in fact a Communist front, and on this point the State Department rejoinder is as follows:

"Senator McCarthy's allegation that *Far Eastern Survey* followed the Communist Party originates in discredited contentions made by one Alfred Kohlberg in 1944. The American Council of the Institute of Pacific Relations investigated Kohlberg's charges. In a document circulated to its members, it was demonstrated that Kohlberg had ignored the overwhelming number of facts that did not support his contention. The document showed, among other things, that Kohlberg had quoted, in connection with *Far Eastern Survey*, and other publications, from less than 2 percent of the articles published and from less than .002 percent of the books published. In April, 1947, the membership of the American Council of the Institute of Pacific Relations in a vote of 1163 to 66 overwhelmingly repudiated Kohlberg's charges as "inaccurate and irresponsible." [8]

This answer was published on May 20, but in subsequent speeches McCarthy made no effort to deal with it; he simply repeated his charges. He had, however, one other piece of evidence against the Institute of Pacific Relations. Let us again use the exact language:

"I am going to leave here on the table a number of photostats of checks representing Communist money — thousands of dollars — which was paid to his [Jessup's] organization . . . The Communists knew what those thousands of dollars were being paid for." [9] Senator McCarthy produced photostats of checks from Frederick Vanderbilt Field totaling $3500, and later he produced more, until the total was $6000. [10] When McCarthy made this statement, the following remarks by Jessup had been public for over two weeks, in answer to an earlier insinuation:

"I believe a comment is appropriate on Senator McCarthy's latest insinuations that the American Council of the Institute of Pacific Relations, in accepting donations from Frederick Vanderbilt Field, had shown that it was being paid to peddle the Communist Party line.

"But first, it is again necessary to correct a misstatement of fact by Senator McCarthy. Senator McCarthy said that the American Council of the Institute of Pacific Relations 'was largely controlled by Mr. Jessup.'

[8] *Bulletin*, XXII, p. 968.   [9] *Bulletin*, XXII, p. 964.
[10] Over a period of fifteen years Field contributed about $60,000, according to his own later testimony to the McCarran subcommittee. His money still remained a very small proportion of the total.

Actually, during the years in which these donations were made, 1942 and 1943, I had ceased to be chairman of the American Council of the Institute of Pacific Relations. I was still a member of the Board of Trustees which had about 50 members.

"At that time, Dr. Robert Gordon Sproul, president of the University of California, was chairman of the American Council of the Institute of Pacific Relations; Francis Harmon was treasurer; and William R. Herod, now president of the International General Electric Company, was chairman of the Finance Committee. During that period, Juan Trippe, president of Pan-American Airways, and Henry Luce of *Time* and *Life*, were sponsors of a drive for funds on behalf of the American Council of the Institute of Pacific Relations. Surely these gentlemen would never have accepted payments from Mr. Field or anyone else for 'selling the Communist Party line.' Neither would I if I had been in control.

"These contributions, according to Senator McCarthy's own figures, total only $3500 as compared with total expenses for the two-year period of approximately $200,000. About half of the amount was met by contributions from the Rockefeller Foundation and Carnegie Corporation. Generous donations by large industrial concerns made up a large portion of the remainder." [11]

Senator McCarthy has never contested this statement, except as to the figure $3500.

We are now in a position to rewrite Senator McCarthy's statements about Mr. Jessup and the Institute of Pacific Relations; they should read like this:

"Mr. Jessup has been a leading member of the Institute of Pacific Relations, along with Ray Lyman Wilbur, Robert G. Sproul, Gerard Swope, Juan Trippe, and Henry R. Luce. This Institute, according to Alfred Kohlberg, followed a line parallel to that of the Communists in a few of its magazine articles and books. It was mainly supported in 1942 and 1943 by the Rockefeller Foundation, the Carnegie Corporation, and large industrial concerns, but it also received money from Frederick Vanderbilt Field. I have no evidence whatever that the small percentage of articles, books, and money which are pro-Communist have anything to do with any of the men named in the first sentence."

It is fair to add that while Mr. Jessup and the Department of State adequately answered Senator McCarthy's specific charges against the Institute of Pacific Relations, they did not tell the whole story. It is certainly true

[11] *Bulletin,* XXII, p. 623.

that the I.P.R. was an object of infiltration by Communists and Communist sympathizers in the 1930's and 1940's, like so many other American institutions — the Government, the C.I.O., the A.F.L., the universities, the Army, the Navy, and even some branches of the Christian Church.

In 1951 a subcommittee under Senator McCarran has been conducting a detailed inquiry into the I.P.R., and while the inquiry has not had the impartial and judicial character to which it has pretended, it has nevertheless shown clearly that there was infiltration by far left-wingers, and further that high officers of the I.P.R., Mr. Jessup among them, were for a time incompletely alive to this danger. I have myself studied with some care the back file of the *Far Eastern Survey* from 1943 to 1947, and I think it plain that while it was far from being a Communist-line paper — it printed defense of Chiang as well as attack — it was distinctly biassed in favor of a soft and optimistic view of the Chinese Reds and did not honestly follow its own announced policy of impartial objectivity. Mr. Jessup undoubtedly erred in permitting his name to be used in defense of this situation, and in its defense of the magazine the State Department also erred; it should not have assumed that because McCarthy and Kohlberg wildly overstated their charges, the *Far Eastern Survey* must be all its defenders claimed.

Yet when every reservation has been made, this case of the I.P.R., by far the most significant part of McCarthy's attack against Jessup, shows the enormous difference between fair criticism and McCarthyism. It is fair to say that in his relationship with the I.P.R. Mr. Jessup was, for a time and to a limited degree, taken in by "progressives" — some of them possibly Communists — who aimed to make the *Far Eastern Survey* a sounding board for their point of view. But Senator McCarthy did not charge that some partyliners infiltrated the I.P.R. for a limited time before 1948. He called it a Communist front, which is something entirely different. The difference between his charge and the truth can perhaps be clarified by remarking that the actual error of the officers of the I.P.R. was very like the one committed in the same period by General MacArthur's Headquarters in Japan. From 1945 to 1948 this headquarters tolerated among its subordinates a group of economic extremists, some of whom were clearly sympathetic to Communism. This of course does not make General MacArthur a Communist sympathizer or his headquarters a Communist front.

We have now dealt with the American-Russian Institute and the Institute of Pacific Relations, insofar as they concern Mr. Jessup. Let us proceed to the remainder of McCarthy's charges.

On May 15, 1950, Senator McCarthy announced in a speech at Atlantic City that Mr. Jessup "belonged, that he was affiliated with, not one, but five Communist-front organizations, and that he not only belonged to, but was a director, a director of one of the worst of the lot named as such by the Attorney General." [12] Of these five, two were the American-Russian Institute and the Institute of Pacific Relations, which we have already discussed. Let us turn now to "one of the worst of the lot," which Senator McCarthy identified in a statement to the press as "the China Aid Council of the American League for Peace and Democracy." Here is the State Department's answer to this charge, made public on the same day:

"Ambassador Jessup is not and has never been a director of the China Aid Council. This charge evidently is based — intentionally or carelessly — on the fact that not Mr. Jessup but his wife was listed in 1944 as a director of the China Aid Council. However, at that time, Mrs. Jessup was taking no active part in the work of the Council and attended no meetings. Prior to 1942, Mrs. Jessup had been active in the American Committee for Chinese War Orphans, formed under the sponsorship of Mme. Chiang Kai-shek to raise money for orphanages in China. This organization has never been cited by the Attorney General or the House Committee on Un-American Activities. In 1942, Mrs. Jessup turned her attention to the American Friends Service Committee in Philadelphia, for which she worked full time until 1946. Meanwhile, however, the China Aid Council absorbed the American Committee for Chinese War Orphans and continued as of 1944 to carry Mrs. Jessup's name on its letterhead." [13]

So much for the China Aid Council. It is fair to say that in subsequent speeches McCarthy revised this part of his attack, charging now that Mrs. Jessup's name on the letterhead showed "the close affiliation of Philip Jessup with this organization too." The reader may judge for himself the accuracy of the words "close affiliation."

At Atlantic City, on May 15, Senator McCarthy did not name the other front organizations with which he claimed Mr. Jessup was associated. Not until May 25 at Rochester did he reveal the rest of his evidence, producing photostats of what he called "five Communist-front organizations with which Jessup was affiliated" and a sixth photostat of the China Aid Council, on the ground of "close affiliation" noted above.[14] Some of these photostats dealt with old charges and some with new, but Senator McCarthy treated

[12] *Bulletin*, XXII, p. 969.　　　　　　　[13] *Bulletin*, XXII, pp. 969–970.
[14] *Bulletin*, XXII, p. 1013.

them all on a level — he simply called them Communist fronts, and asserted that Jessup was affiliated with them.   The State Department promptly answered in detail, and the meat of its answer follows — except that I have omitted those parts which merely repeat answers already discussed.

"At Atlantic City, Senator McCarthy asserted that he had presented photostatic proof of such affiliations to the Tydings Subcommittee but counsel of the Subcommittee informed the Department of State that such proof had not been submitted.   The following analysis of the photostats produced by the Senator at Rochester reveals:

"(1) *American Council, Institute of Pacific Relations.*   Dr. Jessup has been prominently connected with the activities of this organization.   It is not a Communist front. . . .

"(2) *Coordinating Committee, to Lift the Spanish Embargo.*   Ambassador Jessup has never been affiliated with this organization in any way.   At Rochester, Senator McCarthy presented reproductions of three full pages and a part of a fourth page of a brochure entitled, 'These Americans Say: "Lift the Embargo against Republican Spain."'   The full 20-page document is and purports to be merely a compendium of public opinion concerning the Spanish embargo.

"The only reference to Ambassador Jessup in the 'photo-reproductions' presented by Senator McCarthy was a seven-line quotation from a statement by Charles C. Burlingham and Ambassador Jessup in the *New York Times* of January 31, 1939.   A week earlier, the *Times* had printed a three-column letter from Henry L. Stimson recommending the lifting of the Spanish embargo.   On January 26, the *Times* published a letter of rebuttal by Martin Conboy.   It was from a three-column statement which the *Times* headlined as 'Text of Reply of Burlingham and Jessup to Conboy's letter' that the Burlingham-Jessup quotation was taken.   The quotation in question reads:

It [lifting the embargo] would further mark a return to our historic policy of avoiding intervention in European civil wars by following a strict hands-off policy instead of taking the affirmative action which, as events have demonstrated, inevitably affects the outcome of a struggle in which we profess not to be concerned.

"The Burlingham-Jessup quotation was 'photo-reproduced' by Senator McCarthy in such a way as to indicate that it constituted a full page of the brochure; whereas, it was actually only one among eleven similar statements by private individuals included on the page in question of the original brochure. Furthermore, it was only one of a total of thirty-one such quotations in the brochure as a whole, including statements by Henry L. Stimson, John Dewey, Helen Keller, Raymond Leslie Buell, Dorothy Thompson, A. F. Whitney, and William E. Dodd.

"(3) *National Emergency Conference and National Emergency Conference for Democratic Rights.* Senator McCarthy's 'photo-reproductions' show that Ambassador Jessup, along with more than 280 other private citizens, was listed as a sponsor of a 'call' for a National Emergency Conference, to discuss matters of alien registration, in 1939. They also show that Ambassador Jessup's name was carried on the letter head of the National Emergency Conference for Democratic Rights, as a sponsor, in February, 1940.

"With regard to the National Emergency Conference, Ambassador Jessup testified before the Tydings Subcommittee that he had no recollection of the conference, that he did not attend the meeting for which the 'call' was issued and that he 'certainly had no knowledge at the time that it was subversive.' It was not until four years later that the Conference was first cited by the House Committee on Un-American Activities.

"With regard to the National Emergency Conference for Democratic Rights, Ambassador Jessup testified that he did not recall the organization or any participation in it. This organization was first cited in 1943.

"(4) *American-Russian Institute.* Ambassador Jessup has never been a member, sponsor, or officer of this organization. . . .

"(5) *American Law Students Association.* This organization, which Ambassador Jessup served as a faculty adviser for about two years, was a perfectly innocent group. It was not and has never been cited as a Communist front.

"As 'evidence' to the contrary, Senator McCarthy produced at Rochester a photostat of a letterhead of the association carrying the customary union shop printer's label. The label was identified by Senator McCarthy in a typewritten notation as 'Union label no. 209 which is the Communist print shop label.'

"He also handed out at Rochester a mimeographed statement in which he flatly asserted, without giving any supporting evidence, that the association was 'affiliated' with three organizations cited as Communist or Communist front. He then devoted three single-spaced type-written pages to a listing of various citations, not against the American Law Students Association, but against the three organizations with which he asserted it was 'affiliated.'

"The fact that the association has never been cited in any way by any agency speaks for itself.

"(6) *China Aid Council.* Ambassador Jessup has never been affiliated with this organization. . . ." [15]

And the State Department, in concluding on this particular charge, summarized the facts as Senator McCarthy should have stated them in the first place:

"It will be noted that, of the six organizations in question, two are not Communist fronts, and two are organizations with which Dr. Jessup has had no connection. For the fifth organization, Dr. Jessup was a sponsor of two dinners which he did not attend. He signed a 'call' which resulted in the formation of the sixth organization but had no further connection with it." [16]

This is the whole story of Senator McCarthy's charges of Mr. Jessup's affiliation with Communist fronts, and one might suppose that after this rebuttal he would either change his statements or introduce some additional evidence; he did neither; a month later he was still asserting that "the documentary evidence shows that Jessup belonged to five organizations which had been officially declared as fronts for and doing the work of the Communist Party," [17] and a year later he was still making similar charges.

But perhaps Senator McCarthy recognized that these charges were not wholly persuasive, for back on March 20th, the day of Mr. Jessup's appearance before the Senate Committee, he wrote a letter to Senator Tydings in which he said that Mr. Jessup's opinions on Communism, his anti-Communist speeches, the support of his friends, and his good intentions were not the issue. "The issues are: (1) Will he continue running with the same pack that has to date done everything in the Far East that Russia wants, and (2) will he continue to be the 'voice of Lattimore'?" [18]

The first of these issues, as it happened, was disposed of by Mr. Jessup in his statement before the Senate Committee; he pointed out, as we have noted, that he had repeatedly opposed the Russian position on Far Eastern matters, Korean, Chinese, and Indonesian, and for this opposition he had earned Communist curses in a dozen languages; he could hardly continue running with a pack to which he was already opposed. The second question is whether Mr. Jessup was or is the "voice of Lattimore."

We may start on this one by asking what evidence Senator McCarthy produced to support his suggestion that Mr. Jessup was controlled by Owen

---

[15] *Bulletin*, XXII, pp. 1013–14.
[17] *Bulletin*, XXIII, p. 109.
[16] *Bulletin*, XXII, p. 1014.
[18] *New York Times*, March 21, 1950, p. 24.

Lattimore. We find this claim: "that Owen Lattimore had been requested by Acheson to, and did, furnish to the State Department a document to act as a guide for Ambassador-at-Large Jessup insofar as Asiatic policy was concerned." [19] Senator McCarthy also called this document "Lattimore's instructions to Jessup," and went on to assert that it outlined a policy which the Department followed which was now "Jessup's program."

The facts about this claim, as promptly stated by the Department of State and never contested by Senator McCarthy, are as follows: Mr. Lattimore was one of thirty-one persons who submitted memoranda to the Department of State in response to a request from Mr. Jessup in August, 1949. Among those submitting memoranda were such men as Joseph W. Ballantine, William Bullitt, Joseph C. Grew, Roger Lapham, and Admiral Yarnell. None of these memoranda contained any instructions to anybody; they were background material for a general study then being made of policy toward Asia. Mr. Lattimore was also a member of a group of twenty-odd citizens who attended a round table on Far Eastern policy in Ocober; his table-mates were such men as George Marshall, John D. Rockefeller II, and Harold Stassen. Again at the round table no one issued any instructions to anybody.

But Senator McCarthy had a further claim: that the Lattimore document was "Jessup's program." He further stated that the document paralleled the Communist line. In McCarthy's language: "Here is Jessup's program, in this document [the Lattimore memorandum]. . . . What does Mr. Lattimore advocate as a foreign policy for Asia? (1) Abandon Chiang Kai-shek, (2) Get out of Korea, (3) Get out of Japan, (4) Deny the need for a Pacific Pact." [20]

To this claim the State Department answered as follows, in a statement never contested by Senator McCarthy:

"There is no 'Jessup program' distinct from United States foreign policy. The United States' record and policy in the Far East, as it relates to the points made by Senator McCarthy, is well-known. In the light of the Senator's charges, however, it may be summarized:

"(1) The United States poured tremendous amounts of aid into China in efforts to bolster the government of Chiang Kai-shek.

"(2) The United States has led the fight for a free, democratic Korea; took its case to the United Nations; and, since the establishment of this Government, has contributed substantial economic and military support.

[19] *Bulletin*, XXII, p. 965.　　　　[20] *Bulletin*, XXII, p. 966.

[A few weeks later, of course, the United States firmly met the great challenge of June 25, 1950.]

"(3) The United States as the principal occupying power in Japan will not enter into any peace treaty which makes impossible adequate protection of United States' security interests in the Western Pacific. [And the Treaty of 1951 carries out this assurance.]

"(4) The United States has publicly indicated that it would look with sympathy upon a regional alliance of Pacific nations, provided the impetus for such an association came from the nations themselves." [21] [In 1951 an alliance was in fact organized with Australia and New Zealand and another with the Philippines].

Let us now rewrite Senator McCarthy's charge that Mr. Jessup was the "voice of Lattimore." It should read as follows: "Mr. Jessup has had available to him the views of Owen Lattimore, along with those of dozens of other Americans who have a special knowledge of the Far East. Whatever Mr. Jessup and the State Department may have done in the Far East, and whatever advice they may have accepted, it is clear from my own description of Mr. Lattimore's policy that the State Department has not listened to him."

We have now dealt with all of Senator McCarthy's original series of attacks on Mr. Jessup, made in 1950. In the summer of 1951 he returned to the fray with another set of denunciations. In the main these were slightly tailored and modified repetitions of the charges we have already considered — the same so-called "affiliation" with the same five so-called "fronts," and the same so-called "control" of a so-called "front" magazine. Some of the more obvious misstatements disappeared, and the emphasis shifted toward the I.P.R., which we have already considered in sufficient detail. But three themes not used before appear in the 1951 attacks; two of them had been thoroughly discussed by Mr. Jessup before the Tydings Subcommittee the year before, so that the evidence for the defense is readily available. The third can be dealt with from the records of the United States Senate.

The first of the new charges was a claim that "I have in my hand a copy of a petition — and listen to this if you will — signed by Jessup urging that we destroy all atomic bomb material — and I quote — by appropriate means such as dumping it into the ocean." [22]

This small sentence contains two misstatements and a basic distortion.

[21] *Bulletin*, XXII, p. 966.

[22] Radio Address of August 22, 1951, entered in the *Congressional Record* by Senator Malone, August 23, 1951 (*Congressional Record*, 82d Congress, 1st Session, p. A5620).

Taken at its face value it sounds as if McCarthy had somehow tracked down an effort by Jessup to get the basic American weapon destroyed, and that is certainly how McCarthy meant it to sound. The facts are different. It was not a petition to some amenable high officer, but a letter to the *New York Times* published February 16, 1946 — and of course Senator McCarthy does not mention the date, which is vital to an understanding of the letter. It did not urge that all atomic bomb material be destroyed; it urged that *for one year*, while the UN worked for a basic world-wide control of atomic energy, no *new* bombs should be made; the existing stockpile would of course be kept until real agreement was reached. In order to keep the production plants in good shape during this year, however, it would be necessary to run them at a certain minimum rate, and it was the material that would be produced in this operation that Mr. Jessup and his co-signers were ready to dump in the ocean. The co-signers, incidentally, were all professors of different subjects at Columbia, a distinguished group of American democrats, two of them men who had played large parts in creating the bomb. As Ambassador Jessup explained in March, 1950, the proposal was made at a time when the American people and government had great hopes for a genuine international agreement to eliminate the danger of atomic war, and the proposal was intended as a contribution to that national purpose. Obviously it was no longer applicable, nor did it represent Mr. Jessup's own opinion four years later, when experience had so clearly shown that the Russians were not prepared to accept any feasible scheme of inspection and control. What Senator McCarthy should have said, then, was that in 1946 Mr. Jessup was one of twelve Columbia professors who thought that effective international agreement would be easier to achieve if no new bombs were made for a year. To put it this way would have had the disadvantage that it would frighten no one, but it would have had the advantage of truth. Unfortunately, it is a characteristic of Senator McCarthy's method that he prefers false fear to unfrightening truth.

The second new charge in McCarthy's 1951 speeches was that Mr. Jessup had testified as a character witness for Alger Hiss. This of course was no secret, but as Senator McCarthy stated his charge, he made it sound as if Mr. Jessup's testimony included an estimate of the reputation of Hiss in the light of the accusations and evidence that led to his trial. In fact, of course, Mr. Jessup's testimony was given at the second trial, and character witnesses are required to testify *without regard* to the specific charges being tried, a fact which lawyer McCarthy undoubtedly knows. When Mr. Jessup said that the reputation of Alger Hiss was excellent, aside from the charges for which he was being tried, he was merely stating the bald and obvious truth. It was the excellence of his original reputation that made his trial and conviction so sensational.

The last of Senator McCarthy's new charges was that Mr. Jessup had followed the Communist line toward World War II, switching from isolationism to interventionism after Russia was attacked in June, 1941. If true, this would be a grave accusation, for the flip-flop of that month is one of the most reliable tests available for discovering men who followed the party line. The only trouble with the charge is that it is not true, and indeed Senator McCarthy was unable to offer any evidence at all to support it, claiming merely that his investigators had found nothing to show that it was *not* true. If his investigators had bothered to consult the *Congressional Record* for October 29, 1941, or the hearings conducted by the Senate Foreign Relations Committee at the same period, they would have found that Mr. Jessup, who opposed entry into World War II right up to Pearl Harbor, was still acting in support of his convictions by providing legal ammunition to Senator Hiram Johnson at the request of Senator Robert A. Taft. No Communist or party-liner could have taken the stand he took at this time in a long letter opposing President Roosevelt's scheme for arming American merchant vessels.[23]

It remains to consider the general escape clause which Senator McCarthy sought for himself. Whenever he was unable to give evidence for one of his charges, and whenever he was caught in a lie, he would assert that it could all be proved in the files of the State Department and the Federal Bureau of Investigation. The President refused, as all his predecessors had always refused, to surrender the confidential files of the Executive branch, and Senator McCarthy was left in the position of asking for something which by long constitutional precedent he could not get; the President in the end allowed the Tydings Subcommittee to see the State Department files, but those of the FBI, in accordance with the strong recommendation of J. Edgar Hoover, were withheld. So McCarthy had an escape clause, and its validity

---

[23] This letter appears in Hearings, *Modification of the Neutrality Act of 1939*, Senate, Committee on Foreign Relations, 77th Congress, 1st Session, October 24, 1939, pp. 251–52. It is quoted at length by Senator Johnson in the *Congressional Record*, vol. 87, pt. 8, p. 8321. In testimony not fully available at this writing, Mr. Jessup further expanded his account of isolationist activities after June, 1951. I must add that I do not myself think it was good to be an isolationist at *any* time in 1941, but since Mr. Jessup was accused of a party-line flip-flop, his only recourse was to demonstrate his consistent isolationism.

is worth considering for a moment. If Senator McCarthy's theory is accepted, I can accuse you of anything from adultery to witchery, and if you don't let me see all your personal and private papers, I can claim that my accusation holds good.

In the case of Mr. Jessup the sum total of the truth that remained in Senator McCarthy's charges was that Mr. Jessup had been a leader in an organization which Communists at one time infiltrated and from which they had been expelled, that he had once agreed to sponsor two dinners he did not attend, and that he had joined in a "call" for an unimportant group which turned out years later to be Communist-controlled, and with which he had nothing further to do. All the rest was without a shred of Communist-fronting in it. Against these items, and dismissed by McCarthy as irrelevant, was a career of great distinction, a long public record of strong opposition to Communism, and the energetic good opinion of American leaders from Elihu Root to Dwight D. Eisenhower. All of McCarthy's charges were publicly answered; Senator McCarthy never dealt with the answers; the assertions with which he began were the ones with which he continued. I submit that no fair observer could avoid the conclusion that Senator McCarthy was not interested in the truth, or in finding Communists; he was interested in gaining political advantage from an elaborate and intensive campaign of falsehood. Fortunately, in the case of Mr. Jessup, he attacked a man who could fight back and count on his friends, and we may conclude this inquiry with the resolution of Utica Post #229, adopted on April 9, 1950, and never publicly referred to by Senator McCarthy:

"WHEREAS, Utica Post #229 American Legion is proud to number among the list of its Past Commanders a distinguished comrade, friend, and charter member, Ambassador Philip C. Jessup, whose record of patriotic devotion and continued helpfulness to our Country over a period of many years is a source of great satisfaction, pride and distinction to Utica Post and to its entire membership; and

"WHEREAS, the sterling character, splendid reputation, and unquestionable loyalty and patriotism of Past Commander Philip C. Jessup, both privately and in his public capacity as U.S. Ambassador-at-Large, have recently been subjected to scurrilous, unprincipled, and wholly unjustifiable attack by one Joseph McCarthy, who in so doing has sullied the office of U.S. Senator which he presently holds,

"*Now, therefore, be it resolved* that Utica Post #229 American Legion and its entire membership shall and do strongly resent, condemn and decry the

unprincipled, unjustified, unsportsmanlike, un-American and intolerable
conduct of Senator Joseph McCarthy in his wanton attempt without proof
or reason to smear and destroy the good reputation and high standing of so
devoted and patriotic a citizen as our esteemed and valued friend and comrade, the Honorable Philip C. Jessup, U.S. Ambassador-at-Large; and be
it further

"*Resolved*, that Utica Post #229 American Legion and its members in
meeting duly assembled feel privileged at this time to reaffirm their continued trust and confidence in, their esteem and devotion to, and their lasting
friendship for a distinguished public servant, a loyal patriot, and a great
citizen, the Hon. Philip C. Jessup, a Past Commander of this Post; and be it
further

"*Resolved* that this resolution be inscribed upon the Minutes of this meeting, that a copy thereof be delivered to our comrade, Ambassador Jessup; that
a second copy be delivered to the public press; and that a third copy be mailed
to Senator McCarthy with the admonition that his reckless and despicable
conduct in this instance cannot be condoned by any right thinking American
and should never be repeated if he hopes to retain a shred of public respect." [24]

Acheson and Alger Hiss

It is possible to persuade the reasonable student that there is alertness
against Communism in the State Department; it is relatively easy to show
that Senator McCarthy is a charlatan. Yet sooner or later, in discussions of
Acheson and this issue, attention will come back to Alger Hiss. Here is a
man convicted of perjury in such circumstances that the conviction is tanta-
mount to a judicial determination that he was a spy for the Soviet Union;
he has had the best of defense and a manifestly fair trial, in fact two. Yet
immediately after the conviction the Secretary of State deliberately and
publicly announced, "I do not intend to turn my back on Alger Hiss." On
the surface it appears that Mr. Acheson has gone out of his way to give public
support to a man whose conduct has touched his country on its raw nerve,
and those who are surprised at the violent feeling which this remark has
aroused need only ask themselves how they would have felt if Cordell Hull
had publicly announced in 1941 that he would not turn his back on the Nazi
Bund Leader Kuhn. The circumstances are not at all the same, but to many
citizens they *appear* to be the same.

[24] *Bulletin*, XXII, pp. 971–72.

Since in this case the circumstances are everything, the honest student must look to the record that came before and after this one remark which is so gleefully quoted by Acheson's enemies. After looking at the record he may feel that it should not have been said, or that it should have been said some other way, but at least he will understand it, and he is likely to look with some suspicion on anyone who brandishes this single statement as a proof that Dean Acheson is a supporter of Communist spies.[25]

The Hearing on Nomination

The first point to be noted is that when Alger Hiss was convicted, in January, 1950, there was already a considerable official record on his relationship to Acheson. The question of this relationship had been raised at the time of Acheson's nomination to be Secretary, and he had been called on, *as a part of his demonstration of fitness for office*, to explain in detail what that relationship was. It was the questioners, and not Acheson, who first connected this question with the official status of the Secretary of State. Since the discussion of the Hiss matter at this hearing is an essential part of the story, it is presented in full:

THE CHAIRMAN. You were first Assistant Secretary of State, were you not, before you became Under Secretary?

MR. ACHESON. Yes, Senator Connally.

THE CHAIRMAN. It has been charged over the radio and in the press and by word of mouth that, while you were Assistant Secretary, Mr. Alger Hiss was your chief of staff or was your special assistant. Is that true?

MR. ACHESON. It is true that that has been stated. It is not true that that is the fact.

[25] The suggestion that Acheson might be a security risk was once made to his face by Senator Bridges, and the suggestion and reply, however little they may reflect credit on Mr. Bridges' good taste, do at least give us Acheson's approval for a restatement of his relations with Hiss:

SENATOR BRIDGES. Mr. Secretary, would you consider a friend of a person convicted of, say, perjury in connection with a treasonable act and found guilty, a security risk?

SECRETARY ACHESON. I think it would be a matter that you would look into. (Hearings, *State, Justice, Commerce, Judiciary Appropriations, 1951*, Senate, Subcommittee of the Committee on Appropriations, February 28, 1950, p. 601.)

THE CHAIRMAN. That is what I am asking you. Is the statement correct?

MR. ACHESON. Senator, I have waited a long time for the opportunity to answer that question; and, if you will bear with me, I would like to answer it in some detail.

THE CHAIRMAN. That is right.

MR. ACHESON. As a preliminary matter, I should like to state to the committee that my friendship is not easily given, and it is not easily withdrawn. In this instance, Mr. Donald Hiss was my assistant during the years that I was Assistant Secretary of State. He served me and he served the country with complete fidelity and loyalty. He and I became, and we remain, close and intimate friends. He is now my partner, with everything that that relationship implies.

Mr. Alger Hiss was an officer of the Department of State during most of the time that I served there. During that time he and I became friends, and we remain friends. I do not wish to detract in any way from that statement when I point out, as I shall have to point out in a moment, that he was not my assistant; he was never my assistant, and, except for the last few months of his service when I was Acting Secretary of State, he never reported to me in any way.

With that preliminary statement, may I go into the facts?

THE CHAIRMAN. Yes.

MR. ACHESON. As you stated, I became Assistant Secretary of State on February 1, 1941. At that time Mr. Alger Hiss was the assistant to Dr. Stanley Hornbeck, in the Far Eastern Division of the State Department. He continued in that work until May of 1944, when he was transferred to do work in another division of the State Department, again not connected in any way with me, on the preparation for the Dumbarton Oaks Conferences and later on for the Mexico City Conference and the San Francisco Conference.

After he completed that work, he attended the first session of the United Nations in London in the winter of 1945–46. On his return to the State Department he was put in charge of a division which had to do with our relations with the United Nations. That was, I think, sometime in April or May, 1946. That division reported to the Secretary of State, Mr. Byrnes, and to me.

SENATOR WILEY. Who arranged it?

MR. ACHESON. Who arranged what?

SENATOR WILEY. Who arranged this new appointment?

MR. ACHESON. This was the division in which Mr. Hiss was working at the time. He had been working in it since May 1944. He became the head of it on the retirement of Dr. Pasvolsky, who had been the head of that division. This was the first time, in April or May 1946, that Mr. Hiss fell under my jurisdiction in any way. He continued in that office until he resigned at the end of 1946 or the beginning of 1947.

Now, Mr. Chairman, this whole matter of the confusion of two men has arisen out of the testimony of a former colleague of mine in the State Department, Assistant Secretary Berle. Mr. Berle testified before the Un-American Activities Committee and stated — and I read from the transcript of the record — after referring to a conversation which he had had with Mr. Chambers in 1939:

"I checked on the two Hiss boys. Specifically, I checked with Dean Acheson, and later I checked when Acheson became the Assistant Secretary of State, and Alger Hiss became his executive assistant. That, to the best of my knowledge, was the first time when Hiss would have been in a position to do anything effectively. Acheson said that he had known the family and these two boys from childhood, and could vouch for them absolutely."

Mr. Berle's memory has gone badly astray. As I pointed out, Mr. Alger Hiss was not my executive assistant, my assistant of any sort whatever; he was not in any branch of the Department which reported to me or was under me in any way of any sort. Therefore Mr. Berle's memory is quite wrong when he says that Mr. Alger Hiss became my executive assistant, and that, to the best of Mr. Berle's knowledge, was the first time when he could do anything effective.

He then says, speaking apparently as of 1939:

"I checked on the two Hiss boys. Specifically, I checked with Dean Acheson and later I checked when Acheson became Assistant Secretary of State."

May I give you the facts in regard to that matter?

As I say, on entering the State Department, where I was a stranger, it seemed to me highly desirable that I should have attached to me an officer of the Department of State who was well liked and experienced in the Department as a junior assistant to me.   I had met Mr. Donald Hiss, as I had met his brother, when he served as law clerk and secretary to Mr. Justice Oliver Wendell Holmes.   Donald Hiss was a contemporary and friend of the sons of my two senior partners.   I saw him frequently through the late thirties, and came to have a strong liking for him and an admiration for his ability, particularly his ability to get along with people.

I inquired at the State Department whether it would be agreeable and in accordance with the regulations to have this officer assigned to me as a personal assistant, particularly to work on briefing me for meetings, both which I was going to hold and which I was going to attend, on a subject matter which was quite new to me.   The Department told me it was entirely agreeable, and that from their point of view he was well suited for this work.   At that time he was on loan to the Office of Production Management, where he was assisting the general counsel, Mr. Blackwell Smith.   I telephoned Mr. Smith and arranged with him to have Mr. Hiss retransferred back to the Department of State.   That was done.

He had been in my office only a few days or a few weeks when, sometime in February or March of 1941, Mr. Berle asked me to come and see him.   Mr. Berle then said to me that he understood that I had one of the Hiss brothers as my assistant.   I explained to him that I had Donald Hiss as my assistant.   Mr. Berle then said that information had come to his attention that one of the Hiss brothers had had associations which would make his presence in my office embarrassing to me and to the Department.   I explained to Mr. Berle that it was of importance which brother he was talking about, because I had responsibility only for Donald Hiss, and his brother was not under me in any way whatever.

Mr. Berle said he could not tell me which brother it was.   At the time I understood that to mean that he did not know.   It may well have been that he meant he was not at liberty to tell me.   At any rate, he did not.

I then asked him what the nature of this information was, and he said that for security reasons he could not tell me that.   I then said to Mr. Berle that I would question Donald Hiss to find out whether he had any associations which would be embarrassing to me or the Department.   If he told me that he did not, I had complete confidence in him and I was not prepared to change the arrangements which I had made on any such vague information as Mr. Berle had given me.

I then questioned Donald Hiss, asked him to take time to reflect and let me know whether he had ever had any associations which would embarrass me. He did take time to reflect. He told me that he had no such associations and he did not know to what my question referred, but he said that since I had asked the question, there must be some reason that I feared embarrassment from him, and if I had such a feeling, he would go back to his other work.

I told him that I would not permit that to happen, that I had complete confidence in him and so far as I was concerned, the matter was closed. It was closed, and it was never referred to again by him or me.

I should like to add a few further words about Mr. Donald Hiss. During 1941 he served as my assistant. Our principal task during that year was the institution of the financial controls which were applied to the Axis countries, first in Europe and later in Asia. Mr. Hiss represented me in all of that work. We worked with the Treasury Department and with the Administrator of Export Control. In July of 1941, drastic restrictions were imposed on Germany, Italy, the occupied countries, and the Soviet Union. Mr. Hiss assisted in the drafting of those regulations. The regulations continued in effect against the Soviet Union until after the invasion of Russia by Germany.

The Governments of the United States and Great Britain announced their full support of the Russian military effort. At that time, under instructions from the President, the restrictions were lifted as to the Soviet Union.

In January of 1942 this work had taken on such dimensions that a division had to be organized to carry on the work in the State Department. I put Mr. Donald Hiss, with the approval of Secretary Hull, at the head of that office. He worked ably in that position throughout 1942 conducting negotiations with the other American Republics by which they put similar restrictions into effect against our enemies and their enemies.

After the invasion of North Africa, Mr. Donald Hiss, who was a semi-invalid on account of stomach trouble which had required surgical treatment, and thereafter was not fit for military service, became so restless at being absent from the scene of military action that he finally persuaded me to let him go to North Africa to work with other civilian members of General Eisenhower's staff in setting up the supply arrangements for the civilian population and the economic warfare arrangements in North Africa. He went over there in November or December, I think it was, 1942, and stayed until his health broke down and he returned in the spring of 1943. He then returned to me as my executive assistant and stayed there, with frequent break-downs of his health, until March, 1944.

At that time a new office, the Office of Economic Affairs, was organized in the State Department, and Mr. Harry Hawkins, the head of it, asked me whether he could have Donald Hiss as his Deputy. It seemed to me that that work would be less strenuous than the somewhat hectic activities of my own office, and I agreed to that. Mr. Hiss left my office in March, 1944. In November, 1944, he suffered a complete break-down in health. One of his lungs collapsed, and he had to retire from Government service and take a very considerable rest.

At that time my former partners, who were very much overworked because of the departure of their junior partners for military service, asked Mr. Hiss, when he recovered, to join them, which he did, and he has thereafter been an associate, and later a member, of that firm.

I go into this at some length, Mr. Chairman, because of the second statement made by Mr. Berle. In his testimony he was asked by Mr. Stribling, "Were you ever at any time suspicious of Mr. Hiss?" He is now talking about Mr. Alger Hiss.

"Mr. Berle. A better way of saying it is, I was worried. I ought to begin by confessing a prejudice here, so that you can discount whatever I say. As I think many people know, in the fall of 1944 there was a difference of opinion in the State Department. I felt that the Russians were not going to be sympathetic and cooperative. Victory was then assured, though not complete, and the intelligence reports which were in my charge, among other things, indicated a very aggressive policy, not at all in line with the kind of cooperation everyone was hoping for, and I was pressing for a pretty clean-cut showdown when our position was strongest.

The opposite group in the State Department was largely the men in Mr. Acheson's group, of course, with Mr. Hiss as his principal assistant in the matter. Whether that was a difference on foreign policy — and the question could be argued both ways; it wasn't clean-cut — was a problem, but at that time Mr. Hiss did take what you would call today the pro-Russian point of view. That was a cause for worry. It is not necessarily a reason to draw the conclusion that he was a disloyal man, because many people were quite loyal, including a good many of the Army officers, who felt the Russian Army would be important in case of an invasion of Japan, and that by consequence it was desirable not to raise any issues until later.

I may say in Mr. Hiss' defense, although I got trimmed in that fight and as a result went to Brazil, and that ended my diplomatic career, I mention that because I did have a biased view."

Now, Mr. Chairman, in the fall of 1944, throughout 1944 and all preceding years, as I have repeatedly said, Mr. Alger Hiss was not my assistant. In the fall of 1944 he was not in my office. In the fall of 1944 he was working on the Dumbarton Oaks Conferences and preparatory work for Mexico and San Francisco. In the fall of 1944 Mr. Donald Hiss was not in my office. He had left it in March, 1944, and he left the Department of State altogether in November of 1944. In the entire last half of 1944 I had no executive assistant at all for the reason that I was very largely out of Washington attending international conferences. I had no dispute with Mr. Berle of any sort about anything in the fall or summer or other time of 1944. I left Washington in late June, 1944, to attend the Bretton Woods Conference, and was there until August. I then left Washington in early September of 1944 to attend the Montreal Conference and I was there until the middle of October. I returned exactly on the 8th of October, 1944, and Mr. Berle left Washington on the 1st of November, 1944, for the Chicago Air Conference and did not return until the time of his resignation.

Therefore, I want to point out that whoever had any controversy with Mr. Berle at this time, it was not I. Whoever assisted anyone in any controversy with Mr. Berle, it was not either one of the Hisses.

With that, Mr. Chairman, I hope I have answered your question.

The hearing then turned to other matters, returning to the Hiss question later, as follows:

SENATOR SMITH. Mr. Acheson, might I ask you this question: You have given us a very clear story of your relations with Mr. Donald Hiss. I wasn't clear from what you said whether Mr. Alger Hiss during that period was engaged in some other part of the Department of State.

MR. ACHESON. Yes, Senator Smith. I tried to bring out that during the time that I was in the State Department, which begins with February 1, 1941, Mr. Alger Hiss was the assistant to Dr. Stanley Hornbeck in

the Far Eastern Division of the State Department, a division which reported to the Under Secretary, and not to me. He remained there until
May, 1944. At that time he was transferred to another division of the
State Department, again not under me, but which was concerned with
working on the preparation for the United Nations Charter. That involved work in the two Conferences at Dumbarton Oaks, work at the
Conference at Mexico City in which some of these matters came up,
work at San Francisco, where Mr. Alger Hiss was the Secretary General
of the United Nations meeting, and work at London at the first meeting
of the United Nations General Assembly. None of those times did he
work in any part of the Department which was under me or associated
with me in any way.

In 1946, when he returned from London, he then rejoined the Division which reported to the Secretary and Under Secretary, and at that
time I was Under Secretary.

Does that clear it up?

SENATOR SMITH. Yes. I wanted to get that clear. There might be
some confusion between the Hiss brothers. I think you have made that
clear.

There is just this one thought further. We read about his connection
with Mr. Sayre [in 1937, the time of the espionage involved in the Hiss
trial]. What was Mr. Sayre's activity in the State Department at that
time in relation to your position as Under Secretary?

MR. ACHESON. Mr. Sayre was not in the State Department at that
time. Mr. Sayre had been an Assistant Secretary of State. He was
succeeded by Mr. Henry Grady. Mr. Henry Grady was succeeded by
me. At the time I entered the State Department Mr. Sayre was the
High Commissioner of the United States to the Philippines, and was
in Manila.

SENATOR SMITH. As a matter of fact, Mr. Sayre's connection with
State Department was prior to your ever joining it.

MR. ACHESON. That is correct.

SENATOR SMITH. And the events of 1937 we have heard about were
long prior to your connection with the State Department at all?

MR. ACHESON. That is correct, Senator.

SENATOR VANDENBERG. Mr. Acheson, if I may just proceed one step
further; a Senator not a member of the committee asked me to ask you
on whose recommendation did Mr. Alger Hiss enter the Department,

and on whose recommendation was he named Secretary General of the United Nations Conference.

MR. ACHESON. I have no information about that whatever. He entered the Department years before I had any connection with it, and I had nothing to do with the United Nations meeting in San Francisco.[26]

This testimony, together with a short passage already quoted in Chapter One above, was summarized by Senator Vandenberg on the floor of the Senate: "I have asked Mr. Acheson if I might summarize his Hiss attitudes in the following sentences and he agrees: An assertion of personal friendship for the Hiss brothers; staunch defense of Donald Hiss; a preference to leave Alger Hiss to the courts. Total and aggressive hostility to subversion in the State Department." [27]

So it was as the declared friend of Alger Hiss that Acheson was confirmed as Secretary of State, and this declaration had been made as a part of the official proceedings on his nomination. It is against this background that we now turn to see exactly what he said after the conviction of Hiss, a year later. Alger Hiss was found guilty on two counts of perjury on January 21, 1950. Acheson's next press conference was held on January 25. What happened there was clearly and fully described the following morning by the *New York Times* as follows:

"The Secretary was asked if he had any comment on the case.

"After refusing to comment in any way on the evidence, the Secretary edged forward in his chair and with some feeling made the following extemporaneous statement:

I take [it] the purpose of your questions was to bring something other than that out of me. I should like to make it clear to you that, whatever the outcome of any appeal which Mr. Hiss or his lawyer may take in this case, I do not intend to turn my back on Alger Hiss.

I think every person who has known Alger Hiss or has served with him at any time has upon his conscience the very serious task of deciding what his attitude is and what his conduct should be. That must be done by each person in the light of his own standards and his own principles.

For me there is very little doubt of those standards or those principles.

[26] Hearing, *Nomination of Dean G. Acheson*, Senate, Committee on Foreign Relations, 81st Congress, 1st Session, January 13, 1949, pp. 5–12.

[27] *Congressional Record*, vol. 95, pt. 1, p. 460.

I think they were stated for us a very long time ago. They were stated on the Mount of Olives and if you are interested in seeing them you will find them in the Twenty-fifth Chapter of the Gospel according to St. Matthew, beginning at Verse 34." [28]

Verses 34–46 of Matthew 25 read as follows:

Then shall the King say unto them on his right hand, Come, ye blessed of my Father, inherit the kingdom prepared for you from the foundation of the world:

For I was an hungred, and ye gave me meat: I was thirsty, and ye gave me drink: I was a stranger, and ye took me in:

Naked, and ye clothed me: I was sick, and ye visited me: I was in prison, and ye came unto me.

Then shall the righteous answer him, saying, Lord, when saw we thee an hungred, and fed thee? or thirsty, and gave thee drink?

When saw we thee a stranger, and took thee in? or naked, and clothed thee?

Or when saw we thee sick, or in prison, and came unto thee?

And the King shall answer and say unto them, Verily I say unto you, Inasmuch as ye have done it unto one of the least of these my brethren, ye have done it unto me.

Then shall he say also unto them on the left hand, Depart from me, ye cursed, into everlasting fire, prepared for the devil and his angels:

For I was an hungred, and ye gave me no meat: I was thirsty, and ye gave me no drink:

I was a stranger, and ye took me not in: naked, and ye clothed me not: sick, and in prison, and ye visited me not.

Then shall they also answer him, saying, Lord, when saw we thee an hungred, or athirst, or a stranger, or naked, or sick, or in prison, and did not minister unto thee?

Then shall he answer them, saying, Verily I say unto you, Inasmuch as ye did it not to one of the least of these, ye did it not to me.

And these shall go away into everlasting punishment: but the righteous into life eternal.

This is the complete context from which a single clause is regularly quoted. And of course it was the single clause which caused loud noises in

[28] *New York Times*, January 26, 1950, p. 14.

the following month. These noises were so loud and unfriendly that on February 28, 1951, when Acheson appeared before a Senate subcommittee to testify on State Department appropriations, he once more undertook to explain his position. This is his last statement on the matter, and it speaks for itself.

SECRETARY ACHESON. Now, it is quite clear that whatever I say is going to be as misrepresented as what I said before, so I have written down what I would say in this matter, being quite sure that I was going to be questioned about it. I would like to read it, and I hope that this will dispose of this matter for good and all.

I have been asked to explain the statement which I made in regard to Alger Hiss on the 25th of January in the light of various criticisms which have been leveled at it; such as, that it impugned proceedings before a United States court; that it should not have been made, that it condoned the offense for which Mr. Hiss was tried, and so forth.

First, I stated, as clearly as I could, that I would not discuss in any manner whatever the charges against Mr. Hiss, since those charges were then, as they are now, before a court. This is a principle of the most fundamental importance. No one who was brought up in the law, as I was, by Mr. Justice Brandeis and Mr. Justice Holmes, can have the faintest doubt of the transcendent importance of practicing this principle in the strictest possible way. I have been a member of the bar for thirty years. I have never departed from this principle, and I never expect to do so. Therefore, I did not in my former statement, nor shall I now, discuss the charges in this case in any way, either directly or indirectly. The duty of passing upon them rests with the court, and the court should not be, in any manner whatever, embarrassed or prejudiced in performing this duty.

Second. I have been asked why I did not let the matter rest with what I have just said. There seemed to me public and private reasons why this could not be done.

At the time of my confirmation, the Senate committee before which I appeared inquired of me regarding my relations with Mr. Hiss. This is clearly indicative of the committee's belief that the matter was relevant to my fitness for the office. Many of those who have criticized my statement give further ground for this belief. It has been charged, for instance, that what I said indicates that I am not qualified for the office which I hold. I do not agree with this view, but it surely indicates that some persons believe that my views in this matter are relevant to the question of my fitness for the office and that, therefore, the public is entitled to know my views. At any rate, the question which was put to me was directed toward bringing them out, and the issue was, therefore, presented whether I should state them or withhold them.

There were also personal reasons for stating my attitude. One must be true to the things by which one lives. The counsels of discretion and cowardice are appealing. The safe course is to avoid situations which are disagreeable and dangerous. Such a course might get one by the issue of the moment, but it has bitter and evil consequences. In the long days and years which stretch beyond that moment of decision, one must live with one's self; and the consequences of living with a decision which one knows has sprung from timidity and cowardice go to the roots of one's life. It is not merely a question of peace of mind, although that is vital; it is a matter of integrity of character. This is the most fundamental of all considerations.

For these reasons it seemed, and still seems to me that there was no alternative to saying what I said.

Third. The attitude which one who has known and worked with Mr. Hiss will take toward him in his deep trouble is a matter for the individual conscience [to] decide. It isn't a matter which a court, or public opinion, or the Government can decide for one. That is fundamental, not only under our institutions of personal liberty and responsibility but under the Christian ethic. It is not true, for instance, in the Soviet Union. There, all those who have known or worked with a person who has been even charged with the offenses with which Mr. Hiss has been charged must flee from him as from the plague, if they would preserve even the safety of their lives. But that is not true of us; and, indeed, that difference between us and the Soviet Union goes to the very root of the issues which so deeply divide the free world from the Communist world.

Turning then to my personal attitude toward Mr. Hiss, I said that it would be founded upon the principles as stated by Christ in the passages which I cited from the Gospel according to St. Matthew. These passages represent the tradition in which I have been bred, going back beyond the limits of memory. Mr. Hiss is in the greatest trouble in which a man could be. The outcome of his appeal can have little bearing upon his personal tragedy. The court of appeals can either affirm the conviction and sentence, in which case he must go to prison, or, if it finds error in the proceedings below, it can reverse the judgment of the court and remand the case for still another trial in conformity with its opinion. It is in regard to a man in this situation that I referred to Christ's words setting forth compassion as the highest of Christian duties and as the highest quality in the sight of God.

If there is anything in what I have said which casts doubt upon the proceedings of a United States court, I fail to see it. And I do not believe that any fair mind, brought up in the principles which I have discussed, would differ from me. What I have said has nothing whatever to do with the decision of the jury or with the correctness of the rulings of the trial judge. It would be equally valid whether the conviction is affirmed or reversed.

Fourth. Similarly, what I have said would not, I believe, carry to any fair mind the implication that I was condoning the offenses with which Mr. Hiss was charged and of which he has been convicted. It seems fantastic in the light of the facts of my life, which have been a matter of most public record, that any such insinuation should be made. Over the past thirty years I have repeatedly served the United States, and have done so almost continuously for the past ten years. No one can be found to say that I have not done this faithfully and to the best of my ability. Few can doubt that on all of these occasions there were far easier and more profitable courses open to me. So far as public avowals of loyalty are concerned, I have on numerous occasions taken the most solemn oath of allegiance and loyalty to my country and to its Constitution. But for the benefit of those who would create doubt where none existed, I will accept the humiliation of stating what should be obvious: that I did not and do not condone in any way the offenses charged, whether committed by a friend or by a total stranger, and that I would never knowingly tolerate any disloyal person in the Department of State.[29]

Acheson's Defense of the Department

The remarks which follow were made to the American Society of Newspaper Editors on April 22, 1950, at the height of Senator McCarthy's hue-and-cry. They were extemporaneous and heartfelt, and they speak for them-

[29] Hearings, *State, Justice, Commerce, Judiciary Appropriations, 1951*, Senate, Subcommittee of the Committee on Appropriations, February 28, 1950, pp. 636–38.

selves. I have added only a few bracketed notes to fill out the description of the top personnel of the Department.

I should like to clear away some trash which has gathered about the Department of State.

Now, in doing this, I feel that I have a qualification which is so unique that it almost amounts to a disqualification. That is, that I know what I am talking about. I have given ten years of my life to the Department of State, and before that I served in two other Departments of the Government. During the course of that time, I served on two commissions appointed by the President to study the operations of the Government of the United States. I have served under four Secretaries of State and under two Presidents. So I think I am entitled to say that I know something about the Department of State.

The first thing that I should like to say is in the nature of a categorical affirmation. I should like to say that never in its long and honorable history has the Department of State ever been in better shape than it is today.

The Department is manned today, as it has been manned in the past, by able, by honorable, by loyal, and by clean-living American men and women.

It is also a representative department. People who serve in the Department are drawn from all over the United States.

There is no need for anyone to be defensive about the Department of State. What I want you to consider with me are facts.

First of all, when we are talking about this Department, let us look at its top command, let us see who the people are who are controlling and operating and directing the Department of State.

First of all, I don't have to tell you about the Under Secretary of State, Jim Webb. You know he comes from North Carolina. You know his record in the Budget Bureau and in the Treasury. You know what he did in organizing the Sperry Company before the war, when it grew from a little place of 800 people to a great corporation of 30,000 employees. You know what he did in the Marine flying service.

But, the important point that I want to bring out tonight is that I do not know any man in the entire United States, in the Government or out of the Government, who has a greater genius for organization, a genius for understanding how to take a great mass of people and bring them together; so that he pulls out of them all the knowledge and all the competence that they have; so that each person is doing what he ought to be doing; so that efforts of this vast group are pulled together to get a tremendously powerful result. And that is absolutely essential in the Department of State.

When Thomas Jefferson started the State Department it had 6 employees, including himself. Today we have 19,000 employees all over the world, and all of those 19,000 are being pulled by Jim Webb into one great consolidated effort, through a top command.

The third ranking officer in the Department is [Counselor] George Kennan. I don't need to tell you about George Kennan. You have read what he has written. You know his record. He comes from Wisconsin. . . . [Mr. Kennan is a distinguished student and opponent of Soviet imperialism. He has since resigned as Counselor for personal reasons, and his place has been taken by Charles Bohlen, another professional student of the Soviet Union. These two men, to judge by the epithets heaped on them, are known and feared by the Kremlin beyond any other professional diplomats.]

Then we go to another area of the top command, Assistant Secretary Jack Peurifoy of South Carolina. [A few months later, after conducting a vigorous defense of his work as officer in charge of administration and security, Mr. Peurifoy was nominated and confirmed by the Senate as Ambassador to Greece, a country of critical importance — and not even Senator McCarthy opposed his confirmation. He was succeeded by Carlisle Humelsine.] I don't need to tell you about him, except one thing, perhaps, and that is that in all the years that I have been in the State Department he has been with me. When he came to the State Department after he had been in West Point and had to leave on account of disease of the lungs. . . . he very soon became my assistant. He is now the Deputy Under Secretary for Administration. He is in charge of administration. I shall come back to him again in a little while.

Then we have [Assistant Secretary] Jack Hickerson of Texas, a Foreign Service officer of twenty-five years' experience, whom we have taken out of European affairs and put into something which we want to stress, and that is the work of the United Nations.

Then we have [Assistant Secretary] George McGhee of Texas, a former oil man who worked with the Government through the war . . . who took charge of the administration of our Greek-Turkish aid; whom the

President, at my recommendation, put in charge of our Near East and African work; and who, with incredible energy has now visited every one of the areas under his control. . . .

It would be foolish for me to tell you about [Assistant Secretary] Ed Barrett who came from Alabama. He belongs to your profession. [Mr. Barrett is a journalist who came to the Department of State from an editorial desk on *Newsweek*.] You know him. You know the great job which he is doing in overseas information which the President has picked out for such vitally important concentration.

We have put into the Far Eastern work [Assistant Secretary] Dean Rusk of Georgia. He was our Deputy Under Secretary for Political Affairs, and we thought that the whole Far Eastern matter was so critical that we would take our senior political officer and put him into that work.

Walton Butterworth of Louisiana, who had been in that work, we also put in charge particularly of working out some progress on a solution of Japanese matters, one of the most essential things that we must do. In him we have picked out an officer who has the confidence of General MacArthur, who has worked with the military establishment, who is a man of superb integrity and courage.

In case you don't know as much about Walton Butterworth as you do about some of these others, I will remind you that he is the man who had charge of our economic warfare activities during the war in Spain and Portugal. It was he who was in that plane that fell into the river and broke apart at Lisbon; it was Walton who was in the sinking part of the plane in which most of the passengers were trapped; who broke the window through; who pushed his fellow passengers out of the window while the plane was filling up; who then got himself out, kept those who could not swim very well afloat, and helped them onto a wing that was floating. Finally, when the boats came out and picked them up after a very long time and Walton was taken ashore, what do you suppose he had in his hand? It was his briefcase containing his secret papers. That is the type of officer in the State Department.

Then we have as our Legal Adviser, ranking with the Assistant Secretaries, Adrian Fisher of Tennessee. And I note, as I go along here, that we seem to be loaded up with old-fashioned southern "Communists" — no doubt of the Cordell Hull, Walter George, Tom Connally type.

Adrian Fisher was a bomber navigator during the war; later Solicitor with the Department of Commerce; Legal Adviser to the Atomic Energy

Commission, and now the Legal Adviser in the Department of State.

I suggest to people, in the interest of their own security, not to fool with Adrian Fisher. Not only was he a former bomber navigator, but he was a former captain of the Princeton football team. Charges lightly made about him might have serious personal consequences.

[Assistant Secretary] Eddie Miller of New York was born in Puerto Rico, brought up in Cuba, and then in New York. He speaks Portuguese and Spanish as easily as he speaks English. He is a former partner of Mr. Dulles. He has just returned from two trips to South America in which he has put our relations with the Southern Hemisphere on a basis on which I think they have never been before. They are on a sensible, sound basis of mutual advantage, and both they and we know that we both really mean business when we talk, and when we talk we want to talk business.

[Assistant Secretary] George Perkins of New York is a businessman of distinction, who had gone with Paul Hoffman and was working with him in Paris. Paul, with great generosity, let me take him to be in charge of our European affairs.

[Assistant Secretary] Willard Thorp of New York is in charge of economic matters. He is an economic expert; a former director of the Bureau of Foreign and Domestic Commerce in the Department of Commerce; a former partner of Dun & Bradstreet.

[Assistant Secretary] Jack McFall of Colorado and Indiana has charge of our relations with Congress. He has spent fifteen years as the assistant clerk of the Appropriations Committee of the House. If there is anybody who understands, and really understands deeply, the necessities of close relationships between the House and the Senate and the Department of State, it is Jack McFall.

Then in charge of a very important branch of our work, dealing with the new government of Germany and German problems, we have a regular colonel from the United States Army, Colonel Henry Byroade, who was lent to us by the Army — and whom I wish I could steal permanently for the State Department.

In charge of the planning staff is Paul Nitze of Massachusetts, former partner of Dillon Read, a man who went all through the war and was awarded the Medal of Merit for his economic-warfare work.

In charge of our press relations, we have that old friend of yours, Mike McDermott — and you know what sort of a "Communist" he is. [Mr. McDermott has been in charge of press relations since 1927.]

In charge of intelligence work is Park Armstrong of New Jersey, a man who all through the war was dealing with this incredibly important business of the evaluation of intelligence. Don't for a moment believe that the important thing to do is to send someone out with rubbers, dark glasses and a false mustache, to try to steal some paper or find out something. The important business is the evaluation of what you get, either by secret operations or, much more importantly, the material which just pours in on you. Secret material is a dime a dozen. We had, not so long ago, a most interesting and exciting paper planted on us by one of our enthusiastic friends abroad, and it caused a little flurry. But it was Park Armstrong's cool people who discovered in a short time that it was a phony from top to bottom and saved us from the obvious purposes of their planting it on us.

In charge of the great military program for which we and the Defense Department are jointly responsible, we had Jim Bruce of Maryland. Now that he has resigned, Jack Ohly of New York is taking it over. [This program is now under Thomas D. Cabot, formerly President of the United Fruit Company.]

Now, we have also brought in Phil Jessup, Senator Dulles of New York, and Senator Cooper of Kentucky. You can imagine how helpful they would be in covering up all "subversive" activities.

Here in this top command, I say to you, we have men as distinguished, as able, as powerful and as vigorous as any of my great predecessors, from John Marshall to George Marshall, ever had in the Department of State.

Furthermore, we have carried out a reorganization which is based on these men being the operators of the State Department. They are not people who sit around and argue with one another. Each one of them is responsible for carrying out a job, and the policy under which he carries it out is worked out through the planning staff, with the cooperation of all of these men. The policy is laid down and they are given their authority.

I don't sit behind them and pull their coat tails or look over their shoulders. I am kept informed, by the central secretariat, of anything that happens. I am permitted to get in, if I wish to, before something is done, but I don't wish to do that. These men are too good. They cannot hesitate. They cannot be saying, "what does the Secretary think?" They know what the policy is, and they go out and operate. Then, we post-audit the operations; we change the policy if it is not working, but they are given responsibility, and they are well able to carry it.

So I say to you — this is something very, very important, and I suggest that you ask your correspondents in Washington whether what I say to you is true — that today, as rarely before in the State Department, there is no backbiting, there is no jealousy, there is no undercutting. You have an organization of people which is loyal to those within it, which is loyal to the President of the United States and which is loyal to the United States of America.

Let us turn for a moment to the career service. The career service, made up of the Foreign Service and departmental offices, is equally in good shape. This is a service of men and women who are giving their entire lives to the United States, not for a few years, not even ten years, as I have given, but their entire lives, from the time they are young men until they retire at the end of their service. They are giving their whole lives to the United States. They are competent, they are courageous, and they are devoted.

Only this past week, two of our missions were bombed. That is not a pleasant experience. Have any of you ever had it? Have any of you ever had a bomb tossed in the window of your house and had it go off and injure people? Two of our missions have been through that this week. Fortunately, no one was killed, but many people were hurt. Do these people want to come home? Do they say, "This is too dangerous"? Not at all. This is in line of duty. They know their duty. They perform it. It is quite likely that they may be killed, but there is no squeak out of them.

We have just had an officer home who had been held by the Chinese Communists for a year, many months of which he spent in jail, under conditions of incredible hardship and torture. At the direction and request of President Truman, he is going about the United States telling people of what was done to him. Does he ask to retire? Not at all. With great difficulty, we are keeping him in the United States doing this. He wants to go back to the most difficult area that we can find for him. He is not asking to quit. He is not asking for sympathy. This is his duty. He likes it. He wants to go into it again.

We have scores of our people who are now in Chinese cities which are being bombed by the Chinese Nationalists. Are they whimpering about it? Not in the least. They were ordered home because the President decided that was the wise policy. They were perfectly willing to stay there and take whatever came to them.

We have scores of people through southeastern Asia who are in areas of hot war — Indochina, the Philippines, Malaya, Indonesia. Bullets are flying all the time. It is not a cold war in those areas; it is a hot war. And these men and their wives and their children are there, and they are doing their duty. They don't ask to be transferred. They know it is their duty, and they are performing it.

And in other places, in Africa and other parts of the world, we have men with their wives and children who are in situations of the greatest danger, so far as their health is concerned. They are living under very unhealthful conditions. If they are ill, they take their chances under the most primitive medical conditions. There are no schools. There are no oculists to take care of the children's eyes. There are no doctors to give them all the inoculations which your children take. None of those things is available. They don't complain. This is their duty. This is their life. All they ask is that occasionally they be transferred to some situation which is not quite so tough.

Then there are others who are behind the Iron Curtain, and there they are treated as criminals. They cannot have any association with anybody. They cannot have any of the ordinary pleasant relations that all of you have. Anyone who meets them or talks with them will be in jail the next day and possibly hang the day after that. They have to live in a little circle, seeing the same few people day after day. But that is their duty, and they are carrying it out.

Here, again, there are no schools. And if you have a toothache and you want to go to a dentist, you don't call up a dentist; you call up the Foreign Office, and the Foreign Office calls up the secret police, and the secret policeman makes an engagement and comes and sits right beside you in the dentist chair to be absolutely sure that the dentist does not take a message out of your tooth and give it to somebody else.

Those are the circumstances under which these people live.

I don't have to defend these people. There is no reason in the world why they need any defense.

I should like to suggest to you that you would find it a very interesting exercise to try, in your papers, an open letter to these Foreign Service officers of the United States, who are now your front line of defense, who are serving you in these dangerous and difficult parts of the world. Explain to them the attacks which are being made upon them and upon the

Service of which they are just as proud as you are proud of the profession to which you belong. Explain to them, if you can, what is happening to this country behind them. Explain to them why it was that during the war we had USO's and the letter-writing campaigns and everything in the world for the soldiers at the front to show them that the country was behind them and recognized the sacrifice that they were making; and try to explain what is happening now when it comes to these "soldiers," these people who are in the front line of the defense of their country. Explain that to them if you can. You will find it difficult to do.

That is the Department of State as it exists today.

It is not strange that efforts should be made to penetrate this department. Efforts of that sort have been made throughout the history of the United States, and they are being made today.

In the past, these efforts have been made by professionals. But with the spread of this fanatical doctrine of communism, the old profession of professional spies is under competition from amateurs.

Now, this creates difficulty. We are familiar with the methods of counterespionage and the security methods which we have used in the past to protect ourselves from professional spies. In the last few years, we have had a new problem to solve — and we have gone about solving it.

There is a right way to solve that problem, and there is a wrong way to solve it. The right way to solve the problem is to go at it from the point of view of meeting the evil which confronts you and preserving the institution which you are trying to protect. The wrong way is one in which you do not meet the evil that you are attempting to meet, but you destroy the institution that you are trying to protect. Not only do you destroy that, but you destroy the faith of the country in its government and its institutions. You destroy the faith of our allies in us, and you delight our enemies. Those are the right and wrong ways.

The right way was set up by General Marshall in 1947 in the State Department. It was set up under the directive of the President setting up the whole loyalty program. I have never known a man I thought had a surer judgment about people than General Marshall has.

And General Marshall picked out Jack Peurifoy [at Acheson's recommendation] to take charge of the loyalty program in the State Department. He took charge of it. He worked at it through General Marshall's administration. When I came, it seemed to me that there was absolutely nothing better that I could possibly think of to do than to confirm Jack Peurifoy in that particular job. I did, and I have never had occasion to doubt that I did the right thing.

He is not trying to do all this by himself. He has a security staff under a former FBI agent, who is recognized as one of the ablest men ever trained in the service of the FBI. He has a staff of 74 investigators who carry on our investigation work. That is not the only staff that does it. Mr. Hoover's FBI cooperates fully in the whole process. By one method or another, all people who come into the Department and all those who are in it have gone through a thorough screening process. This is a process which is not based on the idea that all these people are crooks. It is a process which is based, first, on protecting the United States but, at the same time, protecting the individuals' rights, protecting their reputations, urging and permitting them to continue to serve the United States with enthusiasm.

Searching examinations are made, so that if we find anything which causes trouble in our minds, we then put it into another level of screening. It goes to the Loyalty Board in the State Department.

General Conrad Snow is the Chairman of that Board. He is an old-fashioned New Hampshire Republican "Communist," a man who, incidentally, is vouched for by Senator Bridges.

That Board, and the people who work on it, have gone through every single case about which any doubt has arisen.

When they get through with it, whatever recommendation is made — whether it is that the man be cleared or that he is not cleared — the whole matter goes on again to the President's Loyalty Board, headed by Seth Richardson, a former Assistant Attorney General under President Hoover, with a group of associates not one of whom works for the Government of the United States. [Mr. Richardson was later succeeded by Hiram Bingham, formerly a Republican Senator from Connecticut.] All of these people are private citizens who are giving their time, their effort and their devotion to the Government.

That is the right way. The wrong way is to smear everybody's reputation; to make charges on the basis that, if one is not right, you try to find another one you hope will stick; to try to destroy the confidence of people in their Foreign Office and in their Government in one of the most critical hours of this nation's history — to do all of those things, and to make it absolutely certain, as a result, that under no circumstances could you ever possibly find a spy in the whole place. It is as though you said to yourself that the best way to find a fire is to ring every fire alarm in the city; not that you know of any fire, but if you get all the apparatus out and have it wheeling around through the city, you might find one.

But I think what is going on is much madder and much more vicious than that. It reminds me more of that horrible episode in Camden, New Jersey, which happened not so long ago, when a madman came out on the street in the morning with his revolver. With no purpose and with no plan, as he walked down the street, he just shot people; one was a woman coming out of a store; a man with his wife in an automobile. That automobile happened to stop because the light turned red. The car ahead of him went on. The car behind him was not where the madman was. So the madman just walked up and shot everybody in the car, without sense, without purpose, without direction.

You remember, I am sure, that poem of Browning's called *Caliban Upon Setebos*. Caliban is talking about this horrible amoral god of his. He says that his god operates in the way that Caliban himself does on the beach. Along comes, says Caliban, a procession of crabs going down to the sea across the sand. And he says something like this: "I stand there and I let twenty go by. The twenty-first I pick up and tear off a flipper. I let three more go by. The next one I crush in order to watch it wiggle in agony on the sand," and so on. It is that degree of vicious madness which has been going on here.

Now I don't ask you for sympathy. I don't ask you for help. You are in a worse situation than I am. I and my associates are only the intended victims of this mad and vicious operation. But you, unhappily — you by reason of your calling — are participants. You are unwilling participants, disgusted participants, but, nevertheless, participants, and your position is far more serious than mine.

As I leave this filthy business, and I hope never to speak of it again, I should like to leave in your minds the words of John Donne in his "Meditations," in which he says:

"Any man's death diminishes me, because I am involved in mankind.
And therefore do not send to know for whom the bell tolls;
It tolls for thee." [30]

[30] Extemporaneous remarks to the American Society of Newspaper Editors, April 22, 1950 (*Bulletin*, XXII, pp. 711–16).

CHAPTER TEN

Korea

THE OPERATION *in Korea has been a success.*[1]

The action of the United States in Korea is certainly the most important single event which has occurred while Acheson has been Secretary of State. The original decision to resist aggression was a great and critical turning point, perhaps one of those moments where the human will really bends the course of history, and the undertaking as a whole has had its great effect on many aspects of policy, while its prosecution has required a complex balancing of many major factors. We have already noted that the resort to open aggression in Korea greatly stimulated the effort to construct a common defense in Europe, that it produced a major modification of the German policy of the United States, and that it sharpened the division between the Soviet and the non-Soviet world. No American needs to be told that in this country it produced the first major effort at rearmament since the demobilization after V-J Day. Yet all these are in a sense collateral effects, vitally important though they are. In this chapter we must concern ourselves with the more immediate problems and policies that grew out of the attack and defense in Korea. And for this purpose we can divide the story into two phases. The first runs from June to October, 1950, and is the phase of collective action against North Korea; the second is from October to July, 1951, and is the phase of Chinese intervention, limited response, and truce negotiations. In considering these two phases it is important to repeat an earlier reminder; we are working with and around the statements and actions

[1] Opening statement to the Senate Committee Hearings investigating the relief of General MacArthur, June 1, 1951 (Hearings, *Military Situation in the Far East*, Senate, Committee on Foreign Relations and Committee on Armed Services, 82d Congress, 1st Session, p. 1716, and *Bulletin*, XXIV, p. 924).

of the Secretary of State, and this method is necessarily incomplete; the reader must constantly bear in mind that these statements and actions are made by a man who is only one member, however important, of President Truman's Administration. In dealing with a set of events largely military in nature, this warning obviously increases in importance.

1. June to October

Korea has become the symbol of resistance against aggression.[2]

At four o'clock in the morning of June 25, 1950, Korean time, the armed forces of the Soviet satellite government in North Korea began a full-scale armed attack across the 38th parallel of north latitude, with the object of destroying the government of the Republic of Korea. Thus for the first time Soviet pressure against the free world took the form of open aggression. At four o'clock in the Korean morning it is two o'clock in the preceding afternoon in Washington and New York. Twenty-four hours later, at 2 P.M., June 25, local time, the Security Council of the United Nations met at American call to take action. The delegate of the Soviet Union, together with his power of veto, was absent — in disdainful boycott of an organization which refused to recognize the Communist régime of China. The American government acted; the Security Council acted, and in a day or two it was plain that a major effort to repel aggression was under way. It was a busy time, and Acheson himself described it dramatically a few days later:

On Saturday afternoon [June 24] — it was just before daybreak of Sunday morning in Korea — without warning and without provocation, Communist forces of the North launched a coordinated full-scale assault on the Republic of Korea. After heavy artillery fire, Communist infantry began crossing the 38th Parallel at three points, while amphibious forces were landing at several points on the east coast, some twenty miles to the south.

First reports to reach the capital at Seoul, thirty miles below the 38th Parallel, were fragmentary and confused. There had been small border forays on many previous occasions, and the magnitude of this attack was not immediately clear.

[2] Address to the General Assembly of the United Nations, September 20, 1950 (*Bulletin* XXIII, p. 528).

Our Ambassador at Seoul, John Muccio, immediately got in touch with Korean Army Headquarters, through our Military Advisory Group, and as soon as it became evident that this was more than another border incident, he cabled the State Department.

Ambassador Muccio's cable reached the State Department code room at 9.26 Saturday night, having crossed an inquiry the Department had sent to him a few minutes before, based on the first press flash on the action.

Within a matter of minutes, the message was decoded and the Department was alerted for action.

By 10.30, our Assistant Secretary for Far Eastern Affairs, Dean Rusk, and the Secretary of the Army, Frank Pace, were conferring at the Department.

By 11 P.M. Secretary Pace had alerted the Department of Defense; a full operating staff was on duty at our Bureau of Far Eastern Affairs; and I had discussed the situation by phone with the President.

Action developed along two fronts in the State Department during the night.

One group of Department officers worked through the night preparing for a meeting of the Security Council which we had immediately requested. The United Nations had established the Republic of Korea and had, since early 1948, maintained a Commission in Korea. We therefore felt a primary responsibility to bring this matter to the immediate attention of the United Nations.

By Sunday afternoon [June 25], within twenty hours of the time the first official word of this invasion was received here, the Security Council had taken its first action. Representatives of ten member nations of the Security Council had been assembled from their Sunday places of rest — the eleventh was the representative of the Soviet Union, who stayed away. After hearing the report of the United Nations Commission concerning the unprovoked act of aggression, the Security Council passed a resolution which called for an immediate end to the fighting and for the assistance of all members in restoring the peace. All actions taken by the United States to restore the peace in Korea have been under the aegis of the United Nations.

Another group of Department officers, meanwhile, were working with their colleagues in the Defense Department, consulting on measures to be taken within the framework of existing policy and plans, and the emergency orders of the President.

The President flew to Washington [from a weekend visit to his home in Independence, Missouri]. By the time he had arrived at 7.20 Sunday evening, completed staff work and recommendations had been prepared and were laid before him. The Departments of State and Defense had worked as one department, with complete agreement and coordination of effort.

During Sunday night and early Monday morning, actions flowing from the conference with the President were set in motion. General MacArthur was authorized to respond at once to urgent appeals from the Government of Korea for additional supplies of ammunition and, in a matter of hours, was flying into Korea loaded transport planes with fighter protection to assure their safe arrival. At about the same time, the Seventh Fleet with all men aboard was steaming north out of Subic Bay, to be on hand in case of need.

It became possible on Monday to get a clearer picture of the military situation, by sifting the fragmentary and sometimes conflicting reports we had been receiving from many different sources.

From the size and speed of the Communist attack, it was evident that it was a premeditated action; that it had been carefully plotted for many weeks before. The initial thrust, supported by planes and tanks, had clearly caught the Korean Government troops by surprise. Although the defending forces rallied and launched several small counteractions, it did not appear that they were in a position to bar the tank-and-plane-supported Communist thrust down the corridor to the capital city.

By Monday night, in the light of this situation, recommendations were prepared by the President's civil and military advisers on the course of action to be taken. In preparing these recommendations, it was clear to all concerned that this act of aggression had brought in issue the authority and indeed the continued existence of the United Nations, and the security of the nations of the free world, including the United States and its forces in the Pacific. These recommendations were prepared with the sober realization of the issues involved, and with the full agreement of all the President's advisers.

As in many other situations which have arisen in the years in which I have served as Under Secretary and Secretary, the President was faced with difficult decisions which had to be made quickly. And as in the previous cases, the President assumed the responsibility, made the decisions, and has given leadership and direction to the entire action of the Government of the United States.

Consultations with Congressional leaders on Tuesday morning demonstrated a complete unity in understanding the problem and the course of action which needed to be taken.

At Tuesday noon, the President announced the actions which this Government would take to support the United Nations and uphold a rule of law in the Pacific area.

In the interval between the meetings of the Security Council on Sunday and again on Tuesday the United Nations Commission on Korea had confirmed the fact that the Communist authorities in North Korea had ignored the cease-fire order and defied the authority of the United Nations. Therefore, the Security Council recommended at its meeting Tuesday night that member nations give aid to the Republic of Korea, and help to restore the peace and security to the area.

Four days after the fighting began, the fall of Seoul was confirmed, but American air and sea support for Korean Government troops was beginning to make itself felt, and peace-loving nations the world over were able to hope that this act of brutal, unprovoked, and naked aggression would not be allowed to succeed.[3]

On the day after this speech, June 30, the President announced that in addition to air and sea forces, General MacArthur had been authorized to use "certain supporting ground units." The battle was fully engaged.

The considerations that moved the American government in these great decisions cannot be fully known at this stage in history, but the basic elements of their thought are fairly plain. They are three. First was the fact that the Republic of Korea was in a special sense a responsibility of both the United States and the United Nations. The background of this responsibility was clearly discussed by Acheson in the same speech of June 29:

Since the nineteenth century, American missionaries, doctors, and educators have been especially active in Korea, so that through the years of Japanese occupation, which began in the first decade of this century, the Korean people came to regard the United States as a symbol of the freedom and independence to which they aspired.

In the Cairo Declaration of December 1943, the United States, the

[3] Address to the American Newspaper Guild, June 29, 1950 (*Bulletin*, XXIII, p. 43).

United Kingdom, and China pledged their determination that Korea would become free and independent. This pledge was reaffirmed in the Potsdam Declaration of July 26, 1945, and was subscribed to by the Soviet Union when it entered the war against Japan 13 days later.

The defeat of Japan made it possible for Korea to look forward to the realization of its desire for independence.

On the day following the first Japanese offer of surrender, which was made on August 10, 1945, the Secretary of War submitted to the Secretary of State a plan for the arrangements to be followed in accepting the surrender of Japanese troops in various places. To meet the immediate problem, it was proposed that the nearby Soviet troops accept the surrender of Japanese armed forces in Korea down to the 38th Parallel, and that American troops be brought up from Okinawa and the Philippines to accept the surrender of Japanese troops in the southern part of Korea. This arrangement was approved by the Joint Chiefs of Staff, the State-War-Navy Coordinating Committee, and the President, and, after it had been accepted by Generalissimo Stalin, was incorporated in the first General Order to be issued by General MacArthur as Supreme Commander for the Allied Powers on September 2, 1945.

Soviet troops had occupied the northern part of Korea on August 12. The Soviet desire and intention to put troops into Korea had been made evident at the Potsdam discussions, one month before. On September 8 American troops had been landed to accept the surrender of the Japanese in the southern part of Korea, and we began efforts to negotiate with the Soviet Union for the unification and independence of the country.

We soon found that the Soviet Union considered the 38th parallel not as a line drawn on a map for the sake of administrative convenience, but as a wall around their preserve.

At the Moscow meeting of Foreign Ministers in December, 1945, a joint commission for the unity and independence of Korea was agreed to between the Soviet Union and ourselves, but we found that every effort to give effect to this agreement and previous agreements was blocked by Soviet intransigence.

The United States was unwilling to permit this situation to delay further realization of Korean independence.

This Government therefore laid the question of Korean independence before the United Nations. The General Assembly of the United Nations, in November, 1947, called for an election in Korea, under the observation of a United Nations Commission, to choose a representative national assembly for the purpose of drafting a democratic constitution and establishing a national government.

The Soviet Union refused to allow the United Nations Commission to enter its zone. Consequently, the right of the Korean people to participate in a free election to establish a free government was confined to southern Korea. The election was held there, and the Government of the Republic of Korea was established on August 15, 1948.

It has been the aim of the United States to provide the people of the Republic of Korea with sufficient assistance and support to enable them to progress through their own efforts toward freedom and independence. The transfer of functions from the United States Army Military Government to Korean agencies was carried out progressively from the moment of the establishment of the Republic. The United States has continued to give assistance and support to the Republic, both within the framework of the United Nations and directly. We have trained and equipped Korean defense forces, we have extended economic aid and technical advice, fostered exchange of students and professors, and, in general, done everything possible to help the people of Korea in establishing a democratic political and economic structure responsive to their needs.

The Government of the Republic of Korea was accepted by the United Nations in December, 1948, as the validly elected, lawful Government of the area in which elections were permitted — and the only such Government in Korea. The General Assembly established a reconstituted commission to continue to work for unification and a representative government for the entire country.

The United States recognized the new government on January 1, 1949. Many other members of the United Nations have since done the same. Membership of the Republic of Korea in the United Nations had been blocked by the Soviet veto.

Meanwhile, the 38th Parallel had become a part of the Iron Curtain. Behind that Curtain, the Soviet Union established a Communist régime. . . . This régime has lived, as it was created, in complete defiance of the United Nations.[4]

Thus the U.S. and the UN had both played major parts in the birth of the Korean Republic; clearly if it were to be abandoned without a struggle,

[4] Same source, pp. 43-44.

both would stand convicted of weakness; both would lose standing, and neither would have much chance of influencing the decisions and actions of other nations faced with the threat of similar Communist attack.

Yet the specific responsibility posed by the history of Korea was only a reinforcement to a second and perhaps still more significant aspect of the matter. This was not merely an action against the interest of the U.S. and the UN. It was an act of outright military aggression. If South Korea had been undermined by internal subversion; if the government had been less attractive to the Korean people than Communist promises; if the government itself had given way to Soviet pressure or had wilted under Soviet blandishments — in any of these cases South Korea might have passed gradually under Communist domination, and both the United States and the United Nations, especially the former, would have lost prestige; both of them would have been weakened in further efforts to assist in the establishment of free and independent governments. But the challenge would have been a very different one, simply another round in a contest short of armed force. This was different; this was *aggression*.

To both the United States and the United Nations the word aggression is more than an abstraction.[5]

Korea was a special responsibility; Korea was a victim of aggression. These were two persuasive elements in the great decision. But in themselves they were insufficient. There was a third consideration: the United States and the United Nations, more by accident than by foresight, were in a position to act; there was force available to maintain the right. In nearby Japan was a large proportion of the operating armed forces of the United States; these forces were less completely battle-ready, it turned out, than they might have been, but nevertheless they were able to fight.

In addition to these three elements, which may be discerned as a part of the thought that led to the decision to resist in Korea, we may note one further element which was *not* present, and it is well to clarify this point at the start, for a tendency to forget or ignore it clouded much of the later discussion. The issue was not joined in Korea on military or strategic grounds. Although all the witnesses who later testified before the Russell Committee were in agreement that the military chiefs supported the decision, none of them suggested that this support had been based on purely military

[5] I use the word here to mean an armed attack across a recognized boundary; this is its usual meaning, though the reader may recall that Acheson has also used it more generally, to apply to all the techniques of Soviet Imperialism. See Chapter Two.

considerations. Korea was a place where they could fight if it seemed right;
it was not the place they would have chosen. This distinction is of major
importance; it means that right from the beginning this was a use of military force to support a basically political decision, not the other way around.
And it is therefore not surprising that it was Acheson who took the lead, as
witnesses later agreed, in urging the decision. And in the following passage
most of the considerations we have been examining were rolled into a few
sentences; once again it is characteristic of the man that in summarizing
the purpose he also draws the moral of the event.

> The great single fact which stands out from this summary history is
> that a peaceful people, ruled by a sovereign independent government of
> their own choosing, brought into being by the United Nations, and
> recognized by the great majority of the free nations of the world, was
> attacked in a cynical and brutal act of aggression.
>
> We are confronted with a direct challenge to the United Nations.
> Whether this organization, which embodies our hopes for an inter-
> national order based on peace with justice and freedom, can survive this
> test will depend upon the vigor with which it answers the challenge
> and the support which it receives from free nations. . . .
>
> The action of this Government in Korea is taken in support of the
> authority of the United Nations. It is taken to restore peace and secu-
> rity to the Pacific area.
>
> It is taken in the conviction that peace and security cannot be ob-
> tained by sacrificing the independence of nations to aggression. . . .
>
> It is now clear to all — if indeed it was not clear before — that free
> nations must be united, they must be determined, and they must be
> strong, if they are to preserve their freedom and maintain a righteous
> peace. There is no other way.[6]

The following year was to show all too plainly the trials and complexities
of the undertaking so bravely and unanimously faced in the last days of
June. As we examine these trials, it may be well to bear in mind that there
were others which the free world was spared. A year later, in summarizing
the results of the resistance in Korea, Acheson found a number of positive
accomplishments and gains to set against the tragic toll of casualties and the
great financial cost; one of the greatest of these accomplishments was in hand
the moment the first decision was taken:

[6] Address to the American Newspaper Guild, June 29, 1950 (*Bulletin*, XXIII, p. 43).

The alluring prospect for the Communist conspiracy in June, 1950 — the prospect of a quick and easy success which would not only win Korea for the Kremlin but shake the free nations of Asia and paralyze the defense of Europe — all this has evaporated.[7]

Once the great decision had been made, the focus of attention necessarily turned to the battlefield in Korea. The bet had been made, but the battle would be the pay-off. As Acheson later put it in a broadcast to the American armed forces, "the entire world was electrified" by the original decision to stand and deliver, but "I want you to know that all who participated in making that decision fully realize that it would have been meaningless if you had not been able to rush into the breach." And for that reason, "Here at home, you hold first place in our hearts. Your courage and your heroism have won the admiration of the free world." [8]

But while the fighting proceeded, from the first gallant delaying retreat, to the battle of the Pusan perimeter, and in September to the brilliant stroke by General MacArthur at Inchon, the political and diplomatic agencies of the government were not inactive. One large set of activities was the effort to keep the war localized, and in particular to prevent the entrance of Red China. This effort, and its failure, will require further attention later. Chronologically — and perhaps logically too — it is preceded by two other major undertakings: the successful move to add to the peace-keeping machinery of the United Nations, and a reshaping of American policy for Pacific security.

2. Collective and Regional Security

The world waits to see whether we can build on the start we have made.[9]

In facing and opposing by force the North Korean aggression of June, the United Nations, with American leadership, had struck a great blow for the concept of collective security. The first satisfaction of the free world arose in large part from a sort of pleased surprise at its own nerve and courage. It

[7] Opening statement to the Senate Committee investigating the relief of General MacArthur, June 1, 1951 (*Hearings*, p. 1717, and *Bulletin*, XXIV, p. 924).
[8] Statement recorded for broadcast to the U.S. Armed Forces on United Nations Day, October 24, 1950 (Department Press Release No. 1086, 1950).
[9] Address to the General Assembly of the United Nations, September 20, 1950 (*Bulletin*, XXIII, p. 524).

had avoided the feeling of helpless shame which is associated with the name of Munich, and even in the darker days of the first withdrawal there was a recognition that defeat would be less painful than inaction would have been. And as the tide turned there was no limit to men's hopes and to their satisfaction. This seemed a magnificent vindication and reinforcement of the concept of collective security.

Sober second thought was not less hopeful, perhaps, but it was better aware of the fact that a single success would not end the threat of aggression. As Acheson put it afterward, "Collective security is not something which is established once and for all by some dramatic gesture." It was, he continued, "like a bank account . . . kept alive by the resources which are put into it. In Korea the Russians presented a check which was drawn on the bank account of collective security. The Russians thought the check would bounce. They thought it was a bad check. But to their great surprise, the teller paid it. The important thing was that the check was paid, [but] the importance will be nothing if the next check is not paid and if the bank account is not kept strong and sufficient to cover all checks which are drawn upon it." [10] So while their troops were meeting the Soviet draft on Korea, the political leaders of the United Nations, and particularly those of the United States were considering their account. Was it ready for any new charges, and if not, what could be done about it?

The larger part of the answer to this question, as Acheson has repeatedly pointed out, was to be found in the straightforward but greatly demanding task of building strength — in this instance military strength. And of course the first reflex of the free world after Korea was a redoubling of military efforts. Without strength, no policy or unity or courage could do the job.

Yet strength alone was not enough. What gave the defense in Korea its larger meaning was the fact that it was under the flag of the United Nations; and what gave it a chance of success was the accident of present and available forces. Neither of these great advantages was foreordained; both were of enormous value, and it was necessary for statesmen to consider whether they could always count on such luck. A quick and easy look was enough to show that as things stood in the summer of 1950 they could not. The effectiveness of the United Nations had been dependent on the absence of the Russian delegate to the Security Council during the critical days of decision; and the availability of force had been the result of the fact that

[10] Transcript of remarks made to a group of magazine and book publishers, June 29, 1951 (*Bulletin*, XXV, p. 125).

Korea is near Japan. When the Russian delegate returned to the Council in August, it was evident at once that he had not come to help, and when the Red Chinese expanded their influence into Tibet later in the year, it was evident that where there was no force there could not be resistance; and these were not new lessons. What could be done to make the United Nations an effective instrument, in spite of the Russian veto? What could be done to increase the chance that there would be force at hand to deal with future acts of aggression? These questions were given particular weight and urgency by the surge of satisfaction that came with successful resistance to the North Koreans. It was a good time for new departures.

On September 20 Acheson presented, for the United States, a far-reaching set of recommendations "designed to increase the effectiveness of United Nations action against aggression." The recommendations as he presented them were promptly dubbed the "Acheson Plan," and when the General Assembly finally passed its "Uniting for Peace" Resolution in November, it was generally recognized that the Acheson Plan had been adopted. The name was flattering, but in reality it was the American Plan that had been adopted, and the burden of the argument in the General Assembly had been born by John Foster Dulles, Republican adviser to the Secretary of State.

In essence, the "Uniting for Peace" Resolution contains four provisions. First, and most important, it provides that if the Security Council should be prevented by the veto from taking action to maintain international peace and security, the General Assembly shall consider the matter and make recommendations to members for collective measures, including force if necessary. Since the General Assembly acts by a two-thirds vote and is not subject to the veto, this provision in effect enables the United Nations to take the lead in maintaining collective security in spite of Soviet opposition. This part of the resolution, then, deals with the probability that the Soviet Union will not again allow the Security Council to take a major step while the Russian delegate sulks in his tent. The Security Council may be blocked by Soviet veto, but the issue can now be brought to a decision in the General Assembly. This is certainly the most important development in the application of the Charter since it was signed at San Francisco in 1945.[11] For although the

[11] It is also probably the least known of major developments in foreign policy since Acheson became Secretary of State. This is the one aspect of the resolution which has troubled this student. The complex legal arguments against the resolution, though important, are not controlling, in my view, but it does seem unfortunate that this major development of the Charter's implications could not have had public debate and acceptance, by the American people, at least partly commensurate with the discussion given the Charter itself in

General Assembly is limited to the power of recommendation, the thrust of this new provision is to invest these recommendations with the same moral authority that attached to the Security Council's initial action in the case of Korea, and it follows that just as the United States has led the way in circumventing the Soviet veto, *it has weakened its own veto*; to the degree that this clause of the "Uniting for Peace" Resolution becomes effective, the basic authority of the United Nations in organizing collective action against aggression now rests with any two-thirds of its members. This is a measure of the degree to which the United States Government is prepared to entrust itself to the weight of the indefinable but important force called world opinion.

A second part of the resolution established a permanent Peace Observation Commission with power, in Acheson's words, "to provide immediate and independent observation and reporting from any area in which international conflict threatens, upon the invitation or with the consent of the state visited." [12] In effect, this provision aims to ensure on all future occasions the kind of independent reporting which the United Nations got in the Korean case from its Commission which happened to be on the spot. Since in cases of aggression impartial on-the-spot evidence is indispensable to a conscientious decision, the Peace Observation Commission is a major addition to the effectiveness of the United Nations.

The remaining two provisions of the resolution are less immediately effective and will certainly require much time before they begin to have active meaning. They set up a Collective Measures Committee to study and report on the whole problem of action under the United Nations in behalf of collective security, and invite members of the organization to set aside elements within their own forces which can be used promptly at the call of the Council or the General Assembly. These two resolutions clearly aim toward the establishment of a system under which *any* act of aggression would find the United Nations able to call on existing force as quickly as geography let it do in Korea; at the same time they aim to fill the gap left

1945. It is entirely true that the resolution had bi-partisan support, and was the outgrowth of considerable discussion among interested and informed circles; there are also the Vandenberg Resolution and other manifestations of Congressional backing. It remains a fact that a great change was very little noticed, and the new departure still lacks the support of an explicit decision in the public arena. Time may repair this weakness, and we must hope that it will. But it is also possible that a check presented against this imperfectly understood commitment might bounce.

[12] *Bulletin*, XXIII, p. 525.

by Soviet obstruction of all efforts to establish the collective force originally contemplated in the Charter. It was not too soon to begin this task, but 1951 has been a year in which most of the peace-loving members of the United Nations have been busier building and using their armed forces than in earmarking them against future contingencies.[13]

The Acheson Plan is not a year old at this writing, and it is clearly too soon to estimate its long-range meaning. There is, however, one point which may be made about it, for its significance as to the mind and purpose of the man who launched the plan. Until the Korean episode Acheson had been distinctly cool toward large-scale schemes for remaking the United Nations. More than that, he had been inclined to emphasize the limitations of the UN rather more than many of its ardent supporters liked. The reader may recall that in 1946 he had remarked that "the ass that went to Mecca remained an ass, and a policy has little added to it by its place of utterance."[14] In 1947 he was not greatly impressed by public clamor to make at least a bow to the UN in the Greek-Turkish program. In 1949 his first great task was to complete the negotiations for the North Atlantic Treaty, a regional undertaking which did not command enthusiasm among those who thought of the UN as the one great hope. Yet here in 1950 we find him taking the lead in a most striking development, one based on the highest assessment of the value of the United Nations, one closely related to plans advanced earlier by such men as Hamilton Fish Armstrong, and coolly received in the Department of State. Are we to say that Acheson learned from experience, or that changing circumstances changed his opportunities?[15] Perhaps we may answer a little of both; in any event both possibilities lead to a single conclusion — that this man, so much abused as a theorist, is in fact of an intensely practical disposition.

At all events, it seems clear that at least since the beginning of the Korean affair, Acheson has placed a very high value on the United Nations as an institution. While he freely admits, as all its honest friends must, that it has not done all that optimists hoped for, he does not count that as a ground

[13] The machinery of the Collective Measures Committee was, however, used to some effect in dealing with the Chinese intervention in Korea.

[14] See page 17 above.

[15] This latter view is supported by the fact that during the previous winter Deputy Under Secretary Rusk and Assistant Secretary Hickerson had indicated in Senate hearings that the Department considered that the Charter left room for much addition to the powers of the General Assembly in dealing with aggression. Perhaps the Acheson Plan was ready and waiting when the Korean episode gave it life and support among other members.

for throwing it out or starting a new organization. And since this is our one chance to express his general views of the UN, we may end this section with two representative quotations. The first is a set statement to the General Assembly, in September, 1950.

It is the firm belief of the people and the Government of the United States that the United Nations will play an increasingly important role in the world during the period ahead as we try to move safely through the present tensions.

I have already stressed the importance we attach to the United Nations as the framework of an effective system of collective security. The steps we take to strengthen our collective security are not only essential to the survival of the United Nations, but will contribute positively toward its development. The close ties of a common defense are developing an added cohesion among regional groups. This is a significant step toward a closer relationship among nations and is part of the process of growth by which we are moving toward a larger sense of community under the United Nations.

The United States also attaches importance to the universal character of the United Nations, which enables it to serve as a point of contact between the Soviet Union and the rest of the world during this period of tension.

As our efforts to strengthen the collective security system become more and more effective, and as tensions begin to ease, we believe that the United Nations will be increasingly important as a means of facilitating and encouraging productive negotiation.[16]

The second passage is less formal and requires a brief introduction. Acheson is talking here about the great danger that the United States would run if it tried to dictate to its friends and allies. "If we take that attitude, then we are creating a relationship indistinguishable from that which exists between the Soviet Union and countries associated with it." And more than that, the narrow view is self-destructive. "Great Empires have risen in this world and have collapsed because they took too narrow a view." What is needed is some means to institutionalize a sense of responsibility to "interests broader than our own," and he continued:

[16] Address to the United Nations General Assembly, September 20, 1950 (*Bulletin*, XXIII, pp. 525–26).

The means are at hand, have been used, and must continue to be used. The means lies in the United Nations. There is much talk these days that the United Nations has proved itself ineffective — it does not do this, it does not do that, we must scrap it in favor of some other kind of coercive machinery. I do not agree with any of those views.

I don't think anyone is more conscious than I am, unless it be General Bradley, of the difficulties of working within a coalition as large as the group in the United Nations who are associated together in Korea. There are a thousand problems in working with so many nations, considering their points of view, and modifying your own so that you may maintain a true friend. But I assure you that it is worth it a million times. Whatever loss there is in efficiency of operation is gained a million times by the strength which comes from the group's believing that the leader is paying attention to other people's points of view. We should be forever grateful to the United Nations for furnishing a forum where the United States of America, to maintain its leadership, must enter and must explain itself to the rest of the world, and do so in terms which are so persuasive that countries will be convinced, do so under circumstances where the United States and its representatives listen to the representative of the smallest country in the world who has a point of view which he wishes to express, do so under circumstances where we make every effort to harmonize the views, adjust views, and may not force views down other people's throats. If we do that, then I believe the United States will lead into a new course in which the free nations will continue to be free nations, freely associated, freely, willingly, and eagerly accepting leadership which they believe considers their interests as deeply as it does its own.[17]

The effort to strengthen the United Nations was paralleled, in 1950 and 1951, by a new urgency in constructing a workable pattern of defense in the Pacific area; this effort centered around the negotiation of a peace treaty with Japan. Work toward a peace treaty had begun before the attack in Korea, but the effort was greatly accelerated and much affected in direction by that attack. For Communist aggression made it plain that the United States could no longer afford to wait for agreement with Reds, whether in Moscow or Peiping.

[17] Stenographic transcript of remarks to a group of magazine and book publishers, June 29, 1951 (*Bulletin*, XXV, p. 128).

Partly because there was in this whole area no strong disagreement on the American interest, and partly because of remarkably skillful labors by John Foster Dulles, the gradual emergence of a draft of the peace treaty and matching security arrangements was accomplished with almost no complaint and confusion.   Both the absence of major disagreement and the presence of Mr. Dulles as the principal American negotiator make it appropriate that in this record these great developments should be treated very briefly.   So with the warning that this brevity is not a measure of their importance, we may content ourselves with the following statement by Acheson, made in April, 1951, when the pattern of Mr. Dulles' negotiations had begun to emerge clearly:

We are moving rapidly ahead to make a prompt and enduring peace with the Japanese and to join with them as well as with other nations in the Pacific in creating the essentials of security in that area.

We believe that, on these matters, we shall find a large, if not a complete, range of agreement and a minimum of divergence on basic points of view. . . .

The peace should be, as Mr. Dulles said, "a peace of reconciliation."

The peace should restore Japan as an equal in the world community.

The peace should afford Japan a chance to earn her own way in the world and to become self-sustaining.

The peace should encourage close cultural relations between Japan and the West.

The peace should enable Japan to obtain a reasonable degree of security.

We want this kind of peace because the great energy and abilities of the Japanese people can make a major contribution to the peace and well-being not only of the Pacific but of the entire world.   We know that Japan can make this contribution only as a full and free member of the family of nations.   We know that the Japanese themselves are anxious to assume their proper international role; that they are in a mood to reject militarism in all its aspects and to seek fellowship with peace-loving nations through collective security and the cooperative activity of the United Nations.

So far as our own country is concerned, these principles of policy have been worked out under the direction and with the approval of the

President. They have been fully discussed by Mr. Dulles with the Japanese and with other governments who are as ready as we to make an early peace. They reflect the views of General MacArthur and have had his full support. They have had detailed consideration in both Senate and House Committees and with the leadership of both of our political parties. . . .

Another important forward step in the great constructive task of building security in the Pacific . . . has to do with security arrangements which we already have or which we expect to have with Japan, the Philippines, Australia, and with New Zealand.

The United States has been chiefly responsible for the security of Japan since the autumn of 1945, by reason of our role as the principal occupying power. Neither we nor the Japanese desire that a vacuum of power should suddenly be created by a peace settlement with an exposed and unarmed Japan, which would tempt the appetites and ambitions of any with aggressive designs. So it is anticipated that the United States and Japan will by mutual agreement arrange for the continued security of that country, whose safety is vital to both of us.

As for the Philippines, no one can be under the slightest misapprehension about our concern for the security of that nation. . . . The United States would not tolerate any aggression against the Philippines from any quarter. . . .

In the case of Australia and New Zealand, we recall with regard and affection our association in World War II. Without formal agreements, it has been clear that our fates have been joined. Discussion of a Japanese peace settlement has raised the desirability of saying more formally what had become an underlying fact. Hence our desire to proceed with more specific plans of this sort. . . .

[These plans] are not a final answer to the organization of security in the Pacific. They will not interfere in any way with such broader agreements as the nations in that area may wish to develop — agreements which we have said would receive the sympathetic interest of the United States.[18]

The Japanese Peace Treaty was signed at San Francisco on September 8, 1951, and the related security treaties were signed shortly before. These

[18] Address to the Women's National Press Club, April 18, 1951 (*Bulletin*, XXIV, pp. 684–85).

signings were the formal seal on diplomatic negotiations and agreements reached in preceding months, and as such they would ordinarily have had no great importance. But the Russians and the invention of television combined to make the San Francisco ceremonies unexpectedly significant. Not only did the meeting become an occasion for a genuine reinforcement of the solidarity of the non-Stalinist world, but it also served to give an extraordinary boost to Acheson's prestige among his countrymen.

It had originally been hoped that as the Soviet Union had refused to participate constructively in the negotiation of the Japanese Treaty, it would boycott the signing ceremonies. When Moscow announced its intention to attend, there was some dismay in Western capitals, for many students and officials feared that the meeting might be tied in bowknots by Gromyko and his seconds from satellite delegations. It turned out that these fears were unfounded, and Gromyko's attempts to make trouble had two useful results. On the one hand, they strengthened the forces opposing him by providing one more demonstration of the basic difference between Soviet and Western diplomacy, and on the other, they showed an enormous American audience, watching on television, that the Secretary of State was fully capable of giving distinguished, firm, and persuasive leadership to the majority in frustrating Soviet attempts to disrupt the proceedings. It is strange, in a way, that this performance should have been the occasion for an outburst of praise, even from old opponents; nothing that Acheson did at San Francisco compared in difficulty or distinction with earlier episodes in which he had matched wits with Soviet opponents, for after all he was called on to do nothing more than carry out a procedure supported by a large majority. Any well-informed student could have predicted with precision that as Chairman at San Francisco he would be all that he was, and Senators who praised him were really less complimentary than they meant to be, for he was only doing his obvious duty. But at least they praised him, and it seems a fair guess that this praise and other applause arose in part from the fact that this time millions of Americans saw him for themselves, and not through other men's distortions.

3. Chinese Intervention

This is a fresh and unprovoked aggressive act, even more immoral than the first.[19]

In mid-October, 1950, it appeared at least possible that the Korean undertaking was about to result in a smashing and complete victory for the forces of the United Nations. The original objective of the Security Council had been reached — the North Korean armies were in full and broken retreat from South Korea. The United Nations had proved itself in action, and the Acheson Plan was proceeding to adoption, so that the UN might be able to carry on in the tradition so well begun. More than this, the General Assembly had authorized, on October 7, the use of UN forces north of the 38th Parallel. In accordance with this resolution General MacArthur's army had crossed the parallel, and it was apparent that if the campaign continued as it was going, its successful completion would not be long delayed. With this prospect in mind, Acheson had made a stirring plea, on September 20, for a rapid and generous United Nations program of reconstruction so that just as Korea had become "the symbol of resistance to aggression," it might also become "the vibrant symbol of the renewal of life."

At this stage the critical question, of course, was whether Red China would intervene. Every effort had been made, from the first moment, to make it plain to the Peiping régime that the action in Korea was in no sense whatever directed against China. Over and over again the Secretary of State and the President emphasized in press conferences and public statements that the United States had no aggressive intentions in China, and that its aim in Korea was purely and simply to repel aggression and help the Koreans to be free, independent, and united. At the same time it had been made plain that the United States would consider it an act of aggression for anyone to join with the North Korean Communists. Yet nothing the American Government said could stem the rising tide of vitriolic denunciation coming from Peiping. At the end of September the Red foreign minister, Chou En-lai, proclaimed that "The United States Government, because of its frenzied and ruthless imperialistic aggression has been proved the most dangerous

[19] Address to the National Council of Churches of Christ in the U.S., November 29, 1950 (*Bulletin*, XXIII, p. 963).

enemy of the People's Republic of China," and he warned that the Chinese would not "supinely tolerate seeing their neighbors being savagely invaded by imperialists."

A particular grievance of the Red Chinese was the change of American policy toward Formosa which occurred at once when the North Koreans attacked in June. The reader will recall that in his statement of the previous January 5 Acheson had warned that "an attack on American forces" would require freedom of action to ensure their security. The attack in Korea did not fall precisely within this description, but it was a Communist attack which American forces were meeting under the flag of the United Nations — an even more persuasive and justified cause for security measures. And so one of the first decisions recommended to the President in the days after June 25 was the neutralization of Formosa by the use of the United States Seventh Fleet. As Acheson described the action, "The President neutralized it by saying that the Seventh Fleet would prevent any attack upon Formosa, and Formosa should not make any attack upon the mainland. There was a fair proposition, and it was meant to work both ways — and it does work both ways." [20]

Moreover, this decision to prevent a settlement by force in Formosa was not intended to foreclose the political future of the island. On that point the United States was prepared to seek a decision in the United Nations. This was, of course, a different position from that taken the previous January, and it implied some modification of the Declaration of Cairo, but as Acheson remarked on this point, the Cairo Declaration "also declares, and this is too often forgotten in these discussions, that Korea should be free and independent . . . both the Chinese and the Russians forget about the Korean part of the Declaration." [21] The political settlement was an open matter; meanwhile the island "must be neutralized in order to protect . . . the left flank of the whole United Nations position." [22]

None of these views was attractive to the Chinese Communists, and a demand for the withdrawal of American force from around Formosa was added to the violent insistence upon admission of Red China to the United Nations.

[20] A television interview on September 10, 1950 (*Bulletin*, XXIII, p. 460). This decision, incidentally, was based on the combined recommendation of the President's advisers, and not on the acceptance of a military recommendation over Acheson's objection (Hearings, *Military Situation in the Far East*, Senate, Committee on Foreign Relations and Committee on Armed Services, 82d Congress, 1st Session, p. 2055).

[21] A television interview on September 10, 1950 (*Bulletin*, XXIII, p. 463).

[22] Same source, p. 463.

Meanwhile nothing in the behavior of the Peiping régime made it more appropriate to extend diplomatic recognition or admission to the UN than it had been before June 25.

But would the Chinese intervene in Korea? The general opinion of the United States Government was that they would not. Acheson's reasoning was stated in the same interview from which we have been quoting:

> I should think it would be sheer madness on the part of the Chinese Communists to do that, and I see no advantage to them in doing it. . . .
>
> The great part of China to the north, which is made up of Sinkiang, Outer Mongolia, and Manchuria, is Chinese at the present moment only nominally. That is where a great cloud from the north, Russian penetration, is operating and it is quite obvious that the plan is to absorb those northern areas of China under Soviet domination.
>
> Now, I give the people of Peiping credit for being intelligent enough to see what is happening to them. Why they should want to further their own dismemberment and destruction by getting at cross purposes with all the free nations of the world who are inherently their friends and have always been friends of the Chinese as against this imperialism coming down from the Soviet Union I cannot see. And since there is nothing in it for them, I don't see why they should yield to what is undoubtedly pressure from the Communist movement to get into this Korean row.[23]

This stand was of course at least partly intended to persuade Peiping not to intervene, but it also indicates Acheson's own estimate of the situation in September. He has never denied that until Chinese intervention actually began, in November, it was considered unlikely by the Department of State. The same estimate was shared in the Pentagon and in General MacArthur's headquarters in Tokyo, and General MacArthur further believed that his command was fully able to control any possible Chinese attack. At Wake Island in October he reported to Mr. Truman that "only 50,000 to 60,000 could be gotten across the Yalu River," and that "if the Chinese tried to get down to Pyongyang, there would be the greatest slaughter." Acheson's remark before the Russell Committee that "that turned out to be an error" must be called an understatement, but the general error was shared by all

[23] Same source, p. 463.

echelons, and when Senator Saltonstall commented, "They really fooled us when it comes right down to it, didn't they?" Acheson's reply was, "Yes sir." [24]

Yet it remains a question whether the United States and the United Nations could have done much differently, between June and October, even if they had estimated the danger of Chinese intervention more accurately. Certain utterances and attitudes of the United Nations commander might have been less provocative, and probably the actual intervention in force could have been rendered less painful if more careful military dispositions had been taken against that threat, but the statements and tactics of General MacArthur were surely not the heart of the matter. A larger question is raised around the decision to cross the 38th Parallel in October. Some senior officers of the State Department are reported to have opposed this decision on the ground that it would lead to Chinese intervention, and even Winston Churchill later said that he would have stopped at the neck of the peninsula north of Pyongyang, keeping clear of the sensitive Yalu River region. We unfortunately have no clear statement from Acheson on his thinking, or that of the United States Government, on this great question. It appeared in testimony before the Russell Committee that the Administration had considered, in late November, the desirability of establishing a buffer zone near the Yalu, but the proposal was still tentative when it became obsolete as a result of the great Chinese counteroffensive.

Neither do we know, from the Chinese side, that it was the crossing of the 38th Parallel or the advance to any particular point which determined the decision in Peiping; we do not even know whether it was a free decision or one largely imposed from Moscow. Nor is it clear, finally, that the United Nations should have stayed below the parallel even if they had put the chances of Chinese intervention much higher than they did. There was always a risk involved in the attempt to follow up the Inchon landing. But there was also a great hope, and the attempt was entirely justified in terms of law and right. Could the United Nations and the United States have stopped in October, merely because of threats and fears? It seems doubtful. One thing at least is certain — if Acheson or the Administration are to be criticized on this count, it must be criticism from sources entirely different from those which were soon to be found lamenting the restraint with which the second stage of the Korean contest was fought.

[24] Hearings, *Military Situation in the Far East*, Senate, Committee on Foreign Relations and Committee on Armed Services, 82d Congress, 1st Session, June 2, 1951, pp. 1832–35.

In any case, the parallel was crossed; the advance to the Yalu was attempted; the war seemed nearly over, and General MacArthur spoke of getting the soldiers back to Japan by Christmas. And then suddenly, in the space of a few short weeks, the hopes of November turned into fears and dangers such as the free world had not known since the end of World War II.

When General MacArthur reported on November 28 that "we face an entirely new war," he was not exaggerating. And while what he said was with reference particularly to the military situation, it was at once apparent that the new war raised diplomatic and political problems of the greatest complexity. It is not too much to say that the framing of policy to meet the Chinese Communist challenge of November, 1950, has been the most complex and difficult task that American statesmen have faced since the end of World War II. And I will venture the personal judgment that this task has been discharged with a remarkable combination of skill, vision, courage, and good luck. To that judgment one must at once add that nothing would have been possible without the extraordinary professional skill and devotion of the forces of the United Nations in Korea, among which the troops of the United States of America stand easily first in numbers and importance.

In order to judge both the problem and its handling we must begin with the dangers that threatened in early December. First, and perhaps most significant of all, there was the danger of general world war. The intervention of major forces of a major nation against an allied force necessarily carried this risk with it, as Mr. Truman pointed out in a nationwide address on December 1. Second, there was an evident threat of major proportions to the newly blooming concept of collective security; if the Chinese aggression should be successful, it was hard to suppose that the hopes of the Acheson Plan would ever become real. Third, the fact that the intervention came from Red China at once introduced a grave strain upon the unity of the non-Stalinist members of the United Nations, for the rights and character of that régime were already a matter of deep-seated difference between the United States and other members. Fourth, there was a serious possibility that American military strength might become dangerously tied down in Far Eastern fighting; the contest with North Korea had already engaged more troops and equipment than military planners liked — would resistance to the new aggressor impose a still heavier burden? Finally, the new contest necessarily involved an intensification of internal debate and division within the United States, for it was already evident that the opposition to the Administration had seized on Far Eastern policy as a burning issue; it was almost certain that for some men at least whatever course was taken would be wrong. Nor was this merely a partisan matter, for any course of action would involve strains and suffering of a new and testing character.

These dangers were interlocking, and to meet any one fully was to run grave danger of failing to deal with the others. To avoid a general war at all costs was obviously to run the risk of rewarding the aggressor; it would also have a devastating effect on the whole coalition of free nations. Yet if a general war should come, on any but the plainest and most persuasive demonstration that it could not be avoided, the coalition would be equally stricken. And since the view of America's partners was not the American view, it might easily happen that what seemed persuasive and plain to Americans might not be so clear to others. Yet to follow the slowest member of the coalition might be to provoke American sentiment beyond endurance. To punish the aggressor would mean fighting. How much, to what end, on what terms, short of general war? The original commitment in Korea had been for political, not strategic ends. How far could the limited strength of the free world be tied down to a contest that engaged not one regiment of Soviet Russian troops? And over all these considerations, coloring them all with feelings not the coolest statesman could avoid, there was the gnawing knowledge of casualties continuing daily, and the sinking possibility, at least at the beginning, that a military defeat might become a military disaster.

It was from a situation with these possibilities and difficulties that the United States emerged, after eight months, with no general war, with an unbroken coalition, with clear military success, without rewarding aggression, with a stronger strategic position, and without any lasting damage to its own body politic.

The first problem, as in the case of the original North Korean attack, was military. A part of the dismay and near panic in Western opinion, in December, may have been the result of fears more imaginary than real, but it was not a paper offensive that pushed the United Nations army in short order from the edge of the Yalu River back south of Seoul. Fighting with great gallantry and after the first shock with increasing effectiveness, the UN forces were able to stabilize a firm position in January and then to begin a slow northward movement. Particularly after the arrival of General Matthew Ridgway as field commander, the troops began to show that hardy professional skill and self-confidence which are the hallmarks of first-rate combat quality in troops and leaders.

While the stubborn and skillful withdrawal was proceeding, in December, the diplomacy of the United States was fully engaged in what turned out to be a two-month task — to bring the United Nations to a clearcut recognition that the Chinese Red régime was guilty of aggression. During this period the patience of the American public was considerably tried, for the fact of Chinese aggression seemed entirely plain to the American people and their leaders from the moment of the massive Chinese attack of November 27. Earlier in the month, when the first signs of Chinese intervention appeared, there had been a more cautious reaction; it seemed possible that this first intervention was limited in scope, and motivated by a concern for the security of the Manchurian frontier. But when the UN army was split and pushed back by a mass attack, there were few Americans who did not share Acheson's view, expressed on November 29:

> An act of brazen aggression has taken place in Korea, the second such act in five months. . . . This is not merely another phase of the Korean campaign. This is a fresh and unprovoked aggressive act, even more immoral than the first.[25]

And he pointed out in the same speech the background from which Americans drew this plain conclusion:

> Now, no possible shred of doubt could have existed in the minds of the Chinese Communist authorities about the intentions of the forces of the United Nations. Repeatedly, and from the very beginning of the action, it had been made clear that the sole mission of the United Nations forces was to repel the aggressors and restore to the people of Korea their independence.
>
> In behalf of the United States, President Truman declared that it is the intention of this country to localize the conflict and to withdraw its forces from Korea as soon as possible. In the Security Council, this Government was one of the sponsors of a proposed resolution which affirmed that the policy of the United Nations was to hold the Chinese

[25] Address to the National Council of Churches of Christ in the U.S., November 29, 1950 (*Bulletin*, XXIII, pp. 962–63).

frontier with Korea inviolate, and that legitimate Chinese and Korean interests in the frontier zone would be fully protected.

The peaceful nations of the world made it unmistakably clear that if the Chinese Communist intervention had a limited motivation, if it sprang from an uncertainty regarding the intentions of the United Nations forces, the matter could be settled without enlarging the conflict.

But, at the very moment when representatives of these Chinese Communist authorities appeared at the headquarters of the United Nations, claiming the right to speak before this world organization in the name of the Chinese people, the cloak of pretense has been thrown off. In great force, the armies of the Chinese Communists have streamed across the Manchurian border, engaging the forces of the United Nations in a new encounter. Against these new, fresh, and numerous forces, our United Nations troops are fighting bravely. But the conditions are difficult; terrain and weather, long lines of supply, and the wear of an arduous campaign have been met with heroic fortitude.[26]

Why then was there so much trouble about getting a solid majority of the United Nations to agree that there was aggression here? An answer to this question is absolutely vital to an understanding of Acheson's work in this period, and it requires us to state briefly the deeply held opinions of other nations. These opinions, in the view of the American Administration, were unjustified, though only too natural; they were also a substantial and extremely important reality, not to be waved away by disagreement or denunciation.

The substance of the feeling of those who hesitated to support the American view of Chinese intervention was that before any such definite condemnation was expressed every possible avenue of peaceful adjustment should be explored. To many it seemed that the Red Chinese had a legitimate grievance against the United States on two issues — Formosa and Chinese admission to the United Nations. Outside the United States and Latin America, there were very few people who had much sympathy for the régime of Chiang Kai-shek, and the general feeling in Europe and Asia was that the United States was merely getting in the way of history when it undertook to protect Formosa. Moreover, the same attitudes in General MacArthur which seemed like splendid patriotism to so many Americans struck other peoples as flamboyant and militaristic nationalism. To these people it

[26] Same source, p. 963.

seemed quite possible that the Red Chinese might have been misled into a genuine fear of American imperialism.

These points of view had behind them more general attitudes. In Asia and among the Arab countries, there was a deep-seated, almost instinctive suspicion of the capitalistic white man and of Asiatics who seemed to rely on white assistance. Thus to the new nations of the East, such rulers as Chiang and Korea's Synghman Rhee were highly suspect, and there was a considerable emotional satisfaction to be derived from suspicion of American motives. In Europe, for somewhat different reasons, there were substantial groups which also liked to find fault with the Americans. And in both continents, especially the European, there was a broad and deep fear of general war. Leaders who could not be accused of hostility or resentment toward America, and who were on record by word and deed as brave opponents of appeasement, were to be found insisting that no faint chance of settlement by negotiation should be ignored. Early in December, after a press conference of the President's had been wildly misreported and misinterpreted, so that for a frantic moment men thought America was about to use the atomic bomb, the British House of Commons, as a unit and without respect to party, cheered the decision of Prime Minister Attlee to fly at once to Washington, and behind this decision was a deep national fear that the Americans might go off half-cocked. With this sentiment prevailing where Americans were best known and most trusted, it can be seen that there was a wide gap between America and her allies. The Attlee mission led to considerably improved emotional understanding, on both sides, and to a general agreement that aggression must be blocked and general war avoided, but the disagreements between the two nations over Formosa and the Chinese UN seat remained as signs of real divergence.

In this situation there was grave danger of a major split between the United States and most of the rest of the free world. There was also a grave danger that the United Nations would not be able to muster the moral force to reassert its devotion to the concept of collective security. If the Americans played their cards wrong, and if the Red Chinese and the Russians played theirs right, the diplomatic test in the UN could result in a resounding rebuff to the United States, to collective security, and to the unity of the free world. This was the problem which the State Department faced in December, and it was a real triumph for American diplomacy when on February 1 the General Assembly of the United Nations, by a vote of 44 to 7, with 9 abstentions, adopted an American resolution plainly stamping the Chinese in

Korea as aggressors, and putting the whole moral and legal authority of the UN behind the American-led resistance to that aggression.

Throughout this period there was a growing concern, not merely among rabid opponents, but among many sober citizens and legislators, lest the Department of State and its Secretary be somehow blind to the reality of Chinese aggression — somehow infected with the attitudes that were held by so many abroad and by a small number of good Americans too. So far as the record reveals, there is no factual justification whatever for this concern. What we have here, I think, is a clear example of the type of difficulty that recurs again and again in the making of foreign policy. The citizen and the Department were agreed on the basic objective; the Department was required to deal with the stubborn facts which the citizen often ignored. If the Department and its Secretary had given public expression to the impatience and even anger which so many Americans felt at the caution and apparent reluctance of other nations, they would have been playing the Communist game, for such expressions could only have increased the difficulty of getting other free and proud peoples to come to agreement on the basic issue of aggression.

A particular instance of this general difficulty came in January, when the UN made its last attempt to get a cease-fire without having to point the finger of accusation at Peiping. A resolution was proposed and passed which, in essence, combined three propositions; first, a cease-fire, second, negotiations for the achievement of an independent and democratic Korea by peaceful means, and third, a discussion of Far Eastern problems at a conference including Red China, Russia, the United States and Great Britain. The American delegation voted for this resolution, which passed by a vote of 50 to 7 (the Soviet bloc, Nationalist China, and El Salvador opposed it), and at once there was a storm of criticism at home; it seemed as if the United States was prepared to go some distance toward granting the Chinese demand for concessions as a price for cease-fire. On January 17, in response to this criticism, Acheson gave a clear account of the problem with which the Government was dealing. He pointed out that the American vote in no way committed the United States to the *acceptance* of Chinese Communist demands; it committed us only to the *discussion* of them, a very different matter. In the same way, the naming of four nations to discuss these matters did not exclude other parties: "It goes without saying that other parties with interests in Far Eastern problems will also participate." But the main point of his remarks was that the American vote in this instance was governed by a regard for the sincere convictions of others:

The proposal was put forward by the Cease-Fire Committee — the President of the General Assembly, Mr. Pearson of Canada, Sir Benegal Rau of India. It had the support of the overwhelming majority of the United Nations members. This support was founded on two principal attitudes. One was the belief of many members that the Chinese Communists might still be prevailed upon to cease their defiance of the United Nations. While we did not share this belief, we recognized that it was sincerely held by many members.

The second attitude was that, even though there might be little prospect of success in the approach to Peiping, the United Nations should leave no stone unturned in its efforts to find a peaceful solution. Holders of each view believed and stated to us that opposition or abstention by the United States would destroy any possibility of success which the proposal might have.

Peaceful settlement is one of the cardinal purposes of the United Nations. The resort to force in Korea came from the North Koreans first and the Chinese Communists second. The United Nations has constantly demanded that this should end and that the United Nations objectives should be attained by peaceful means — we have stood and still stand for this position. Also, it has been our goal to so act as to maintain the unity of the free nations against aggression which has marked the United Nations actions in Korea. Accordingly, we voted for the resolution to demonstrate our adherence to these basic principles even though we did not share the beliefs of other members, mentioned above, that it would achieve its purpose.[27]

It is probably fair to say that American acceptance of the resolution of January 13 was indispensable to the result of February 1. Certainly it is clear that the restraint and accommodating spirit of the Americans were more attractive than the violent and churlish responses given by the Chinese Communists to every proposal of the United Nations. And after the resolution of January 13 was rebuffed on January 17 by a Chinese note in which Peiping reaffirmed its demand that major concessions be a condition of the cease-fire, the United States moved rapidly to reap the harvest of its restraint. Acheson at once announced his view of the matter:

The reply of the Chinese Communists to the United Nations cease-fire proposal is still further evidence of their contemptuous disregard of

[27] Statement released to the press late on January 17, 1951 (*Bulletin*, XXIV, p. 164).

a world-wide demand for peace. Their so-called "counterproposal" is nothing less than an outright rejection.

Once again, the Peiping régime has shown a total lack of interest in a peaceful settlement of the Korean question.

There can no longer be any doubt that the United Nations has explored every possibility of finding a peaceful settlement of the Korean question. Now, we must face squarely and soberly the fact that the Chinese Communists have no intention of ceasing their defiance of the United Nations.

I am confident that the United Nations will do that. The strength of the United Nations will lie in the firmness and unity with which we now move ahead.[28]

Three days later the United States introduced a resolution calling the aggressor what he was, and in defending this resolution Ambassador Austin used a phrase that summed up the American view of the Chinese Communists' impudent demand for a UN seat: "You can't shoot your way into the United Nations." In Washington the Congress backed the American position in two overwhelming votes, and the American lead was followed by the vast majority of the free nations, and in particular by the vitally important partners of the Atlantic Community. The fight in Korea against the Chinese Communists was formally established as a UN undertaking. And in order to understand that this was not merely a matter of words, one has only to consider what would have been the position of the United States, the UN and the coalition of free nations if the American resolution had *not* been accepted.

This whole two-month effort, in its final result, vindicated both the restraint of the United States and its calculation that the Chinese Communists could be forced either to expose themselves or to accept a genuine settlement. Back in November Acheson had warned that "The authorities of Communist China stand before the bar of the judgment of mankind. The world will watch their actions in Korea and at Lake Success. . . . If they defy the United Nations and mock the Charter then no lies, no bluster, and no veto will conceal from the people of the world the evil of their action." [29]

[28] Same source, p. 164; the Chinese note of January 17 arrived after the press conference quoted above.

[29] Address to the National Council of Churches of Christ in the U.S., November 29, 1950 (*Bulletin*, XXIII, p. 963).

The event had justified the prophecy. Indeed the lies and bluster had served to reveal the aggression more plainly than ever to those with honest doubts. And as for the veto, it had been neutralized in advance by the Acheson Plan, and the resolution of February 1 was the first demonstration that the General Assembly was prepared to act as that Plan intended.

4. The MacArthur Debate

I believe that the aggression can best be brought to an end, with a minimum risk and a minimum loss, by continuing the punishing defeat of the Chinese in Korea. This is being done.[30]

In February and March the advances of General Ridgway's forces continued, and for a while public and Congressional attention was fixed on the Great Debate on European policy discussed in Chapter Four. The struggle in Korea remained limited, on both sides — there was no attack by UN forces on Chinese supply lines and air bases across the Manchurian border, and the great United Nations base in Japan also remained outside the theater of combat. General MacArthur's dissatisfaction with this arrangement was made plain in his communiques, but the issue did not become urgent until the end of March and the beginning of April. Here again it was the course of the fighting that determined the political development. While the United Nations forces were advancing steadily and inflicting a growing toll of casualties on the enemy it was possible to suppose that eventually the chosen line of action might produce completely satisfactory results; in any event, the situation was steadily improving, and it was so much better than men had feared at Christmas time that there was no immediate pressure for a change.

But as the UN advance slowed down, and as casualty lists continued to grow, it seemed less clear that the plan in Korea was sound. It was at this point that General MacArthur intensified his public insistence that new decisions were needed, and in two pronouncements, one in an announcement to the enemy, and the other in a letter to Congressman Joe Martin, he indicated clearly what he thought those decisions should be — an extension of the war to Chinese bases and supply lines, and a clear reversal of the neutralization of Formosa to permit Nationalist troops to return to the mainland of

---

[30] Opening statement to the Senate Committee investigating the relief of General MacArthur, June 1, 1951 (*Hearings*, p. 1718, and *Bulletin*, XXIV, p. 925).

China with American logistical support. He made it plain that this attitude rested on "the conventional pattern of meeting force with maximum counterforce as we have never failed to do in the past."

The letter to Congressman Martin appears to have been the immediate cause of Mr. Truman's decision to relieve General MacArthur. For the President this open and energetic advocacy of policies not approved by the Administration, expressed in a letter to a leader of the opposition, marked the end of a long effort to maintain the usefulness of the extraordinary man who was Supreme Commander in the Far East. On April 11, at 1.00 A.M., the White House issued the Presidential announcement that General MacArthur had been relieved of all his commands in the Far East and would be succeeded by General Ridgway.

The relief of General MacArthur is not, in any immediate sense, a part of Acheson's record. The decision was made with the advice and approval of all his senior advisers, civil and military, but it was clearly the President's own decision. In the grand inquest that was held by the Russell Committee it became entirely plain that the differences between General MacArthur and the Administration were large enough to leave no question that the General was not the right man to carry out the policies of his superiors in Washington. It also became plain that it would have been better if the President had stuck to his original arrangement for relieving the General through the agency of a personal visit by Secretary of the Army Pace.[31] What remained as a subject of debate and inquiry were the substantive issues between General MacArthur and the Administration, and these are of the first importance, not only in themselves, but as part of our study.

The Russell Committee took two million words of testimony, and more than four hundred thousand of them were taken during the eight days of Acheson's appearance. The inquiry ranged with unwearied repetition over an extraordinary variety of topics, and of course it was colored by partisan advocacy at nearly every turn, on both sides. One of its more peculiar characteristics was the lack of effectiveness of cross-examination in nearly every case; the result is a record in which the most powerful arguments of the opposing sides were never brought face to face. Supporters of the Administration, in the main, treated General MacArthur with great restraint, and al-

---

[31] The only laughter that is recorded in Acheson's mountainous testimony before the Russell Committee came when he was asked if he would have handled the dismissal of General MacArthur as the President did and he replied, "I think that is quite an unfair question to ask me, Senator." (Same hearings, p. 2125).

though critics tried to deal with Acheson and his colleagues, they were quite clearly outmatched in both mental equipment and grasp of the facts. In order to deal properly with the central issues of the conduct of the contest in Korea, therefore, we must adopt the device of extracting the central arguments made by General MacArthur and confronting them with the replies which Acheson made. It is also necessary to exclude a great many small points, only tangential to the inquiry. Some of these resulted in small scores for the opposition, and some in equally small victories for the Administration. In sum, they are a distraction from the larger issues posed on both sides.

The first and perhaps the most basic difference between General MacArthur and the Administration was the difference over the objective in Korea. To General MacArthur it seemed plain that while war was utterly revolting, "once it is forced upon us, there is no other alternative than to apply every available means to bring it to a swift end. War's very object is victory, not prolonged indecision. In war there is no substitute for victory." [32] Like many of General MacArthur's eloquent statements, this one was probably a little more extreme than he intended, for it would have justified an immediate use of the atomic bomb, which the General never advocated directly. But in essence, this attitude was critically different from that of the Administration and the Secretary of State. For them the objective in Korea was not so narrow, not so simple, and perhaps not so direct in its popular appeal. As Acheson stated it to the Russell Committee, "The objective of our military operation in Korea is to end the aggression, to safeguard against its renewal, and to restore peace." [33] For this purpose the Administration needed a certain amount of military success, obviously, and Acheson constantly emphasized the degree to which the whole policy of the United Nations rested on the valor and skill of the men fighting in Korea. But it was *not* required of these men, or of their compatriots, that they make the further military efforts necessary to produce unconditional victory.

And this was fortunate, because there was a deep and vitally important disagreement between General MacArthur and his military superiors as to the feasibility of achieving such a victory by additional measures beyond those authorized. General MacArthur wished to bomb the Manchurian bases, blockade the China coast, use the Nationalist army on Formosa, and continue the battle in Korea with "major reinforcements." The *military* weakness of these proposals, according to the unanimous view of the Joint

---

[32] Address to Congress, April 19, 1951 (*Congressional Record*, 82d Congress, 1st Session, p. 4235).   [33] *Hearings*, p. 1717.

Chiefs of Staff, was that they would not be effective in producing a victory in Korea unless undertaken in such strength as to involve a totally disproportionate commitment of the strength of the free world in a single theater of war. It simply was not true that merely by changing the rules of the contest for a few weeks or months a total victory could be achieved. The price of such total victory was a general war in China, with all the risks and costs of such an undertaking. In the succinct phrase of the Chairman of the Joint Chiefs of Staff, General Bradley, the policy advocated by opponents of the Administration would involve us in "the wrong war, at the wrong place, at the wrong time, and with the wrong enemy." [34]

The military objections to General MacArthur's position were matched by political objections. The basic political difficulty with the MacArthur position was a simple one: the United States could not afford to govern its entire foreign policy by the single objective of victory in Korea. In addition to the risk of general war with China, Acheson in his opening statement to the Committee argued two propositions which were directly opposed to the conclusions General MacArthur drew from his single-minded and devoted pursuit of his goal. Acheson believed that policy must be shaped with an eye to the attitudes of both the Soviet Union and America's allies.

The General had argued that the expansion of the war in Korea should not be avoided in fear of Soviet intervention; he believed that "the Soviet will not necessarily mesh its actions with our moves. Like a cobra, any new enemy will more likely strike whenever it feels that the relativity in military or other potential is in its favor on a world-wide basis." [35] Acheson's answer was that this assumption was unwarranted by the facts:

As to Soviet reactions, no one can be sure he is forecasting accurately what they would be, but there are certain facts at hand that bear on this question.

We know of Soviet influence in North Korea, of Soviet assistance to the North Koreans and to Communist China, and we know that understandings must have accompanied this assistance. We also know that there is a treaty between the Soviets and the Chinese Communists.

But, even if the treaty did not exist, China is the Soviet Union's largest and most important satellite. Russian self-interest in the Far East

[34] Same hearings, p. 732.

[35] Address to the Congress, April 19, 1951 (*Congressional Record*, 82d Congress, 1st Session, p. 4235). The General's analogy can hardly have been persuasive to those who have had dealings with cobras, for this snake often strikes when stepped on or otherwise annoyed, without stopping to consider the relativity in potential.

and the necessity of maintaining prestige in the Communist sphere make it difficult to see how the Soviet Union could ignore a direct attack upon the Chinese mainland.

I cannot accept the assumption that the Soviet Union will go its way regardless of what we do. I do not think that Russian policy is formed that way any more than our own policy is formed that way. This view is certainly not well enough grounded to justify a gamble with the essential security of our nation.

In response to the proposed course of action, there are a number of courses of counter-action open to the Soviets.

They could turn over to the Chinese large numbers of planes with "volunteer" crews for retaliatory action in Korea and outside. They might participate with the Soviet air force and the submarine fleet.

The Kremlin could elect to parallel the action taken by Peiping and intervene with a half million or more ground force "volunteers"; or it could go the whole way and launch an all-out war.

Singly, or in combination, these reactions contain explosive possibilities, not only for the Far East, but for the rest of the world as well.[36]

The second great political consideration was the importance of maintaining a solid coalition of the free nations. On this point, General MacArthur had argued that victory in Korea was more important than this coalition; "here we fight Europe's war with arms while the diplomats there still fight it with words";[37] under questioning before the Russell Committee he said further that the United States should be prepared to "go it alone" in order to achieve the necessary victory. Since one of the great central premises of American foreign policy was the critical importance of building a partnership of the free nations, Acheson could hardly accept this view.

We should also analyze the effect on our allies of our taking steps to initiate the spread of war beyond Korea. It would severely weaken their ties with us and in some instances it might sever them.

They are understandably reluctant to be drawn into a general war in the Far East — one which holds the possibilities of becoming a world

[36] Opening statement to the Senate Committee investigating the relief of General MacArthur, June 1, 1951 (*Hearings*, pp. 1718–19, and *Bulletin*, XXIV, pp. 925–26).

[37] Letter to Congressman Martin, March 20, 1951, in reply to Congressman Martin's letter of March 8, 1951, requesting that General MacArthur express his views on over-all strategy, "either on a confidential basis or otherwise." Both letters are printed in the *Congressional Record*, 82d Congress, 1st Session, p. 3938.

war — particularly if it developed out of an American impatience with the progress of the effort to repel aggression, an effort which in their belief offers an honorable and far less catastrophic solution.

If we followed the course proposed, we would be increasing our risks and commitments at the same time that we diminished our strength by reducing the strength and determination of our coalition.

We cannot expect that our collective security system will long survive if we take steps which unnecessarily and dangerously expose the people who are in the system with us. They would understandably hesitate to be tied to a partner who leads them to a highly dangerous short-cut across a difficult crevasse.

In relation to the total world threat, our safety requires that we strengthen, not weaken, the bonds of our collective security system.

The power of our coalition to deter an attack depends in part upon the will and the mutual confidence of our partners. If we, by the measures proposed, were to weaken that effect, particularly in the North Atlantic area, we would be jeopardizing the security of an area which is vital to our own national security.[38]

So he believed that both the Russian position and the requirements of collective security argued against an extension of the fighting along the lines MacArthur proposed. And in an earlier speech he had combined the two considerations, pointing out that it was absolutely vital that if general war should come, it should not come in a way that might cloud the issue of fault and blame. To extend the fighting on MacArthur's terms would be to play the Kremlin's game.[39]

In summary, General MacArthur's policy had been rejected because its advantages were less than its disadvantages:

What this adds up to, it seems to me, is that we are being asked to undertake a large risk of general war with China, risk of war with the Soviet Union, and a demonstrable weakening of our collective security system — all this in return for what?

In return for measures whose effectiveness in bringing the conflict to an early conclusion are judged doubtful by our responsible military authorities.[40]

[38] Opening statement to the Senate Committee investigating the relief of General MacArthur, June 1, 1951. (*Hearings*, p. 1719, and *Bulletin*, XXIV, p. 926).

[39] Address to the Women's National Press Club, April 18, 1951 (*Bulletin*, XXIV, p. 687).

[40] Opening statement to the Senate Committee investigating the relief of General MacArthur, June 1, 1951 (*Hearings*, p. 1720, and *Bulletin*, XXIV, p. 926).

If a large part of the debate centered on the gains or losses to be expected from a change of policy, an even larger part centered on the assessment of gains and losses from the policy actually being followed. In his testimony before the Russell Committee General MacArthur constantly resisted efforts to get his full views on the broader issues we have been noting, and as constantly he drew the Committee's attention to what he considered the extremely unsatisfactory situation in Korea; he energetically reiterated his view that American blood was being shed to no useful or honorable purpose, and this cry was taken up by many other critics. For the opponents of the Administration this was, indeed, a more comfortable line of argument, for it did not require them to reach agreement among themselves as to what they would do if the responsibility was theirs.

A major part of Acheson's opening statement, therefore, and a still larger part of his work in answering the questions of Senators, was devoted to assertion and reassertion of the positive advantages being won in Korea. He repeated his standing view that the initial decision to stand in Korea had been a turning point in history; he defended the President's right to make this decision without a Congressional declaration of war; he noted that both the American people and leaders of both parties had supported this decision "because it accorded with the principles by which Americans live." [41]

He rejected entirely and bluntly the charge that nothing was being gained by the sacrifices of the men in Korea.

The operation in Korea has been a success. Both the North Koreans and the Chinese Communists declared it to be their purpose to drive the United Nations forces out of Korea and impose Communist rule throughout the entire peninsula. They have been prevented from accomplishing their objective.

It has been charged that the American and Allied forces fighting in Korea are engaged in a pointless and inconclusive struggle.

Nothing could be farther from the fact. They have been magnificent. Their gallant, determined and successful fight has checked the Communist advance and turned it into a retreat. They have administered terrible defeats to the Communist forces. In so doing, they have scored a powerful victory.

Their victory has dealt Communist imperialist aims in Asia a severe setback.[42]

---

[41] Same hearings, p. 1715, and *Bulletin*, XXIV, p. 924.
[42] *Hearings*, p. 1716, and *Bulletin*, XXIV, p. 924.

Then he pointed out that the Communists had been deprived of the alluring prospect of a quick and easy success.[43] But this negative achievement
was not all; the resistance in Korea had caused the Communist aggression to
have many useful results in the free world:

> Instead of weakening the rest of the world, they have solidified it.
> They have given a powerful impetus to the military preparations of this
> country and its associates in and out of the North Atlantic Treaty Or-
> ganization.
>
> We have doubled the number of our men under arms, and the produc-
> tion of materiel has been boosted to a point where it can begin to have a
> profound effect on the maintenance of the peace.
>
> The idea of collective security has been put to the test, and has been
> sustained. The nations who believe in collective security have shown
> that they can stick together and fight together.
>
> New urgency has been given to the negotiation of a peace treaty with
> Japan, and of initial security arrangements to build strength in the
> Pacific area.
>
> These are some of the results of the attack on Korea, unexpected by
> — and I am sure most unwelcome to — the Kremlin.[44]

This defense covered the question of the value of the stand in Korea.
There remained the insistent question of a solution. However much the
United Nations forces might have gained, it would hardly be pleasant to see
them forced to continue interminably in a seesaw battle back and forth
across the 38th Parallel, and there seemed to be no likelihood that they
could fight their way to the Manchurian border. What end did the Administration see to this venture? In early June Acheson's answer to this question
was necessarily somewhat indefinite. In essence it was that the present
course of the fighting was proving to the Reds that they must abandon their
attempt to conquer South Korea. As military leaders had testified to the
Committee, "Our forces are in excellent shape . . . their morale is high . . .
they are in a good supply position . . . the offensives of the enemy have been
broken and thrown back with enormous enemy casualties." And Acheson
continued:

[43] For this passage, see page 253 above.
[44] *Hearings*, p. 1717, and *Bulletin*, XXIV, p. 924.

These defeats in Korea, together with other consequences of this campaign, present grave problems for the Communist authorities in China.

While the manpower resources of China are vast, its supply of trained men is limited. They cannot cover up their casualties. They cannot gloss over the draft of more and more men for military service.

The Chinese Red leaders have betrayed their long-standing pledge of demobilization and the military demand for manpower has, instead, been increased.

Peiping has also broken its promises of social and economic improvement. In the great cities, dependent on imported materials, unemployment increases. The régime has not lightened the burdens of the people. It has made them heavier.

All of this is reflected in a sharp increase in repressive measures, and in propaganda to whip up the flagging zeal of their own people.

In the light of all these factors, I believe that the aggression can best be brought to an end with a minimum risk and a minimum loss by continuing the punishing defeat of the Chinese in Korea. This is being done.[45]

He concluded this passage by remarking that "no one can predict when the fighting will stop and when the aggression will end." But the same thing had been true in Berlin and in Greece. The course of action in Korea was the best the Administration could design for "stopping hostilities and ending the aggression in Korea."

Finally, and perhaps most urgently, Senators wanted to know exactly what goal would be considered satisfactory by the Administration. General MacArthur said "victory"; the Administration said "end the aggression." What did the Administration mean? Specifically, would the Administration be content to stop fighting short of a unified and democratic Korea? Acheson's prepared statement contained no definite commitment on this point, and the discussions with various Senators gradually brought out a picture which was never continuously stated during the hearings. It seems best, then, to take Acheson's own summary as stated three weeks later to the House Committee on Foreign Affairs. In an appearance before this committee he was asked whether he thought the Korean conflict would be successful "if we are to stop at the 38th Parallel." His answer was "Yes," and he went on to explain it. The central point of this explanation, and of his

[45] *Hearings*, pp. 1717–18, and *Bulletin*, XXIV, p. 925.

discussion before the Russell Committee, is that the object of the fighting was not the same as the overall political objective; the secondary point is that something less than the high hopes of the preceding September would constitute success:

There are two purposes in Korea. One of the military objectives and purposes there grows out of the resolutions of the 25th and 27th of June, 1950. The other is the great continuing purpose which the United States has had ever since the Cairo Declaration and which the United Nations has had ever since 1947, when the General Assembly passed the resolutions looking forward to the unification of Korea.

A year and 2 days ago Korea was divided. It was at peace. There was no idea that the United States or the United Nations should call out troops and go into Korea for the purpose of unifying Korea by armed force. That was not United Nations policy, nor was it United States policy.

The attack on Korea occurred, and the United Nations passed two resolutions in the Security Council. One of them called on the North Koreans to withdraw behind the 38th Parallel and cease their aggression. When they failed to do that, the other resolution branded the attacks as aggression against the Republic of Korea, and called on all nations to furnish forces in order to help South Korea to repel the aggression against them, and to restore peace and security in the area.

From the military point of view what we are doing and have been attempting to do is to repel the aggression and restore peace and security in the area, which remains the policy of the United Nations, [and] to unify Korea, if that can be done. But it is not its policy that it must or should try to unify Korea by armed force.

Now, after the Inchon landing the military operation was such that it was necessary to go into North Korea. With the landing at Inchon the North Korean forces were cut in two. About half of the forces were bottled up in South Korea. The other half withdrew north of the parallel and continued fighting. There were guerrilla operations in South Korea by which the United Nations forces continually reduced this North Korean Army. However, very considerable portions of the enemy would melt away, putting on civilian clothes and throwing away their rifles, and go through those mountains and join up with the remnants that were in the North. General MacArthur went north under the directions of the Joint Chiefs of Staff in order either to capture or destroy this North Korean force, and that had been practically accomplished at the time of the Chinese intervention.

Now, I pointed out that if he had been able to do that, and if there had been no intervention by the Chinese — which were "ifs" of considerable size — then there would probably have been a unification of Korea as a result of the combat; but the combat was not for the purpose of doing that. It was for the purpose of eliminating this aggression by rounding up people who refused to surrender and who refused to lay down their arms and refused to do anything except keep on fighting.

If this aggression is stopped and if you have adequate assurance that it will not be resumed, and if those who are doing it will withdraw so that we know that there is not any immediate danger of resumption, then you would have repelled the aggression and you would have established peace and security so far as that can be done by military means in the area.

Therefore I should think that the United Nations would believe it had accomplished what it set out to do. It would then have before it the same task which it had before it on June 25, 1950, of attempting to unify Korea.[46]

This was the general position of the Administration when the cease-fire negotiations began in July; during those negotiations it was further clarified, and in particular it became clear that Acheson's general acceptance of a cease-fire near the 38th Parallel did not include a willingness to abandon strong positions slightly to the north.

Acheson's basic position before the Russell Committee has now been stated; he believed the operation in Korea to be a success; he believed it could be brought to a satisfactory ending; he believed that to extend the conflict on American initiative would bring no great gain and many serious dangers. And for eight days and four-hundred-thousand words he defended this position. From this mass of discussion I have selected a few passages that seem particularly useful in clarifying important aspects of his position.

One great point made by critics was that the allies of the United States were leaving the main job to American troops. Senator Johnson asked Acheson if he would discuss the contribution the Allies were making in other areas, which might justify their relatively small contribution in Korea. The answer began with a tribute to Allied troops in Korea, and went on to show the basic unfairness of measurements based on that area alone:

[46] Hearings, *Mutual Security Program*, House, Committee on Foreign Affairs, June 26, 1951, pp. 24–5.

I feel badly when I hear these discussions of the inadequate effort of our allies in Korea.

I think all of them are painfully aware that they are not able to do as much as they would like to do, and I think that they are trying hard to do the very best they can. I will come to their other efforts in a minute.

In view of the extraordinary gallantry of the action of their troops in Korea which is up to the very highest standards and I think is regarded by our own troops as something to be very proud of, it seems a little bit unfortunate to be talking about the inadequacy of their effort.

I think the latest example of it is the fight that the battalion of the Gloucestershire troops put on in the recent offensive which is one of the great stories in military history. A battalion of 622 men came out with five officers and 34 people.

Those fellows fought, there are no two ways about that, and they held up the entire advance of the Chinese in the western sector, the First Corps sector, until the rest of the troops could get themselves into position. It was very gallant. It was a superb thing.

And the French have put on their show in the same way, and the Turks, and the others have just been very fine, and I think our troops recognize that these are comrades that they are very, very glad to have.

Now so far as the effort of these countries in other areas, the effort which the British are making in Malaya and the French are making in Indochina if put together is roughly equivalent to the effort which we are making in Korea, that is the United States contribution.[47]

Another question was whether there were not important shipments of strategic materials going to Red China from America's allies. Acheson answered this question in great detail.[48] In essence, he pointed out that under discussions and agreements dating back nearly three years, the United States and her Allies had progressively strengthened the embargo of strategic materials to *all* countries in the Soviet bloc, including Red China, and that as a result of agreements reached early in 1951, "about ninety percent of the items which we regard as being of strategic significance have been put on these lists for embargo." As for oil, on which some extravagant charges had been made, "It can be stated flatly . . . that no significant shipments of

[47] Hearings, *Military Situation in the Far East*, Senate, Committee on Foreign Relations and Committee on Armed Services, 82d Congress, 1st Session, June 3, 1951, p. 1772.

[48] Same hearings, pp. 1724–28.

petroleum products of military usefulness have been exported to Communist China from or through any place in the free world." This basic position taken by the United States, and successfully argued with her allies, had been backed on May 18, by a vote of 45–4, in a General Assembly resolution calling for an embargo on strategic exports to Communist China. Even rubber, on which there had been an important difference with the British, had been embargoed by them on May 10. There remained differences among the Allies, and the United States would have preferred a complete economic blockade, enforced by United Nations naval forces under United Nations sanction, but Acheson denied that America's purpose had been blocked by her allies; on the whole he thought the record showed that "we have had considerable success" in pressing for an economic blockade; after all, "Some of our associates have problems [of trade] which are, for them, serious problems, and ones which we do not have in the same degree." For these reasons the entire Administration, military, naval, and civilian, was agreed that the thing to do was to continue to work for still further agreement on further economic restrictions, rather than to take the high-handed course of imposing by force an American naval blockade.

Much of the discussion in the hearings, as we have already seen, turned upon events that occurred long before General MacArthur was relieved — and some of the criticism was directed at decisions which he had specifically approved when they were made. An example was the questioning on the decision made in early 1949 to withdraw all American occupying troops from Korea. Acheson pointed out that this decision had had the concurrence of General MacArthur, and the energetic support of the Defense Department; it had been repeatedly requested by the Korean Government; it had been recommended by the United Nations; it had been parallel to a Russian withdrawal which had been completed, at least in form, somewhat earlier. It might be true that to have stayed in Korea would have been to deter the attack of June, 1950, but it was also true (Acheson did not spell this out specifically) that to have stayed would have been to defy the United Nations, to give the Communists everywhere a most powerful propaganda position, and to arouse the resentment and perhaps even the hostility of the Korean government. Senator Lodge was undoubtedly right when he spoke of the educational advantages of Monday-morning quarterbacking, but an essential part of that task was surely the weighing of the alternatives available in the situation in which the quarterback made his Saturday decision. As Acheson remarked a few weeks later, "In this particular age in which we live we do not have choices between something that is highly desirable and something that is undesirable. We have choices between undesirables, and we have to pick out the less undesirable." [49]

And on this note we may leave the hearings on the relief of General MacArthur. For in the end the problem of policy in Korea was precisely this problem — the choice of the best possible course in a situation that could never be made wholly agreeable. This is the brutal truth about the whole of foreign policy, and it is never more brutal than in the supreme test of meeting the challenge of aggression.

For Acheson himself, the hearings before the Russell Committee turned into something of a personal triumph. An honest critic, Senator Wiley, told him on the sixth day, "You have had a long chore, sir, and you have done a grand job for yourself, I would say, with that mind of yours."[50] And the magazine *Life*, with splendid logic, said he had done so well he should resign at once. But of course the real test of the Administration's policy was not to be found in any personal triumph, nor in any committee hearing. It was to be found in the future. In the concluding paragraph of his opening statements, Acheson had drawn that moral. One of the arguments implicit in General MacArthur's position was that it was too late for half-measures, that we must force the issue now. Acheson's reply was a brief restatement of his whole purpose as Secretary of State:

I should like to deal briefly with the . . . proposition that we may need to take extreme risks now because time may not be on our side. I believe this is wrong.

The basic premise of our foreign policy is that time is on our side if we make good use of it. This does not necessarily mean that time must bring us to a point where we can match the Soviet Union man-for-man and tank-for-tank.

What it does mean is that we need to use the time we have to build an effective deterrent force. This requires us to create sufficient force-in-being, both in the United States and among our allies, to shield our great potential against the possibility of a quick and easy onslaught, and to ensure that our allies will not suffer occupation and destruction. And

[49] Hearings, *Mutual Security Program*, House, Committee on Foreign Affairs, June 26, 1951, p. 46. Comments on the decision to withdraw troops from Korea in 1949 occur in the Russell Committee hearings at pp. 2008–12, 2082–84, 2168.
[50] Same hearings, p. 2130.

back of this shield we need to have the potential that would enable us to win a war.

This is the measure of the force we need; as we approach it, we approach our objective of preventing war.

Can we do this? I believe we can. We and our allies have the capacity to out-produce the Soviet bloc by a staggering margin. There is no doubt about that. Our capacity to produce has been set in motion and is rapidly getting to the point where its output will be vast and its effect significant.

There is also the critical factor of our will. The future belongs to freedom if free men have the will to make time work on their side. I believe the American people and their allies do have the will, the will to work together when their freedom is threatened. This is the ultimate source of our faith and our confidence. A free society can call upon profound resources among its people in behalf of a righteous cause.[51]

This was the general challenge to Americans, and it would continue indefinitely in the future.

[51] Opening statement to the Senate Committee hearings on the relief of General MacArthur (*Hearings*, p. 1720, and *Bulletin*, XXIV, p. 926).

CHAPTER ELEVEN

Conclusion

THE TIMES *in which we live must be painted in the somber values of Rembrandt. The background is dark, the shadows deep. Outlines are obscure. The central point, however, glows with light: and, though it often brings out the glint of steel, it touches colors of unimaginable beauty.*

For us, that central point is the growing unity of free men the world over. This is our shaft of light, our hope and our promise.[1]

With the cease-fire negotiations in Korea we come to a necessary stopping point in this record. Such a stopping point is wholly arbitrary. In the first weeks after it appeared that there might be an end to the Korean fighting, Acheson repeatedly made such statements as this: "We must not for one second allow any development which may occur in Korea to lull us into a belief that now we have turned the corner."[2] By the nature of the contest in which the United States was engaged there could be no early finishing point which it was possible to call the goal.

In the two and a half years which we have discussed, many great steps have been taken. It is too soon to say what Acheson will be remembered most for: his response to the challenge of Russian Communism; his part in the growth of the North Atlantic Community; his special interest in the focal problem of Germany; his firm and unfrightened moderation in the Far East; his leadership in the stand against aggression in Korea; his part

[1] Address on receiving the Freedom House Award, New York City, October 8, 1950 (*Bulletin*, XXIII, pp. 615–16).

[2] Stenographic transcript of remarks to a group of magazine and book publishers, June 29, 1951 (*Bulletin*, XXV, p. 127).

in a major development of the capacities of the United Nations Charter; or for his integrity under bitter personal attack. At this writing it seems possible that the most striking single phenomenon about his tenure as Secretary of State may be the extraordinary disparity between what he has accomplished and the opinion in which he has been held by a large number of his countrymen. But these speculations are for others. It remains in these concluding paragraphs to summarize if we can the central principles of his policy and then to show briefly what he considers to be the basic implications of this policy for the attitudes of Americans.

On June 26, 1951, Acheson appeared before the House Committee on Foreign Affairs to present and defend a "Mutual Security Program" of eight and one-half billion dollars. In this program there were combined for the first time the economic, military, and technological help which underpinned the active foreign policy of the Government. In his opening statement he made a number of comments which I have extracted and connected as a basic statement of the policy for which he stands. This basic policy as we have seen requires different interpretation in different places and at different times, and yet I think it fair to say that all of what we have been discussing is summarized in these paragraphs:

> This national program is part of a great effort by the free nations to rid the world of war and to make peace secure. That is our present goal. That is the proposition which unifies the free nations.
>
> Weakness invites aggression. Now and in the future, strength is the precondition of peace . . . No nation, including our own, is strong enough to stand alone in the modern world. . . . The Soviet Union wants to see the United States try to "go it alone." . . . That is why our security program requires us to make sure that we have strong and reliable friends and allies.
>
> In reviewing our policy, we might begin with our own country, a center of strength in the free world. . . . The supreme test of our ability to survive is our ability to win if war is forced upon us. We must be prepared for that supreme test, and preparation for it offers the best means of avoiding it. . . . The core of our national policy is a rapid development of strength in our country and the maintenance of that strength so long as the threat continues.
>
> The crucial problem of war and peace centers around the challenge presented to the rest of the world by the policies of the Soviet Govern-

ment. . . . The process of encroachment and consolidation by which Russia has grown in the last five hundred years from the duchy of Muscovy to a vast empire has got to be stopped. . . . We have to hold, if possible, against its drives wherever they may be made . . . against armed attack . . . and equally against internal attack, which is the new weapon added to the Russian arsenal by the Communists.

Free societies can outbuild, outproduce, and outlast societies based on tyrannies and oppression. . . . The free world includes over two-thirds of the total population of the earth . . . nearly three-quarters of the world's land area. . . . The total productivity of the free world is many times that of the Soviet Empire. And, most importantly, the free world has resources of mind and spirit incalculably greater than those under the totalitarian control of the Kremlin. . . . It would be folly for all our nations to invite war by leaving this potential of strength undeveloped and unorganized.

If there can be created unity of purpose, resolution to meet the present danger, and the great strength that can come from mutual security efforts — and this is what we are now doing — then the threat that faces us can be reduced to manageable proportions. Our United States policies are aimed at helping to bring about these conditions.

Deter, defend, and develop. . . . We seek to deter war; for peace, not war, is the only full answer to our present danger. We shall do what we can and shall cooperate with others to defend the free nations against the twin menaces of external and internal attack. We shall do what we can and cooperate with others in the spirit of the Charter of the United Nations to develop the economic, political, and military strength of free men and the extent of free institutions.[3]

If this is the basic policy, what does it mean for Americans? The first and simple answer, one which Acheson repeatedly states, is that it means unwearied effort, but this answer itself has little meaning unless in turn its implications are examined. On June 29, 1951, speaking from notes to a group of magazine and book publishers in the White House, Acheson undertook to examine these implications.

He began by remarking upon the extraordinary volume of information published on the subject of foreign affairs — from the Department of State

[3] Hearings, *Mutual Security Program*, House, Committee on Foreign Affairs, 82d Congress, 1st Session, June 26, 1951, pp. 7–18.

1200 press releases a year, 320,000 words a day on the Voice of America, nearly 300 volumes of documentation each year — and by private citizens and institutions 500 books and literally innumerable press and radio reports. In this mass of words, he remarked, there was no lack of suggested solutions. Every simple solution contradicted every other and each one began with a somewhat different notion of where the problem came from and what made the present what it is. From this discussion he proceeded to consider, "some of the attitudes which seem to me essential for us to have in mind as we struggle with the times in which we live."

The first attitude which seems to me essential is the recognition that whenever the present began and whenever the present will end, it will be with us for a very long time. If we will get that firmly in mind, we will begin to get over the impatience which leads people to try to find magic solutions. If we will recognize that we have before us a long period of work, then we have the beginning of wisdom. Once we understand that we have a long period of work before us then we can see that the object of our efforts is not to remove these problems. They are not removable. The object of our work is to reduce these problems to manageable proportions. . . .

We cannot for a moment believe, if we are really sensible in facing the present, that the problems can be escaped. We must believe over and over again, and understand over and over again — as though we heard them for the first time — Lincoln's great words in his message to Congress of December 1862: "We cannot escape history." We cannot escape the problem of the present. We can only escape it by death or defeat. If we are going to deal with those problems, we must be willing to deal with them for a long time. We must be willing to reduce them from almost impossible problems to manageable problems, and we must have a sense of continuing responsibility in dealing with them.

The second very important attitude for us to take in dealing with the problems of the present is to avoid overdramatizing any particular problem or overemphasizing it. That is always our danger, not peculiar to the United States but common to everybody. The particular problem with which we are dealing seems to us to be the overwhelming problem of all time. Take Korea, for instance, which God knows is important enough. . . .

Korea's significance is not the final crusade. It is not finally making valid the idea of collective security. . . .

The third attitude which I think is important for us to have in mind is a proper sense of proportion about the problems and difficulties which come before us. In getting the proper sense of proportion about our difficulties, the first thing that we must understand is that the present situation is a great deal more serious than the United States as a whole has yet come to realize. We must understand that the Soviet Union is a much tougher adversary than the United States has yet realized. We must not only understand that, but we must understand something else, and that is that the Soviet Union is not the only difficulty we have. Behind and beyond the Soviet Union, and our problems with the Soviet Union, lie other difficulties, perhaps even greater. . . . We must so act in dealing with the immediate difficulty that we manage also the more long-range ones.

What do I mean by those general words? Twice in our lifetime we have dealt with problems before us as though the solution of those problems was the solution of all problems. We dealt with the Kaiser as though the defeat of the Kaiser was the defeat of all such menaces to the world. And yet there immediately grew up after that Hitler and Tojo. Then we dealt with Hitler and Tojo, and then we found looming behind them Stalin and the menace of Communism and the Soviet Union.

Now what lies behind the Soviet Union? I see two problems. I am not saying these are caused by the Soviet Union, but I am saying that here are problems which we must reduce to manageable proportions in our dealing with the present. One is the awakening of the vast populations of Asia, populations which are beginning to feel that they should have and should exercise in the world an influence which is proportionate to their numbers and worthy of their cultures. That force is a force which can be turned to good, or it can be a force which can rend to pieces a world which has imprudently managed its immediate problem and which finds itself weakened, perhaps shattered in facing these upsurging forces of Asia. Therefore, in thinking about the Soviet Union, we must think about this shadow on the rock behind it. We must manage our difficulties so prudently that we have strength and initiative and power left to help shape and guide these emerging forces so that they will not turn out to be forces which rend and destroy.

In addition to the emergence of these peoples of Asia with their ambitions and possible power — which has to be thought about in relation not only to the existing power but also to the power which might be left after some imprudently inaugurated struggle had torn the Western world apart — there are the great problems of the world's growing hunger, of its growing numbers, of its deficient knowledge of the very elemental methods of staying alive.

Another attitude which we must always keep in mind is the need to match our strength with the interests which we must defend. We hear it said — and it is wisely said — that there must be a balancing of commitments and capabilities. Too often people say that when they mean that we should reduce our commitments to meet whatever our capabilities may be at any time. Nothing could be more erroneous than that. What we must do is to be conscious of our national interests. A commitment is a national vital interest of which we have become conscious and for which we have made provision, but we may have national interests, which are just as valid, of which we have not become conscious and for which we have not made provision — about which we should immediately become conscious and about which we should immediately make provision. . . .

It is very important that we should not underestimate ourselves. We have to meet and face limitations and difficulties. But if every time a difficulty comes along somebody says, "Oh, to do that will wreck the economy of the United States," that is underestimating ourselves. I have no doubt that there is a point beyond which the United States cannot go, but I am equally sure that we are not anywhere near that point. Therefore the thing to do is not to be timid about ourselves but to realize that our great strength is there to be used, and to use it wisely and economically and sensibly to create the defenses which we need. . . .

There is no unitary approach . . . We must use all means at our hand, whatever they are, and not say that one is the answer, or one or two are the answers. If you take, for instance, the views of those who urge that propaganda is the sole necessary weapon to survive and win in the modern world, you easily find yourself in the ridiculous position where you may have all the people of a nation on your side, but those people are politically organized as an effective opposition to you. To a very large extent — not completely, but to a very large extent — that is the situation which exists in China. I believe that the vast masses of the people in China are sympathetic to the United States, and yet those masses of people in China are organized effectively against us so that they are a very strong opponent. . . . Propaganda . . . is an important weapon, and . . . we must use it fully but it is not the sole answer.

Neither is dealing with governments alone the sole answer. The idea that we can make arrangements with this, that, or the other government, without regard to popular support founded on free consent would all too probably involve us in excessively brittle alliances. We have a very good illustration of that sort of brittleness in the arrangements which were made between Hitler and Mussolini; they seemed very fine but they were very brittle, and when the pressure was put upon them they broke down. As it turned out, not the nation but only their passing masters proved to be the parties to the alliance.

We must be aware of both the fallacy of recovery without defensive strength and the fallacy of military strength upon a shaky economic foundation. . . . Defensive strength is as integral to recovery as a fence is to a cornfield. Yet in seeking to replenish military strength it is necessary to avoid putting too great a load on our allies or on ourselves, for that matter.

There is no substitute for strength at the center. Alliances are important. It is of vital importance to us that our allies in the North Atlantic Treaty and in the Rio Treaty be strong and that the bonds between them and us be strong. But it is equally important, if not more important, that there be strength at the center of these groups — the strength of the United States, its economic strength, its military strength, which will, in itself, breed strength at the periphery of our associations. The same applies in the United Nations. In that union of nations there is no substitute for the strength of the United States at the heart of the great group of powers which share our determination to uphold the principles of the Charter. . . .

We must believe that time is on our side. I concede to you that in saying this there is an element of faith. There is an element of faith because I believe that we are people who act. Time is not on our side if we merely sit in the shade and fan ourselves. Time is on our side if we go to work. We can do much in time. We can strengthen ourselves, we can strengthen our allies. We have a vast productive power which is now not harnessed, much greater than those opposed to us. We can harness it. There is much we can do and, if we will do it, time is on our side. If we don't do it, it is not.

Therefore we come to the matter of will. We have a strong geographical position. We have people who are skilled in industry, who have courage, who make fine soldiers and producers. We have natural re-

sources. We have the productive plant. All of those things are no good
at all unless they are cemented together and thrown into action by will.
I believe that the American people have that will and that they can put
that will strongly behind everything of a material nature that they have
so that they, along with their allies, will secure for the future the things
they value.

... We must keep constantly before us the goal toward which we are
working. What we are working toward is a situation in which the
normal course of settling disputes will be negotiation. We are enthusiastic people, and occasionally we get so enthusiastic about what we
are doing that we believe that is the end instead of the means. We
must never get ourselves into the state of mind where we say that we
are building this strength in order to use it. We are building this
strength in order that we may never have to use it, in order that we
may get to the point where the normal way to settle things is to sit down,
to argue about them, to negotiate about them, and to find a solution
with which all parties concerned can live, even though it is not ideal for
any of us.

That is not really a hopeless ambition. It seems a long way off —
and it is a long way off when you are dealing with the Soviet Union
under the present imbalance of power — but we have reached a situation in the Western Hemisphere where negotiation is the normal way of
settling disputes. The normal way for the American republics to settle
all their differences — and there are very grave and serious difficulties —
is by negotiation and reasonable settlement. That has taken nearly 60
years to work out. ...

There is one last attitude which I should like to stress: ... We must
deal with these problems within a pattern of responsibility. ... We
must act with the consciousness that our responsibility is to interests
which are broader than our own immediate American interests. Great
empires have risen in this world and have collapsed because they took
too narrow a view. There is no divine command which spares the
United States from the seeds of destruction which have operated in
other great states. There is no instruction to that one of the Fates who
holds the shears that she shall withhold them from the thread of life
of the United States. We must operate in a pattern of responsibility
which is greater than our own interests. We cannot yield to the
temptation, because we are virile and enthusiastic, of thinking that,

because we believe a thing, it just must be right. We must not confuse our own opinions with the will of God.

That is essential for leadership. It is not merely a moral dissertation which I am making. It is essential to leadership among the free nations if we are going to maintain the sort of coalition which we have. We cannot take the attitude that we will coerce nations, that we are so right that if they do not do exactly what we want them to do we will withhold economic aid, or we will withhold military aid, we will do this, we will do that. If we take that attitude, then we are creating a relationship indistinguishable from that which exists between the Soviet Union and countries associated with it. That must never be our attitude. We are the leader. We are accepted as the leader. But we will continue to be accepted as the leader only if the other countries believe that the pattern of responsibility within which we operate is a responsibility to interests which are broader than our own — that we know today what Thomas Jefferson was talking about when he spoke of the need of paying a decent respect to the opinions of mankind.[4]

This is a formidable list of requirements; it sets a severe test for the American people. And in Acheson's view the test is the more severe because as a people we have not asked for nor expected these heavy obligations of leadership. He has made this point in many ways, but never more sympathetically than in the passages which follow. They come from a letter written in February, 1951, to Mr. Clarence Moullette, who had sent on to Acheson, with a thoughtful covering comment, a letter from his Marine son which was bitterly critical of American foreign policy in general and Acheson in particular. Without attacking the sincerity of the young Marine's opinions, Acheson suggested that his bitterness came from the painful contrast between the life he had expected and the one he faced:

The real problem lies deeper than the questioning of particular decisions — even the important ones which distress your son. It lies in the fact — for which we may thank God — that these boys have been brought up in the fundamental decency and rightness of American life. They have lived in communities where they have breathed in with the air truth and tolerance of others' interests, generosity and good nature, hard work, honesty and fairness. To all of them opened the oppor-

[4] Stenographic transcript of remarks to a group of magazine and book publishers, June 29, 1951 (*Bulletin*, XXV, pp. 125–28).

tunity for happy and constructive lives, their own homes and families, work to do, a part to play in the community in a hundred ways. They saw no problems, here at home, that would not yield to effort, ingenuity, and the give-and-take of people who believed in the same right values.

Now, just at the moment when they were about to enter fully as grown men in this world, its promise is dashed. In its place they find hardship, loneliness, uncertainty, danger. They are separated from family and friends. Even worse, they are denied the natural development of their lives. The fact that this happens to them because some distant and shadowy figures in the Kremlin, controlling millions of people far from them, are setting out to make impossible such lives as they had every right and hope to have, does not help their frustration and bitterness.

This agony of spirit, so understandable and right, makes it hard to believe that so monstrous an evil can exist in a world based upon infinite mercy and justice.

But the fact is that it does exist. The fact is that it twists and tortures all our lives. And, I believe, to each of us in this case as in so many others, the great thing is not what happens to us but how we bear what happens to us.

For our country, and for most of us as individuals, the period which has passed since V-E and V-J Days has been one of cruel disappointment, slowly forming resolution, and, finally, great determination and effort. The high hopes, for which great sacrifices were made during the war, did not come to ready fruition. That did not mean that these hopes — for peace, and for a good life for all — were wrong, or that the principles of freedom and justice on which they were based were not worthy of these sacrifices.

What it did mean was that it was going to be a good deal harder to build the kind of world we wanted than we thought it was going to be. . . .

In some ways, this is an ancient problem. Our forebears on this continent had it cruelly impressed upon them that the liberty we enjoy is not won and preserved without unremitting effort, without sacrifice, without "eternal vigilance." But we had for so long enjoyed the blessings of freedom that we had come to accept this condition as automatically assured. It has fallen to us — to your son's generation, and to ours — to take up again the defense of freedom against the challenge of tyranny.

In other ways, this is a new problem. Our country, which has risen to a position of unprecedented power and eminence in the world, is seeking to use that power in such a way as to help bring about a peaceful international order. This means that we have to be doing two things at once: while we move ahead in our efforts to build the kind of a world in which we can all live together peacefully and in common helpfulness, we are at the same time protecting ourselves from being overrun by the tyranny which is run from Moscow. I have sometimes compared this two-pronged effort as being like the way our ancestors had to have some men drilling and keeping watch from the blockhouses, while others went on, tilling the fields.

In a sense, we are standing with one foot in the world of our hopes for a future order among nations, and the other foot in the world of power. Both of these are part of the present reality. Unless we are strong enough — we and the other free nations — to prevent the Soviet rulers from extending their control over the entire world, then we shall never have the chance to help build the kind of a world we all want.[5]

So the problem, as Acheson saw it, was whether or not Americans would deal with the realities. This did not mean agreement on specific policies; it was rather a matter of facing facts without losing faith.

I know that these thoughts I have written to you will not answer all the questions which you have touched on . . . What I am concerned about is not that your son should feel that I, or the Administration, or the Government is right on any particular issue. It is good that he should question whether the steps we are taking are right or are wrong. But what is important is that he feel, and that all our young people feel, a strong faith in the validity and the reality of the ideals on which this country was founded and on which it now endeavors to guide its actions. So long as our young people are steadfast in this faith, we can be assured of the vitality of our society, and its ability to go on meeting the challenges of the future.[6]

And on this final issue of faith, Acheson's position is simple; he is a believer. To show this belief one might quote from a dozen speeches; at different times he has affirmed his central faith in the various but mutually

[5] *Bulletin*, XXIV, p. 450.   [6] Same source, p. 450.

consistent terms of Christianity, patriotism, and freedom. Yet I think the most characteristic of these affirmations is the one which follows:

The fundamental moral value on which our society rests is the brotherhood of man. To the extent that our actions abroad, and our relations among ourselves at home, are expressive of this humanist principle, we shall create a good that will live after us.

It is not in the words we profess, but in what we do, and in how we do it, that our ends will be found.

Justice Holmes expressed it:

"Man is born a predestined idealist, for he is born to act. To act is to affirm the worth of an end, and to persist in affirming the worth of an end is to make an ideal." [7]

[7] Address to the Harvard Alumni Association, June 22, 1950 (*Bulletin*, XXIII, p. 38).

INDEX